26/24

EDWARD CARPENTER AND
LATE VICTORIAN RADICALISM

EDWARD CARPENTER

AND

LATE VICTORIAN RADICALISM

Edited by

TONY BROWN
University College of North Wales,
Bangor

FRANK CASS

First published 1990 in Great Britain by
FRANK CASS & CO. LTD.
Gainsborough House, Gainsborough Road,
London E11 1RS, England

and in the United States of America by
FRANK CASS
c/o International Specialized Book Services, Inc.
5602 N.E. Hassalo Street, Portland, Oregon 97213

British Library Cataloguing in Publication Data

Edward Carpenter and late Victorian radicalism.
   1. Socialism. Carpenter, Edward, 1844–1929. Great Britain
   I. Brown, Tony
   335.0092
   ISBN 0-7146-3400-X

Library of Congress Cataloging-in-Publication Data

Edward Carpenter and late Victorian radicalism / edited
   by Tony Brown.
      p.   cm.
   ISBN 0-7146-3400-X
   1. Carpenter, Edward, 1844–1929. 2. Carpenter, Edward, 1844–1929–
   –Friends and associates. 3. Carpenter, Edward, 1844–1929—Political
   and social views. 4. Politics and literature—Great Britain–
   –History—19th century. 5. English literature—19th century-
   –History and criticism. 6. Great Britain—Politics and
   government—1837–1901. 7. Radicalism—Great Britain—History—19th
   century. 8. Socialism—Great Britain—Biography. 10. Authors,
   English—19th century—Biography. I. Carpenter, Edward,
   1844–1929. II. Brown, Tony.
   PR4451.Z5E39   1990
   828'.809—dc20   90–35726
                                                        CIP

This group of studies first appeared in a special issue on "Edward
Carpenter and Late Victorian Radicalism" of *Prose Studies*, Vol.
13, No. 1, published by Frank Cass & Co. Ltd.

Printed in Great Britain by
Antony Rowe Ltd, Chippenham

Contents

Notes on Contributors

Parminder Kaur Bakshi lectured in English at the University of Delhi before studying for a Ph.D. on E.M. Forster at the University of Warwick. She is currently working in the Centre for Research in Ethnic Relations at the University of Warwick.

Tony Brown is a lecturer in English at the University College of North Wales, Bangor. His publications include articles on the influence of Carpenter's ideas on early-twentieth-century writers, especially E.M. Forster. His "Annotated Bibliography of Edward Carpenter" was published in *English Literature in Transition* in 1989.

Marie-Françoise Cachin is Maître de Conférences (Senior Lecturer) in the Department of English at the Université de Paris 7 and is the author of a doctoral thesis on Edward Carpenter and the British socialist movement.

Laura Chrisman is a lecturer in English in the School of African and Asian Studies at the University of Sussex. Her work on Olive Schreiner began with her doctoral research on the relations between South African imperialism and English literature, 1880–1920.

Scott McCracken is a lecturer in English in the School of Modern Languages at the University of Salford. He is currently engaged in research on representations of masculinity in literature, 1880–1920.

Keith Nield lectures in Social History at the University of Hull, where he is currently Dean of the School of Economic and European Studies. He is joint editor of the journal *Social History* and his main research interests are in labour history and in critical historiography.

Christopher Shaw is head of the Social Science section at Harrogate College of Arts and Technology. His main research interest is in the history of socialist thought and its interaction with ideas about nature. He is co-editor of *The Imagined Past: History and Nostalgia* (Manchester U.P., 1989).

Beverly Thiele lectures in Women's Studies at Murdoch University, Western Australia, from where she received her Ph.D. for a doctoral thesis which examined works on "the woman question" by five late-nineteenth-century British socialist theorists.

Martin Wright is engaged in research in the History Department at St. David's University College, Lampeter, on British socialist propaganda and strategy, 1884–1914.

Edward Carpenter's Main Publications
(with abbreviations used in this collection)

Towards Democracy, 1883 (Complete Edition in four parts, 1905) (*TD*)

England's Ideal, and Other Papers on Social Subjects, 1887 (*EI*)

Civilisation: its Cause and Cure, and Other Essays, 1889 (*CCC*)

From Adam's Peak to Elephanta: Sketches in Ceylon and India, 1892 (*AP*)

Love's Coming-of-Age: A Series of Papers on the Relations of the Sexes, 1896 (*LCA*)

Angels' Wings: A Series of Essays on Art and its Relation to Life, 1898 (*AW*)

The Art of Creation: Essays on the Self and its Powers, 1904 (*AC*)

Prisons, Police and Punishment: An Enquiry into the Causes and Treatment of Crime and Criminals, 1905 (*PPP*)

Days with Walt Whitman, 1906

Sketches From Life in Town and Country, and Some Verses, 1908

The Intermediate Sex: A Study of Some Transitional Types of Men and Women, 1908 (*IS*)

The Drama of Love and Death: A Study of Human Evolution and Transfiguration, 1912

Intermediate Types Among Primitive Folk: A Study in Social Evolution, 1914

The Healing of Nations, and the Hidden Sources of their Strife, 1915

My Days and Dreams: Being Autobiographical Notes, 1916 (*MDD*)

Towards Industrial Freedom, 1917 (*TIF*)

Pagan and Christian Creeds: Their Origin and Meaning, 1920

Introduction

> Edward Carpenter was the greatest spiritual inspiration of our lives. His *Towards Democracy* was our Bible. ... We read it aloud in the summer evenings when, tired by tramping or games, we rested awhile ... We read it at those moments when we wanted to retire from the excitements of our Socialist work and in quietude seek the calm and power that alone give sustaining strength. ... Carpenter came one evening. I remember him vividly. His head and features were of extraordinary beauty: his face a chiselled statue, clear-cut and of perfect outline; his eyes bright and kindly; there was refinement in his every movement and in the tone of his voice. One admired and loved him at once.[1]

This is Fenner Brockway, writing on Carpenter's death in 1929, illustrating the kind of influence and adulation which Carpenter enjoyed in the labour movement in the years before the First War. His attacks, from the 1880s onwards, on the values which he saw as governing Victorian middle-class life – "cant in religion, pure materialism in science, futility in social conventions, the worship of stocks and shares, the starving of the human heart"[2] – made him a hero of English radicalism in the decades around the turn of the century. On his seventieth birthday, in 1914, he received a congratulatory address, expressing "admiration and gratitude" for his work, signed by some three hundred friends and admirers, including figures as various as R.B. Cunninghame-Graham, Havelock Ellis, Roger Fry, John Galsworthy, Harley Granville-Barker, Keir Hardie, Peter Kropotkin, Jack London, Sidney and Beatrice Webb, and W.B. Yeats.[3] On his eightieth birthday he received the congratulations of the Labour Government, signed by the whole Cabinet. But by then his reputation was fading. E.M. Forster, whose visit to Carpenter in 1913 had inspired *Maurice*, wrote in 1931: "If my impression of him is correct, he is not likely to have much earthly immortality. ... He will not figure in history."[4] Forster's prediction proved for many years to be correct. Only in recent years, as many of the issues on which he wrote have been engaged anew, has interest in Carpenter at all revived, with the publication of several studies of his life and work and the re-issue of some of his books. The present collection is intended as a further contribution to this renewed discussion of Carpenter's writing and the type of radicalism that he represented.

As an endorsement of the causes which he advocated, Carpenter's remarkable life was almost as important as his writings. This man who was to question so many of the values and attitudes of Victorian life was born, in 1844, into the comfort of the Victorian middle classes. His father was a qualified barrister who lived, however, on his private income, the family home being in Brighton which at the time represented all that was fashionable in the leisured world of the English upper middle class. The family was large – Carpenter had six sisters and three brothers – but, as was perhaps not unusual in that class at that time, there was little show of intimate affection between parents and children. It is clear that Carpenter especially adored his mother, but from a distance:

> [She] thought any manifestation of feeling unbecoming. We early learned to suppress and control emotion, and to fight our own battles alone ... and so my abiding recollection of all that time is one of silent concealment and loneliness. (*MDD*, p. 15)

Initially Carpenter fulfilled the expectations of his class: a successful undergraduate career at Cambridge and, in 1868, election to a clerical Fellowship in Mathematics at Trinity Hall, becoming in addition curate at St Edward's, Cambridge. But before long he grew disillusioned with his ministry and the "petty vulgarities and hypocrisies" (*MDD*, p. 53) of his congregation, which was composed mainly of the commercial middle classes. However, at the root of his "insuperable feeling of falsity and dislocation" (*MDD*, p. 58) was, once more, a sense of isolation and emotional unfulfilment. As an undergraduate, Carpenter had realised that he was homosexual. Now, in his loneliness, he became increasingly alienated from Cambridge – "the so-called intellectual life of the University was ... a fraud and a weariness" (*MDD*, p. 72) – and by 1871 Carpenter was on the verge of a nervous breakdown. Periods of leave from his duties provided only temporary relief.

He had first read the poetry of Walt Whitman in 1868, in W. M. Rossetti's edition, and the impact on Carpenter was immediate: "[W]ith a great leap of joy ... I met with the treatment of sex which accorded with my own sentiments" (*MDD*, p. 30). Carpenter had not only found someone who felt as he did, but who did so with no sense of guilt, celebrating "the manly love of comrades" openly and joyously. Moreover, here was a robust social vision which subverted the values of middle-class gentility, values in which Carpenter had felt himself to have been increasingly painfully imprisoned since boyhood. The immediate effect of Carpenter's reading of Whitman at Cambridge was, paradoxically, to exacerbate his sense of isolation, in that such reading emphasised the discrepancy between Whitman's vision and Carpenter's own situation. But further reading of Whitman during the emotional crises of 1871–73 brought about a new realisation, which seems to have struck Carpenter with almost visionary force:

> [I]t suddenly flashed upon me, with a vibration through my whole body, that I would and must somehow go and make my life with the mass of the people and the manual workers. (*MDD*, p. 77)

He sought to do this, after resigning from Holy Orders and from his Fellowship, by going as a University Extension lecturer to the industrial cities of the Midlands and the North. The constant travelling brought its own stresses, but eventually, in 1881, Carpenter settled in the countryside near Sheffield and bought a smallholding at Millthorpe in Derbyshire, not far from Sheffield. He lived there with working-class friends – and, after 1898, with a working-class lover, George Merrill – making a living by selling the produce of the small-holding at Chesterfield market. This simple life of physical labour, "so congenial ... so unrestrained ... seemed to liberate the pent-up emotionality of years" (*MDD*, p.105).

It was at this point, as his whole life changed, that the first part of *Towards Democracy* (1883) was written. It is unashamedly Whitmanesque in style and vision, although that vision is transmuted by Carpenter's own experience and his own view of *English* society. As Scott McCracken's paper demonstrates, the narrating "I" which surveys that society is not a distancing, discriminating "I," but is uninhibited in its inclusiveness, embracing the robust, uncouth world beyond the middle-class pale, unrespectable sexually – as Carpenter celebrates the "shameless lusty unpresentable pal"[5] –

> You fill me with visions, and when the night comes I see the forests upon your flanks and your horns among the stars. I climb upon you and fulfil my desire. (*TD*, p.20)

and unrespectable socially:

> O England, do I not know thee – as in a nightmare strangled tied and bound?
> Thy poverty – when through thy filthy courts from tangles of matted hair gaunt women with venomous faces look upon me? (*TD*, p.24)

> Oaths and curses and obscene jokes; the group of laughing men and girls tumbling out of the doors of the beershop, the haggard old woman under the flaring gas-jet by the butcher's stall ... (*TD*, p.33)

Carpenter celebrates his immersion in a teeming world, free of the constrictions of middle-class life:

> Through the city crowd pushing wrestling shouldering, against the tide, face after face, breath of liquor, money-grubbing eye, infidel skin, shouts, threats, greetings, smiles, eyes and breasts of love, breathless, clutches of lust, limbs, bodies ... (*TD*, p.31)

"Joy" and "freedom" are the words which echo through the opening sections of *Towards Democracy*, but the poem is far from being merely a celebration of personal release; it is also a prophecy of a more universal emancipation: "Freedom at last!/Long sought, long prayed for – ages and ages long" (*TD*, p.3). The recurring theme is whole-ness, the transcendance of division and inhibition both in the indivi-dual and in society. What is offered is a vision of a society that is a transformation, indeed an inversion, of Victorian England, communalism and sexual comradeship in place of class division and sexual inequality, a simple pastoral economy instead of urban industrial capitalism. This is Carpenter's "Democracy," the society of the future:

> ... I saw the joy of free open life under the sun:
> The green sun-delighting earth and rolling sea I saw,
> The free sufficing life – sweet comradeship, few needs and common pleasures – the needless endless burdens all cast aside,
> Not as a sentimental vision, but as a fact and a necessity existing ... (*TD*, p.145)

Meanwhile the old structures, especially the leisured life of the capitalist middle classes which Carpenter knew all too well, are repeatedly attacked:

> Back! Make me a space round me, you kid-gloved rotten-breathed paralytic world, with miserable antics mimicking the appearance of life ... (*TD*, p.20)
> I see deadly Respectability sitting at its dinner table, quaffing its wine, and discussing the rise and fall of stocks ... I see the struggle, the fear, the envy ... (*TD*, p.24)

This "puppet dance of gentility" (*TD*, p.26), which he consistently sees as claustrophobic, unnatural and destructive of its own participants, as well as of the slum-dwelling workers whose labours finance it, Carpenter labels "Civilisation."

The essays which Carpenter wrote in the 1880s, collected in *England's Ideal* (1887) and *Civilisation: its Cause and Cure* (1889), develop the same issues in more discursive terms. The earliest of these, especially "Simplification of Life," "Does It Pay?" and "Trade" (*England's Ideal*) are implicitly an apologia for his new life-style and his rejection of his old one. In turn his attacks on middle-class society and his advocacy of a new, simpler way of life gain force from the fact, made clear to the reader, that Carpenter is not writing out of vague theory but from personal experience: "I do not say this lightly. I know what it is for anyone to have to abandon the forms in which he has been brought up."[6] The life of the English middle classes he sees as fundamentally unhealthy and diseased: "The slow poison and paralysis" of the "great clotted and congested centres which call themselves 'society' .. spread claws of contagion all through the vital organism" (*EI*, p.167). The wealthy do little or no physical work and they over-eat and over-dress. The way in which men's and women's bodies are swathed and imprisoned in layers of heavy clothing epitomises for Carpenter the ways in which their physical nature, including their sexual drives, are denied in "respectable" society, resulting in unhealthiness and neuroses; again we feel the presence of Carpenter's own experience. Middle-class society, artificial, inauthentic, needs to return to its roots, to the sources of vitality:

> To descend, first;
> To feel downwards and downwards through this wretched maze of shams for the solid ground – to come close to the Earth itself and those that live in direct contact with it ... (*TD*, p.28)

In other words, Carpenter's solution to his own spiritual and emotional "dis-ease" is offered as a cure for what he sees as the present unhealthiness of English society as a whole. The middle-class reader is urged to sell up his/her suburban villa, strip off the luxurious trappings of "Civilised" life and go to live and work close to nature.

Carpenter emphasises in *My Days and Dreams* that his own seeking of a life of manual work in the countryside was a personal necessity and not "in pursuance of some great theory or scheme of social salvation" (*MDD*, p.111) and, indeed, *Towards Democracy* and the early essays do not put forward a programme for bringing about social and political change in England. They are concerned, rather, with men's and women's inner lives, with creating new structures of feeling, with self-realisation and modes of personal relationship. But changes in individuals would inevitably bring about changes in the social structure, given Carpenter's vision of society as an aspect of a dynamic, evolutionary process. Christopher Shaw demonstrates in his paper Carpenter's belief that the present Civilisation had evolved from a pre-historic period in which "there had been a connectedness among mankind and a feeling of community between man and nature"; with an argument that owes something to Lewis Morgan's *Ancient Society* (1877), Carpenter sees primitive communalism as having been replaced by a passion for private property, which brought with it the present division into antagonistic social classes, the alienation of the individual from his fellows and from nature, and the contemporary emphasis on materialism and scientific rationalism. As Shaw indicates, the third and final phase was to be "the unification of primitive feeling and intuition with the more recently acquired faculties of rationality and self-consciousness." This is the integration, the unity of "Democracy." In fact, from the title essay of *Civilisation: its Cause and Cure* through to *The Art of Creation* (1904) Carpenter develops a whole metaphysic of cosmic unity, human society, the animal kingdom, the natural world itself all seen as aspects of the "Great Self" or "World Soul"; the awareness of this unity – isolating, alienating individual consciousness being transcended in a "cosmic consciousness" – is, again, that of the Democracy phase.

Human society is thus seen as part of a dynamic universe, evolving, or "exfoliating," not according to the competitive principles of Darwin, but the purposive principles of Lamarck. (See "Exfoliation: Lamarck versus Darwin" in *Civilisation; its Cause and Cure* and "Social Progress and Individual Effort" in *England's Ideal*.) We might note, however, the ways in which Carpenter adapts Lamarck: first, while Lamarck applies his principle of evolution to organisms in the natural world, Carpenter applies Lamarck's pattern of change not only to plants and animals but also to society itself. Repeatedly in *Towards Democracy* and the early essays, human society is seen *as* an organism, evolving like a larva, growing and changing inside its old forms until it bursts out of the constraining chrysalis, the outmoded conventions and social structures, whereupon the process begins again as the social organism evolves to the next stage. Second, while Lamarck sees "necessity" (*besoin*) as the initial stimulus to change, Carpenter uses the word "desire," a word with altogether more conscious, more active, and arguably more personal connotations.[7] In so doing, Carpenter emphasises the capacity of the human individual to "exfoliate" himself/herself, to manifest his/her desires and ideals in external structures or ways of life, in new social structures; "function precedes organisation ... desire precedes function":[8]

> When a new desire has declared itself within the human heart, when a fresh plexus is forming among the nerves – then the revolutions of nations are already decided, and histories unwritten are written. (*TD*, p.45)

Thus, the individuals who follow Carpenter's example and break out of their present life are the growing points of the newly-evolving society, of Democracy.

His critique of the divisive, alienating effects of capitalism almost inevitably led Carpenter towards the emergent Socialist movement. One might trace the roots of his thinking back to Cambridge – he had been F.D. Maurice's curate, he had read Mazzini's *The Duties of Man* (1862), addressed to the working men of Italy, while a member of a radical discussion group at the University, and in the summer of 1871 Carpenter had been in Paris only a few weeks after the fall of the Commune – but it was a reading of H.M. Hyndman's summary of Marxist ideas, *England for All*, in 1883 which brought Carpenter into the movement:

> [T]he mass of floating impressions, sentiments, ideals, etc., in my mind fell into shape ... I saw that the current Socialism afforded an excellent text for an attack upon the existing competitive system, and a good means of rousing the slumbering consciences – especially of the rich; and in that view I have worked for it and the Anarchist ideal consistently. (*MDD*, pp.114–15)

In the same year he visited Hyndman and William Morris at the offices of the Social Democratic Federation in London, and later contributed £300 towards the setting up of the S.D.F.'s journal *Justice*.[9] In 1886 he was one of the founder members of the Sheffield Socialist Society, a group of mainly working-class Socialists; Carpenter drafted the group's manifesto and helped arrange visiting speakers, who included Morris, Hyndman, Annie Besant, Tom Maguire and the anarchist, Peter Kropotkin.[10]

As Martin Wright's essay makes clear, the last two decades of the century saw much factional disagreement within the Socialist movement, but Carpenter managed to a remarkable degree to transcend most of the ideological splits; he consistently emphasised less the divisions than Socialism's "oceanic character" (*MDD*, p.126), seeing all of the groups as working ultimately to the same great end. At the same time, as Marie-Françoise Cachin demonstrates from her analysis of Carpenter's revisions of his essays – and as is underlined by the juxtaposition of Socialism and "the Anarchist ideal" in the passage quoted above – Carpenter was consistently, and increasingly, sceptical about the way in which certain modes of Socialist thinking could lead to a more centralised state, not to the increased liberty of the individual. For we must remember that, as Lowes Dickinson points out in a tribute to Carpenter, "His approach had not been that of economic theory ... He started with the love of men and of nature and in his desire to liberate that became a critic of social institutions."[11] Carpenter's Socialism was not concerned merely with the material conditions of the working classes, with wages or the eight-hour day. He wanted not just a change in the way power was held and wealth distributed, but a transformation in men's and women's ways of feeling, in the ways in which they related to other individuals and to the natural world. The present social and economic structure was ethically wrong; as it was immoral for the middle classes to live on the labours of the workers, so it was immoral to pollute the natural environment and kill living creatures.

Christopher Shaw sees Carpenter's sensibility as being essentially religious and indeed the very language used by Socialists like Carpenter reveals the origin of their concern with personal relationships and their belief that social transformation began with a change in the heart of the human individual. Carpenter's vision, especially in *Towards Democracy*, is frequently expressed in the language and imagery of the Christianity he had supposedly left behind at Cambridge. "Democracy" is "the everlasting life" (*TD*, p.9) in which men and women may "look forth" upon "new heavens and a new earth" (*TD*, p.20); the "voice of the woods" tells the suffering individual to "Come unto me: and I will give you rest" (*TD*, p.185). The Socialist millennium is expressed in the language of salvation.

One way in which Civilisation distorted natural impulses Carpenter had seen at close quarters. He had grown up in Brighton with six sisters. The tedium of the empty lives of these young upper-middle-class women he describes in *My Days and Dreams* (p.32), aware that there are hundreds of thousands like them across England:

I see avenues of young girls and women, with sideway flopping

heads, debarred from Work, debarred from natural Sexuality,
weary to death with nothing to do, (and this thy triumph, O deadly
respectability discussing stocks!) ... (*TD*, p.25)

Capitalist Civilisation imprisoned such women in a social role which
gave them no economic or political power and for the most part denied
them the possibility of choosing their own means of imaginative or
emotional fulfilment. That they had *sexual* needs of their own would
almost certainly have been denied by the women themselves, conditioned as they were by the prevailing sexual mores. As a homosexual,
Carpenter realised from his own experience the toll that emotional and
sexual repression took, not only in terms of personal unhappiness but
also in neuroses, even prostration, and he felt he could identify,
therefore, with the "sufferings which are endured by an immense
number of modern women" (*MDD*, p.97). He discussed these issues
with the growing circle of radical and Socialist friends who visited
Millthorpe, including women friends like Olive Schreiner, Edith Lees
and Kate Salt. The pamphlets which he wrote in the 1890s, and which
are discussed in Beverly Thiele's paper, were the result; they were
collected as *Love's Coming-of-Age* in 1896. Carpenter argues that, as
Civilisation has evolved, men in their lust for material possessions have
not only denied their own sensitivity and capacity for sexual tenderness
– the middle-class male is consistently seen as "ungrown"[12] in matters of
personal affection – but have made chattels of women: "[O]ur marriage
and social institutions ... lumber along over the bodies of women, as
our commercial institutions grind over the bodies of the poor" (*LCA*,
p.31).

Natural sexual impulses had come to be seen as "unclean" (*LCA*,
p.11) and Carpenter argues that relations between the sexes would not
improve until "the body and all its functions" was seen as "pure and
beautiful" (*LCA*, p.19), that it was accepted that a woman *had* such
impulses and was allowed "to face man on an equality; to find, self-
balanced, her natural relation to him; and to dispose of herself and of
her sex perfectly freely, and not as a thrall must do" (*LCA*, p.53). The
"Free Society" in which this would be possible is essentially the
comradely Democracy visualised in the earlier writing. In other
words, Carpenter realises that women's freedom – economic as well as
emotional and sexual – and the changes which he desired in sexual
attitudes generally ultimately depended upon wider changes, upon the
evolution of society beyond Civilisation:

> The freedom of Woman must ultimately rest on the Communism
> of Society ... It is evident that no very great change for the better
> in marriage-relations can take place except as the accompaniment
> of deep-lying changes in Society at large. (*LCA*, pp.54, 111)

Moreover, Carpenter's "Free Society" is not only one in which men and
women would be able to love each other openly and freely as equals, as

"comrades," but also one in which people of all varieties of sexual preference would be free to love in their own way. Women would be free, for example, to have a "temporary alliance with a man for the sake of obtaining a much-needed child"; couples might have a relationship "with little of the sexual in it" (*LCA*, p. 142); other couples might "have intimacies with outsiders, and yet ... continue ... perfectly true to each other" (*LCA*, p. 105) – all of which is aimed at liberating men and women from what Carpenter saw as the suffocating "*égoisme à deux*" (*LCA*, p. 87) of Victorian marriage and the repressive sexual attitudes that went with it.

That such a sexually tolerant society would be attractive to a man of Carpenter's own sexual temperament is obvious. In fact, as Dr Thiele demonstrates, the "hidden agenda" in Carpenter's writing on sexual relations is a defence of homosexuality. This leads him ultimately to emphasise the "transmutation" of the sexual impulse onto a spiritual plane, rather than to stress physical sexuality, and also, consequently, to separate sexuality from procreation. This in turn leads, as Dr Thiele shows, to a failure fully to confront the issue of reproduction and child-bearing.[13] Perhaps the most serious flaw in Carpenter's analysis of the relations between the sexes, however, is his failure to transcend the notion of fixed gender characteristics; for all his radicalism, Carpenter is still trapped in the gender stereotypes of his age:

> Woman is the more primitive, the more intuitive, the more emotional ... [W]oman tends more to intuition and man to logic ... Generally it will be admitted, as we are dealing with points of mental and moral difference between the sexes, Man has developed the more active and Woman the more passive qualities. (*LCA*, pp. 40, 50, 52)

Such a view of gender as biologically determined ignores – even as it demonstrates – the social construction of gender, ignores, as Sheila Rowbotham points out, "how all our notions of what a man is and what a woman is are created by the totality of our social relationships and by the circumstances of our own sexual practice."[14]

Despite such limitations, however, *Love's Coming-of-Age* was a challenging early examination not only of the relations between men and women, but also of the ways in which the individual's most private feelings could be conditioned and distorted by social attitudes and the ways in which the sexual conventions of a particular society at a particular time could be erected by the Church and by the legal system into what appeared to be incontrovertible facts of nature. The book proved to be one of Carpenter's most popular and most influential works, going through ten English editions by 1918 and seven editions in the United States, as well as being translated into several European languages. It was read by working-class women active in the women's movement, as well as by middle-class radicals. It provided a context for feminists like Olive Schreiner, whose letters show her to have had a long and close friendship with Carpenter, albeit her own vision of the future for women, as Laura Chrisman shows in her paper, is a bleaker one than his. While he confidently focusses on the "Free Society" of tolerance and equality, Schreiner emphasises the labour, the struggle of bringing it about.

In Carpenter's perception of gender characteristics as biologically determined, we may again sense his "hidden agenda." In *The Intermediate Sex* (1908), with J. A. Symonds' *A Problem in Modern Ethics* (1891) one of the earliest apologies for homosexuality in English, Carpenter argues for homosexuality not as sinful or pathological or even, as Havelock Ellis had argued, as a "sport" or "one of those organic aberrations which we see ... in plants and in animals,"[15] but as perfectly natural, a part of Nature's infinite variety, the diversity and richness of which defies society's crude moral and sexual classifications:

> That there are distinctions and gradations of Soul-material in relation to Sex – that the inner psychical affections and affinities shade off and graduate, in a vast number of instances, most subtly from male to female, and not always in obvious correspondence with the outer bodily sex – is a thing evident enough to anyone who considers the subject ... Before the facts of Nature we have to preserve a certain humility and reverence; not rush in with our pre-conceived and obstinate assumptions. (*IS*, pp. 10–11)

Homosexuality is, Carpenter insists, natural and congenital, not acquired, and the legal sanctions against it, therefore, arbitrary and unjust. Carpenter was familiar with the work of continental workers in the field of sexual research, especially De Joux, Moll, Krafft-Ebing and Karl Ulrichs, and he followed Ulrichs in seeing the male homosexual – or "Uranian" – as a female soul in a male body, *"anima muliebris in corpore virili inclusa"* (*IS*, p. 19). The male homosexual – as Beverly Thiele shows, Carpenter gives little serious attention to lesbianism – is thus at the median between the male and the female, a new type of man; he has "male" strength, courage and practicality and also "female" sensitivity, intuition and tenderness. However questionable the gender labels which Carpenter uses, the character of the Uranian he defines is quite different from the insensitive, emotionally "ungrown" middle-class male described in *Love's Coming-of-Age*, and is perceived by Carpenter as a newly-evolving sexual type, "the outline and draft of the new creature" (*TD*, p. 396).

The Uranian is seen not only as a reconciler of the sexes, breaking down the barriers between male and female – having both male and female elements in his own make-up, he can act as adviser to both men and women in the delicate readjustments in the roles of the sexes which Carpenter saw as slowly taking place in the society around him – but also as one who could help break down the equally rigid barriers which divided the classes in England. Carpenter emphasises the fact that homosexuals exist in all classes, including the working classes; the homosexual is "sometimes a child of the people, without any culture, but almost always with a peculiar inborn refinement" (*IS*, p.33). Uranian love could thus be a means of transcending the divisions of class: "Eros is a great leveller" (*IS*, p.114). (Again there is, manifestly, a personal dimension; it had been Whitman's vision of the love of comrades of different classes which had persuaded Carpenter to make his life "with the mass of the people and the manual workers." In Sheffield he had finally found the working-class comradeship he had sought.) Moreover, Carpenter had a vision of Uranian comradeship not only uniting the classes but helping to undermine the very capitalist system on which the English class structure was based:

> There are cases I have known ... of employers who have managed to attach their workmen ... very personally to themselves, and whose object in running their business was at least as much to provide their employees with a living as themselves; while the latter, feeling this, have responded with their best output. It is possible that something like the guilds and fraternities of the middle ages might thus be reconstructed, but on a more intimate and personal basis than in those days. (*IS*, p.115)[16]

While society continued to be run by the capitalist, who was as insensitive and acquisitive in his virile accumulation of wealth as he was in his sexual relationships, inequality between the classes and the sexes would continue. Comradeship in the economic world, as in the world of personal relationships, could change that society. At the very least it could provide a "counterbalance"[17] to the prevailing materialism. In *The Intermediate Sex*, perhaps even more than in *Towards Democracy*, we can see how Carpenter's Socialism was inseparable from the desire for a new emotional and sexual order, a desire which in turn originated in his own sexual temperament.

Artistic, gentle, emotionally open, uninterested in capitalist and imperialist ambition, sensitive to the feelings of women, anxious for the reconciliation of the classes, the Uranians are seen by Carpenter as the first signs of a new form of human being, who would shape the society of the future in their image; they are

> the advanced guard of that great movement which will one day transform the common life by substituting the bond of personal affection and compassion for the monetary, legal and other external ties which now control and confine society. (*IS*, p.116)

Carpenter develops his argument in his later book, *Intermediate Types Among Primitive Folk: A Study in Social Evolution* (1914), a book which one critic has called "a gay *Golden Bough*."[18] Here Carpenter refers in detail to a wide range of anthropological and sociological studies in seeking to demonstrate not only that homosexuality has existed in all ages and in all cultures, but also the special place which individuals who did not accord with their cultures' conventional gender roles have had in various cultures in the past and have in some contemporary non-European societies.

In India, Parminder Kaur Bakshi shows, Carpenter found, in Hinduism, a culture that did "not comprehend sexuality as problematic." In the *Bhagavad Gita*, which he read in the early 1880s as he changed his whole way of life, Carpenter had found not only a vision of the physical world as part of a great transcendent, all-inclusive Whole, but a unity of which the individual can become aware through love; Krishna tells Arjuna:

> Not by the Vedas, or an austere life, or gifts to the poor, or ritual offerings can I be seen as thou has seen me.
>
> Only by love can men see me, and know me, and come unto me.[19]

Ms Bakshi demonstrates how, in 1890, at a time of personal and political difficulty, Carpenter's passage to India was a liberation from the constraints of England. Anticipating Forster's Adela Quested by over thirty years, Carpenter was determined "to see the real India"[20] and he did so by avoiding the life of British India and immersing himself in the emotionally and sexually sympathetic life of the Indians themselves, mainly those of the lower classes. He repeatedly ventured into areas usually avoided by English visitors; he visited an opium den, a native theatre and a cotton mill, as well as being admitted to a night festival in a Hindu temple (*AP*, Ch. VII). Such experiences, as well as his discussions with ordinary Indians, gave Carpenter a perspective on India which few Englishmen in 1890–91 can have had. An obvious corollary to his sympathy for Indian life is his antipathy towards British imperial rule; for Carpenter the British in India epitomised the Civilisation he had been attacking in his writing for almost a decade and he is particularly aware, both in *From Adam's Peak to Elephanta* and in his later writing on the topic, of the way in which imperialism is rooted in economic exploitation of the native workers. While he felt that there was potentially much good will among Indians towards the British, Carpenter knew his countrymen too well to believe that their own attitudes were likely to change very quickly and this led him to place more importance on the National Indian Congress movement than did many other commentators at this time, predicting that the movement would eventually bring British rule in India to an end, either by violent confrontation or by the British gradually yielding more and more representative power to the people. *From Adam's Peak to Elephanta* is a fascinating and neglected work which deserves to be made available in a modern edition.

Edward Carpenter's reputation was at its height in the years around the turn of the century. Keith Nield has pointed out elsewhere how, especially in the 1890s, "Carpenter sometimes drew as many as two thousand people to a Sunday meeting of a Labour Church or to a lecture in the Sheffield Hall of Science or some other large hall, usually in a provincial town,"[21] and Mr Nield's essay in the present collection indicates something of the popularity and international reputation of Carpenter's books in the period. From the 1880s onwards, Millthorpe became a place of pilgrimage for those in whom Carpenter's writings had struck a chord, those seeking the "simple life," vegetarians, dress-reformers and people experiencing emotional and sexual difficulties. At the same time, Millthorpe became a place where middle-class radicals and intellectuals like William Morris, Havelock Ellis and Edith Lees, Olive Schreiner, Kate and Henry Salt, Goldsworthy Lowes Dickinson, Roger Fry, and C.R. Ashbee could engage in discussion openly and frankly in a sympathetic environment. Millthorpe became in a sense an enclave of the new life; most of the people named stayed for periods of time there, either living in the house itself or renting cottages nearby. It is clear from the accounts in Gilbert Beith's book of recollections and tributes, that Carpenter had the personal impact on audiences and on individuals that today would be called "charisma"; we have already seen Fenner Brockway's reaction, and E.M. Forster writes of Carpenter that "The spell of his personal influence was tremendous. ... It was the influence which used to be called magnetic, and which emanated from religious teachers and seers, it depended on contact and couldn't be written down on paper."[22] Almost inevitably, then, as Carpenter grew old (he was seventy in 1914) and his appearances on public platforms became fewer, his reputation began slowly to decline and by the 1920s a younger generation of Socialists had grown up who knew little of him. By the First War, anyway, the labour movement had taken a different direction; Carpenter's brand of ethical Socialism, concerned with inner transformation of the individual as a prelude to social change, had been marginalised as the Labour Party concerned itself more directly with economic and social issues in its quest for parliamentary power. In fact, Carpenter's writing on sexual matters did not meet with the approval of some leaders within the movement – Beverly Thiele points out Robert Blatchford's reaction to Carpenter's pamphlets and this, of course, pre-dates his books on homosexuality – and there were clearly those who in seeking electoral approval did not want the movement associated with radical sexual ideas.[23] And in any case Carpenter's base had always been Sheffield, not London; he had never been a national leader, his influence being exerted mainly at grass-roots meetings in the north of England. As Keith Nield argues, once Carpenter's reputation had faded, not only the utopian nature of his Socialism but also the fact that he had not had a role in the national leadership and a clear identification with a particular organisation retarded his recovery and re-examination, the earlier phases of the study of labour history tending to concentrate on the biographies of leaders and the study of discrete organisations.

Recent scholarly interest in Carpenter has its origins in the 1960s; Mr

Nield not only suggests historiographic reasons for this, but also points out that that decade saw a re-engagement of issues of sexual and political liberation which were central to Carpenter's vision. It is in this period that the first two contemporary studies of Carpenter were completed, albeit in the form of doctoral theses which remained unpublished.[24] The publication of E.M. Forster's *Maurice* in 1971, with Forster's references to Carpenter in the "Terminal note," and, in the same year, of Emile Delavenay's *D.H. Lawrence and Edward Carpenter*, drew the attention of reviewers and critics to Carpenter and his writing. Other studies have followed, detailed in the essays in this collection, and Gay Men's Press has made *Towards Democracy* and some of Carpenter's writing on sexual issues available once more.[25] Indeed, there is perhaps a certain irony in the fact that it is renewed concern, particularly on the left, with those issues which contributed to Carpenter being marginalised by the labour movement that has contributed significantly to a revival of interest in his work; once more, indeed, it is being asserted that a truly free society is not merely one in which there is greater economic equality, but one in which individuals should be free to follow their own sexual preferences and one which lives in harmony with its natural environment. However, simplistic claims for the "relevance" of a man who advocated sexual freedom and "dropped out" to live a life of self-sufficiency in the countryside with his working-class lover need to be avoided; Carpenter exhibits some characteristic attitudes of his age, for example, in his optimistic faith in the evolutionary progress of mankind and, as we have seen, in his notions of gender. But a study of Carpenter's life and work throws interesting light on a whole nexus of attitudes and ideas current in radical circles in the last decades of the nineteenth century. His writing, moreover, made such ideas familiar to a number of major writers in the Modernist period. The responses of Forster and D.H. Lawrence to Carpenter's work are by now familiar; through Forster, Lowes Dickinson and Roger Fry, as well through his writing, Carpenter's ideas were current in Bloomsbury and, perhaps through Bloomsbury, T.S. Eliot seems to have been aware of his work.[26] Carpenter's writing, especially on personal relations, was also known to Sassoon and Owen, as well as to others who shared the comradeship of the trenches.[27] Indeed, it has been argued that, particularly through *The Art of Creation* (1904), Carpenter's thinking made a contribution to notions of the self and of tradition which we find in literary Modernism; one recent writer, examining the influence of Carpenter's writing, especially his concept of "cosmic consciousness," on the artistic and literary *avant-garde* in America before the First War, goes as far as to assert that "if we are to understand early modern art and theory, as well as literature, we must rediscover the unknown Edward Carpenter."[28] What we can certainly say is that Carpenter's work, however much it has been lost sight of until recent years, made in its time a significant contribution to the gradual shift of ideas, sexual, social and political, which mark the transition from Victorianism into the modern age. In Raymond Williams' words, "Carpenter was, to an extraordinary extent, a prefigurative man."[29]

TONY BROWN

NOTES

1. "A Memory of Edward Carpenter," *New Leader*, 5 July 1929, p.6.
2. Edward Carpenter, *My Days and Dreams: Being Autobiographical Notes* (London: Allen & Unwin, 1916), p.321. Further references are incorporated into the text.
3. See Emile Delavenay, *D.H. Lawrence and Edward Carpenter: A Study in Edwardian Transition* (London: Heinemann, 1971), plate 3, and *MDD*, p.318.
4. "Some Memories" in Gilbert Beith, ed., *Edward Carpenter: In Appreciation* (London: Allen & Unwin, 1931), p.80.
5. *Towards Democracy* (Complete ed., 1905; rpt. London: Allen & Unwin, 1921), p.20. Further references are incorporated into the text.
6. *England's Ideal, and Other Papers on Social Subjects* (1887; rpt. London: Swan Sonnenschein), p.20. Further references are incorporated into the text.
7. On this point see Terence Eagleton, "Nature and Spirit: A Study of Edward Carpenter in his Intellectual Context," Diss. Cambridge University 1968, pp.173–4.
8. *Civilisation: its Cause and Cure* (1889; rpt. Allen & Unwin, 1919), pp.132–3.
9. See Chushichi Tsuzuki, *Edward Carpenter 1844–1929: Prophet of Human Fellowship* (London: Cambridge U.P., 1980), p.54.
10. The fullest accounts of the Sheffield Socialists are to be found in Sheila Rowbotham and Jeffrey Weeks, *Socialism and the New Life: The Personal and Sexual Politics of Edward Carpenter and Havelock Ellis* (London: Pluto P., 1977) and D.K. Baruah, "Edward Carpenter and the Early Sheffield Socialists," *Trans. of the Hunter Archaeological Society*, 10 (1971), 54–62.
11. "Edward Carpenter as a Friend" in Beith, p.36.
12. *Love's Coming-of-Age* (Complete ed., 1906; rpt. London: Methuen, 1914), pp.28–9. Further references are incorporated into the text.
13. There is, perhaps, an additional personal factor behind Carpenter's consistent sentimentalising of motherhood, not just in *LCA* but elsewhere in his writing, especially in *TD*. (See, for example, *TD*, pp.86, 92, 96, 118, 233, 242, 245; in "O Child of Uranus" (*TD*, p.410), "Uranian," or homosexual, love is described as "Passing all partial loves, this one complete – the Mother love and sex-emotion blended.") We should remember not only that Carpenter's own mother died in 1881, as the poem was germinating (*MDD*, pp.105–6), but also the depth of his feelings for her, still clearly evident in his autobiography over thirty years later.
14. Rowbotham and Weeks, p.111.
15. *The Intermediate Sex: A Study of Some Transitional Types of Men and Women* (1908; rpt. Allen & Unwin, 1921), p.61. Further references are incorporated into the text.
16. Carpenter encouraged C.R. Ashbee's Guild of Handicraft from the beginning and visited the Guild in its Chipping Campden years. See Alan Crawford, *C.R. Ashbee, Architect, Designer and Romantic Socialist* (London: Yale U.P., 1985).
17. Whitman, "Democratic Vistas," quoted in *IS*, p.76.
18. Valentine Cunningham, "Sex and the single Victorian," *Sunday Times* [London], 23 Nov. 1980, p.45 (a review of Tsuzuki).
19. *The Bhagavad Gita*, trans. Juan Marasco (Harmondsworth: Penguin, 1962), p.95.
20. *From Adam's Peak to Elephanta: Sketches in Ceylon and India* (1892; rpt. London:

Swan Sonnenschein, 1910), p.262.

21. Keith Nield, "Edward Carpenter" in Joyce Bellamy and John Saville, ed., *Dictionary of Labour Biography, Vol. 2* (London: Macmillan, 1974), p.89.

22. Beith, p.79.

23. For a symptomatic example of the way political opponents associated Socialism and radical sexual ideas, see "Socialism and Sex Relations," *Spectator*, 19 Oct. 1907, pp.558–9, and the letters in response, *Spectator*, 26 Oct. 1907, p.608.

24. Eagleton, cited in note 7, and Dilip Kumar Barua, "The Life and Work of Edward Carpenter in the Light of Intellectual, Religious, Political and Literary Movements of the latter half of the Nineteenth Century," Diss. Sheffield 1966.

25. Edward Carpenter, *Selected Writings, Vol. 1: Sex*, ed. David Fernbach and Noel Greig (London: G.M.P., 1984) and *Towards Democracy* (London: G.M.P., 1985).

26. See, for example, Grover Smith, *The Waste Land* (London: Unwin, 1983), pp.104–6, and Tony Brown, "Edward Carpenter and *The Waste Land*," *Review of English Studies*, NS 34 (1983), 312–15.

27. Sassoon corresponded with Carpenter before and during the War and visited Millthorpe. See Tsuzuki, pp.147–8, 175–6. See also Martin Taylor, ed., *Lads: Love Poetry of the Trenches* (London: Constable, 1989), pp.45–6.

28. Linda Dalrymple Henderson, "Mysticism as 'The Tie That Binds': The Case of Edward Carpenter and Modernism," *Art Journal* [New York], 46 (1987), pp.29–37. Emile Delavenay, pp.154ff., argues that Carpenter's view of the individual ego in relation to the "World-Self" leads him to a new concept of personality, which may have contributed to the portrayal of consciousness as fluid and dynamic which we find in Lawrence and other Modern novelists. Ian F.A. Ball, *The Critic as Scientist: The Modernist Poetics of Ezra Pound* (London: Methuen, 1981), Ch. 5, sees *AC* as a key text in propagating assumptions of "tradition" and racial memory embodied as "gods," which we find in Pound.

29. Raymond Williams, "The little green book," *Guardian*, 20 Nov. 1980, p.18 (a review of Tsuzuki).

Edward Carpenter:
The Uses of Utopia

"There is another world – it is this one."[1]

It is all too easy to write about Edward Carpenter as a pious act of recuperation. His was a literary reputation which peaked modestly and decayed fast. It lasted not much more than thirty years. As a result he makes a perfect target for those who may wish to explore the antiquarian by-ways of literary criticism and rehabilitation. At the same time, his prolonged connection with what might be seen as the heroic phase of the British labour movement – the period between about 1880 and 1924 – remained obscure even to many of his contemporaries, and certainly to subsequent analysts. Moreover, Carpenter's philosophical writings lay in the peculiarly British tradition of Carlyle and Ruskin – that is, less an analytical or disciplined engagement with contemporary work in a particular field, and more an assertion of a critical view of the present and of hopes for a better and freer future. A master of the unfalsifiable proposition, Carpenter's prose writing, like his poetry, was an invitation to his readers to embrace his own view of the world and the possibility of its improvement. His was a kind of writing which can make a modern reader uneasy in ways that some of Carpenter's own contemporaries shared.

The extraordinary range of his interests over some forty years of writing compounds this unease: vegetarianism, sex-reform, anti-vivisectionism, pantheism, economic organisation, socialism, anarchism, Marxism, biological theory, music, poetry and so on. This range, and, until recently, the sheer unfamiliarity of this grouping of concerns, makes Carpenter elusive as an object of recuperation. The puzzle which he presented to his contemporaries, though in some cases it did not delay them very long, remains a problem for present-day observers. Locating Carpenter, without editing away the contradictions and difficulties inherent in his work and life, is an exceedingly difficult task. It is certainly not one which this article will attempt. But reducing him by some selective and extraneous principle of "relevance" – this is all too easy.

For example, in his survey of *Socialism in England* in 1890, Sidney Webb referred (briefly) to Edward Carpenter and the Sheffield Socialists, a society which Carpenter had helped to found in 1886. With characteristic flatness of tone, Webb described their position as a kind of "Ruskinian Socialism ... not free from influences akin to those emanating from Thoreau on the one hand, and from Tolstoi on the other." Nevertheless, he continued, "The duties of citizenship are not neglected, and here a second socialist was elected on the School Board in 1889."[2] As far as Webb was concerned, while Carpenter's head might be in the clouds, or in the woods of distant Concord, his feet were planted, for all the world a Fabian, on the Town Hall steps. Webb's flat, half-comprehending account unintentionally captured something of the reality of Carpenter's position – if only by a caricature of its extremes. Engaged from around 1882 in the reforming activities of socialists, Carpenter also had a wider context. That part of his life and work visible to Webb in 1890 had its counterpart in his poetry and theoretical interests as well as in his extensive reputation in the labour movement generally, especially outside London. Only partly, in his role of social reformer, did Carpenter occupy a finite position in the Fabian political schema, and, seeing only a fraction of the world, Sidney Webb disposed of Carpenter in a couple of paragraphs. Bernard Shaw achieved the same effect more quickly in his life-long reference to Carpenter as the "Noble Savage" – a hostile judgement on the allegedly simple-minded "back-to-nature" tendencies of Carpenter's rural retreat in Derbyshire. William Morris, as might be expected, was kinder. But, in the main, important figures in the labour movement saw Carpenter as something of a crank: a vegetarian and a principled tee-totaller; a sandal-wearing devotee of the doctrine of three acres and a cow, a man who, struggling to shake off the culture of his class, set himself up comfortably in a therapeutically secluded cottage between Sheffield and Chesterfield, from which he contemplated the horrors of a world he never really touched nor which, after his "retreat," ever touched him. With characteristic negligence and contempt, it was George Orwell who offered, in anger, the last rites to this alleged tendency when he wrote of the "magnetic force" with which the mere words "Socialism and Communism draw towards them ... every fruit-juice drinker, nudist, sandal-wearer, sex-maniac, Quaker, "Nature cure" quack, pacifist, and feminist in England."[3] Orwell's list is symptomatic and self-revealing.

It is true that Carpenter's cottage, "Millthorpe" in the Cordwell valley, became a popular place of Sunday "pilgrimage" for the West Riding labour movement, as well as for sex and diet and dress reformers, for spiritualists, for "ethicists," and for adherents of the Labour Churches. His voluminous correspondence reveals many approaches made to him concerned with securing his support for nudism as a way of life, for woodcraft as a means of making "earth-contact," and for the setting up of anarchist and other communities devoted to the pursuit and practice of the good life. Carpenter, too, more than most, was victimised by single-minded enthusiasts and proselytisers, whose anodyne solutions for the problems of modern life lay, to the exclusion of all else, in a single dietary regime or sexual predilection.[4]

Even in death, Carpenter's reputation was not well served by his principal obituarists, especially in a volume of commemorative essays edited by his friend and executor, Gilbert Beith, in 1931.[5] Empty of analysis, the 28 essays in the main trivialise their subject in unrestrained panegyrics on Carpenter's character, or in a sentimentalism so excessive as to invite comparative consideration of Carpenter's influence and Jesus Christ's. One of the few attempts in them to present Carpenter as something other than a saintly socialist poet is a cavilling piece by Henry S. Salt, who merely vented his mild animus against a friend of 40 years.[6]

If Carpenter has suffered, both during his lifetime and posthumously, at the hands of his friends and admirers, until very recent times he has done no better among historians. Henry Pelling took the view that Carpenter's work was "too subtle, amorphous and intangible for the ordinary mind to grasp";[7] G. D. H. Cole that he was of little importance though well-known;[8] and even E.P. Thompson tends to confine himself to stressing the difference between Carpenter's retreat to "Millthorpe" in repudiation of the styles of thought and feeling of his class and the subsequent retreat of stockbrokers in flight from the social pressure of suburbia.[9] More recently, important work by Chushichi Tsuzuki, Sheila Rowbotham and Jeffrey Weeks,[10] in quite different ways, has done something to restore a balance. But Frederic Vanson's plea for a Carpenter revival shows no sign of fulfilment.[11] As a literary figure, Carpenter remains incorrigibly obscure, emerging only intermittently in studies of nineteenth-century literary culture, and only then as an example of a tendency or common response.

Even in his own day, Carpenter's literary work evoked only a small response in the literary press. Except for a couple of spectacularly hostile reviews, *Towards Democracy*, Carpenter's principal poetic work, was barely noticed at first. Published separately in four parts in the 20 years after 1883, and as a palpable imitation of Whitman's *Leaves of Grass*, it drew its admirers from a small circle of writers and critics in England at the turn of the century who were also receptive to Whitman. Havelock Ellis – although he subsequently revised his judgement – referred to it as "Whitman and water."[12] Such, then, is the case against Carpenter: that he was an eccentric, isolated figure on the fringes of the labour movement and the late-nineteenth-century literary scene, whose work was amorphous, intangible and therefore inconsequential, and whose life was devoted fundamentally, if not continuously, to the subsequently stereotyped pursuits of the wealthy progressive.

But Carpenter's books sold in thousands for more than a quarter of a century, and not just in the United Kingdom. *Towards Democracy*, for example, whose first part was written between 1881 and 1883, at first could find no publisher. Eventually Carpenter took it to John Heywood, a small printer in Manchester, offering to cover the costs himself. Heywood printed two editions before it was included in the list of T. Fisher Unwin in 1892. In turn, this arrangement lasted only three years, when the effects of the trials of Oscar Wilde were deeply felt in

Bloomsbury, and *Towards Democracy* was removed from the list. Unwin had also published a volume of Carpenter's essays on sex questions entitled *Love's Coming-of-Age*, but, hearing of a further pamphlet of Carpenter's in private circulation entitled "Homogenic Love," Unwin acted quickly. For the next seven or eight years, Carpenter was thrown back on a small labour press in Manchester, in which he had a small financial interest. *Towards Democracy* continued to sell slowly until 1902, when Swan Sonnenschein, conscious of the relative success of Carpenter's other work, took over its publication. By 1916, *Towards Democracy*, now complete in four parts, reached its sixteenth thousand. The thirtieth reprint of the complete edition appeared in 1926. Mitchell Kennerley published the first of four American editions in 1912, and it was translated, in whole or in part, into German, French, Italian, Russian and Japanese. Practically unnoticed by the literary press throughout this whole period, *Towards Democracy* eventually, slowly, found a considerable audience in the United Kingdom and overseas.

Fairly full details of the editions and translations of Carpenter's books, together with some sales figures for Britain up to 1916, can readily be found.[13] Two of his texts were re-issued, and occasionally noticed, as late as 1967. Outside Britain, Carpenter's books enjoyed greatest success in German translation. Of the seven which were published in German editions, *Love's Coming-of-Age* had a circulation which Carpenter himself described as phenomenal; and in 1912, its German translator, Karl Federn, wrote to him:

> The House of Wilhelm Borngräber Verlag Neues Leben – new but financially sound – wants to publish a 'fine edition' of 'Love's Coming-of-Age' ... fourty [sic] thousand copies have been published and yet publishers think of a new edition. I do not think another modern English book has had a similar success in Germany.[14]

It seems probable that this book alone enjoyed an international circulation of at least a hundred thousand copies, possibly many more. Besides the German editions, it was issued in Britain sixteen times after 1896, three times in 1915 alone. In the USA it had seven editions, and single editions in France, Italy, Sweden and Holland. 1915 and 1916 were Carpenter's best years, some ten of his books being re-issued or newly-published in those years, together with the publication of a large study of his work.[15] Publishers around this period evidently had considerable confidence in Carpenter's name and reputation when it came to selling books; and, if only for a short, intense period, it can hardly be questioned that Carpenter's popularity as a writer was extensive.

The disjunction between Carpenter's popularity as an author, and the often severe, sometimes even contemptuous judgement of literary and political contemporaries as well as later commentators, is worth a little exploration. The question must at least be put as to whether the

disjunction is somehow inherent in the *quality* of Carpenter's work —
i.e. insufficient to withstand the test of time and generation — or
whether it is a function of the *procedures* and assumptions of literary
criticism, the history of ideas, and, perhaps most important of all in this
case, British labour history. Each of them in certain modes is driven by
a tissue of unargued assumption — what R. G. Collingwood referred to
as "absolute pre-suppositions." A Leavisite focus on the text and its
interior, largely at the expense of other forms of analysis, might be
adduced as an example.[16] Another lies in the history of ideas understood as tracing the development of important theories of all kinds via a
close consideration of their internal structure and their relationships of
"influence" with other systems and theories, usually of the first order.

Fifty years ago, Karl Mannheim designated this kind of study
"immanent intellectual history": the concentration upon ideas articulated at the highest levels of abstraction and considered largely in
isolation from the social and other conditions of their formation. By
this method the explanation of change remains at the level of ideas. "...
the fact seems to be perfectly clear," Mannheim wrote in the 1930s,
"that the ... method of intellectual history which was oriented towards
the *a priori* conception that changes in ideas were to be understood at
the level of ideas, blocked recognition of the penetration of the social
process into the intellectual sphere."[17] The practice, arguably, resulted
in two further losses to historical analysis. This sort of intellectual
history tends, in its own assumption and pre-supposition, to put a
premium on the *quality* and *coherence* of systems of ideas, as well as on
their longevity, their ability to influence other intellectuals across time
and place. As a result, systems of thought and bodies of writing which
do not meet certain criteria of quality and influence are pressed to the
margin of the account, even where their popularity, their apparent
"appropriateness" to a particular historical context, is acknowledged.
Yet even bad ideas have some sort of place in legitimate historical
analysis — the history of Nazism would not be much without such a
recognition. But it is hard to see how conventional intellectual history
could cope with it adequately, relying, at least in part, on what Talcott
Parsons referred to as

> some kind of idealist metaphysics of the sort from which it has so
> often been inferred that ideas must arise through some process
> of "immaculate conception" unsullied by social and economic
> forces, or that they influence action by some automatic and
> mysterious process of self-realization or "emanation" without
> relation to other elements of the social system.[18]

More than twenty years ago, writing "On the Limits of Historical
Explanation," Quentin Skinner, too, attacked the standing of that sort
of historical work which he characterised as the study of "linked
abstractions." "The mistake," he asserted, "lies in supposing that the
history of an idea or event can ever be adequately written in terms of its

leading actors ... [and] in failing to concede that the qualities of intelligence and presentation which make a writer the best illustration in a philosophical picture will make him in an historical picture the worst. ..." Intensive social research and "... countless minor social and intellectual biographies ... would ... at least promise histories of real entities and activities. ..."[19]

The implications of all this for a consideration of the work of Edward Carpenter should by now be obvious. There is no need of his recuperation, of the restoration of his literary reputation by an assertion of the *quality* of his writing, or a revelation of its *coherence* as an *oeuvre*. Nor, from the point of view of historical analysis, is there any need to defend him from literary critics and others who, *de haut en bas*, handed down contemptuous or dismissive judgement upon him.

There is no need, as Edward Thompson perfectly expresses it in another context, to rescue him from the condescension of posterity. The need, amongst others, is to explain his popularity in his own generation, and, in so doing, perhaps to reveal unexpected dimensions of the labour and progressive movements of the late-Victorian and Edwardian periods. But the historiography of those movements, as it developed in the twenty years after 1945, perhaps offers still another obstacle to this project, an obstacle once again inscribed in the procedures and presuppositions of this scholarly field. There is no space here to develop this argument fully, though the (no doubt tendentious) comments which follow might not be thought entirely inappropriate to the argument. They will be developed more fully elsewhere.

No full account exists of the development of British labour history as a field of study. This does not so much reflect a lack of self-consciousness peculiar to this kind of historical work alone, but a neglect of critical historiography, of the history of history-writing, much more widely throughout the discipline. Few undergraduate courses in history include a critical account of the development of the subject, such as would be compulsory in sociology or in social anthropology. In common with other historical practices, labour history has devoted itself over the years, and with an astonishing rigour and discipline, to accumulative, empirical procedures. The output of the field, for some thirty years or more, has been exceptional, reconstructing, *via* biography and studies of particular institutions, the interior of a complex labour movement over time which more conventional bodies of history writing have tended to neglect or systematically to ignore. At first, the most important of these was a highly developed *economic* historiography, whose principal focus of interest and published output centred on the question of industrialisation and its consequences – that is, precisely on the period and the economic conditions pertinent to the formation of modern labour movements. Yet in this historiography, the history of labour was neglected as a legitimate object of scholarly enquiry. Labour tended to be classified as merely one of a number of factors of production, all relevant to the analysis of the industrialising process, in the manner of the neo-classical theories on which, in the main, economic historians depended. Labour history, by contrast, was to emphasise the human and political side of the development of labour movements, their historical complexity, authenticity and legitimacy as an object of study. This was a project which went far beyond an analysis iron-bound by the assumptions of conventional economics. But it was not without its own organising ideas, and some of these at least can be read off from labour history writing of the last decades, others inferred from moments of decisive shift in the field. Two might usefully be identified here.

The first is reflected in the intense concentration of labour historiography on leaders and on organisation. Biographies of individual leaders, of discrete labour organisations – parties, fractions, trade unions – and of symptomatic or spectacular events in the history of British labour, make up the principal focus of writing in the early years. In the main, wider questions of economic and social development were left to others to address. As a consequence, a dense labour historiography developed, focussed on the movement and its principal activists at the expense of the study of the *detailed* conditions of its formation, the wider context of power, politics, state, economy and social formation. Moreover, the early concentration on leadership and organisation in the labour movement in Britain strongly suggests the presence, perhaps subterranean, of a tissue of "centralist," not necessarily Leninist, assumptions. It suggests a preference for elements of labour organisation and development which were anti-capitalist, tightly organised, with a clear picture of a socialist future, and a sense of agency, revolutionary or not. Prolonged arguments about the degree to which William Morris might or might not be considered a Marxist are symptomatic here;[20] as is the recurrent counterfactual of labour historiography: why did the English working-class movement fail to generate an indigenous revolutionary tradition? In general, however, it should be noted here that the development of labour history was hardly congenial to a sympathetic re-consideration of the work of Edward Carpenter. He was no leader of an organising kind; his work was something less than "scientific" and, at its worst, plainly "utopian"; his critique of capitalism was generalised, moral, firmly in the romantic tradition and, consequently, might tend towards a conservative nostalgia for a pre-capitalist past in the manner of Thomas Carlyle. Labour history, in its conventional notation, makes a poor point of departure for the study of Carpenter.

A point of decisive shift in the preoccupations of labour history came in 1963 with the publication of Edward Thompson's *The Making of the English Working Class*. This text has been the object of so much commentary in the years since that there is no need here to rehearse its main arguments – save for two that might be pertinent. First, the book's often neglected sub-theme is an excoriating attack upon the conventional economic history of the post-war period for some of the reasons outlined above as well as for much else, including its inherent procedural and methodological bias in favour of the social and economic *status quo*. *The Making of the English Working Class* is still probably the finest polemic against the genre of economic history in England which the original turn towards labour history has produced. Second, the book self-consciously turned its face against studies of leaders and of labour organisations. Thompson sought to reconstruct the self-making of a whole class in the period of early industrialisation, a whole element of a new social formation. It was an ambition which trespassed confidently outside the hitherto existing limits of labour historiography and, in so doing, Thompson produced a text which proved pivotal in the modern development of social history in England. In dealing with the poor and the exploited, the neglected and the forgotten, Thompson was able to restore to a place of significance the masses of mankind who made up the class, and to rescue from *ex post* condescension and neglect all sorts of defeated movements, even the followers of Joanna Southcott. In Thompson's account the victory, and therefore the historical interest, did not always go to the big battalions. He transformed the intellectual environment in a way which made it infinitely more congenial for a study of Edward Carpenter, and others, once significant, who failed some arbitrary test of time or teleological relevance. It is no accident that much of the scholarly writing on Carpenter dates from the middle of the 1960s.

But a congenial environment is not an explanatory or analytical practice. It does not in itself address the central problem of Carpenter's intense, but brief, popularity as an author and his subsequent, relatively sudden neglect. It does not offer even the beginnings of an explanation of the hiatus in the public prominence of the tissue of moral and political concerns which motivated Carpenter in the early part of this century, and which returned in a somewhat different form in the mid-1960s. Here is not the place to develop this connection, except to say that the "moment" of 1968 remains largely unreflected, underanalysed, even sentimentalised. But no advanced capitalist country at that time was free of movements of individual liberation, of release from capitalist work disciplines, from sexual stereotypes and suffocating moralities, and from the social and political disciplines inherent in war and state violence. The modes of self-assertion of these movements were seldom "political" in a party sense or formally revolutionary in intent, though this was present too. Rather the assertion took the forms of mysticism, of sexual liberationism, of extreme democracy in acknowledgment of the rights of others, hatred of the state, of war, and of the ideologically and morally chloroformed world of the Cold War and the 1950s. At the time it seemed, to all sides, no less subversive for that, probably more so. But, strikingly, in different dress, some of the principal concerns of 1968 were remarkably similar to the tissue of Carpenter's concerns fifty years before and, by extension, the concerns of his now anonymous readership. Subversive? Not conservative nostalgia for a non-existent pre-capitalist idyll? Not inconsequential utopianism with no purchase on the real world? Not diversionary dreaming in the path of the political struggle? Tell it to the Marines.

In both contexts, what tends to be underestimated is the strength and density of the specific historical form of cultural and political hegemony, as well as its capacity for self-renewal, self-defence and regular adjustment. The great liberal-capitalist consensus of Victorian and Edwardian Britain was not the product of some conspiratorial committee of public safety, determined at all costs to preserve the authority of the state, and the profitability of industry and empire. Rather it was inscribed in institutions, state and other – the Home Office, the factory, the Established Church, and so on. It suffused the social formation and its discourses as well as the formal political structures. It served to create and to re-create conditions in which the relations of production and power themselves could reproduce,[21] a vast obstacle to fundamental change, curtailing the ability even to think about it creatively at the same time as suppressing by force movements publicly committed to it.[22] An effective cultural hegemony imposes silences; inhibits the thinking of alternatives; renders opposition intellectually difficult; mobilises an unco-ordinated tissue of institutions and intellectual positions of great power – established religion, education, nationalism, imperialism, communications, official culture, polite society, sexual stereotypes, acceptable behaviour, and even high culture. Breaking into the cultural hegemony, and breaking its imposed silences, is not a matter of simple organisation, political or otherwise.[23] And, in any case, behind all, lies the power of the state.

In the face of such power, some simple, not to say facile, analytical dichotomies seem inadequate. The easy couplets – utopian/scientific; idealist/materialist; organised/unorganised – deployed in reference to the life and work of a single man, let alone a social movement, do not, even confidently ascribed, define value or purpose once for all. They tend, used as judgements, to by-pass the question of *context*, the "penetration," as Mannheim expressed it, "of the social process into the intellectual sphere." They sometimes miss the point. At any rate, I think they do in the case of Edward Carpenter.

This is not to argue, however, for a revival of Carpenter's work, or to assert its relevance in our own times, or even to claim that its qualities have been unjustly neglected by posterity. All this may well be true, but the argument of this paper so far has not been concerned with the question of Carpenter's *quality* as a writer and a poet. On the contrary, it has been concerned with two quite different matters. The first has been to dispose of those easy dismissals of Carpenter's historical significance which have been based simply in a critical reading of his work. The second is to invite attention to the question of *context*, by suggesting that the *form* of his writing – its utopianism, its mysticism, even its "diffuseness" – may result from something other than an implied intellectual dereliction or vacuity on his part. It may have much more to do with the power, density, and historical specificity of the cultural hegemony which he and his contemporaries confronted. It is in this context that may be found the reasons for Carpenter's considerable but contingent popularity as a political figure and temporary success as a writer and a poet.

This emphasis on context is crucial to the argument. It permits at least the suggestion that "utopianism" may have its uses after all, and in certain historical conjunctures these might not be negligible. The construction of a counter to an intellectual and cultural hegemony as severe as that in Carpenter's period is not a simple matter of taking down and dusting off some blueprint for socialist or other opposition. It is not a question of devising plans for alternative social and economic organisation and of, single-mindedly, applying some routines of political action and agency.

Each historical conjuncture has its own specificity, each stable hegemony its own particularity. Arguably, it may only be challenged in specific and particular ways, sometimes in conjunctures where the state, the mechanism of economic distribution, and the cultural forms of class domination evince no signs of crisis. Rather they seem fluidly and mutually to reproduce the conditions of their own survival. It was in a conjuncture such as this that Gramsci wrote his *Prison Notebooks*. A conjuncture profoundly different but just as difficult drew Edward Carpenter, and it must be supposed, thousands of his readers, towards mysticism and utopianism as the means to express a tissue of alternative values. To subject his work to a close, critical *literary* reading, without attention to its context, is to miss the point that this paper is seeking to make. To seek to evaluate his work as a contribution to the organisation of labour will result in failure and/or condescension.

Socialist and anarchist by turns, recluse and public lecturer, utopian and provider of finance for socialist journals,[24] dreamer and down-to-earth commentator on the need for birth control, mystic and public supporter of the Walsall Anarchists in their disgraceful trial of 1892,[25] aesthete and organiser of a provincial socialist society, Carpenter's contradictions seem endless. Certainly they make him hard to classify in the manner of scholarly protocol. Sometimes, too, it should be noted that they may well have conduced to his appropriation into styles of thought and action of which, had he lived long enough, he could scarcely have approved. This is particularly true in German translation, where some of his books and articles were made to converge to "*völkisch*" structures of thought and feeling.[26]

However, in general terms, it has to be stressed that a recognition of the diffuseness and utopian character of Carpenter's work does not lead inexorably to the conclusion that it was therefore inconsequential. So what did it offer in its own time, and to whom? Gestures of gratitude to Carpenter in the autobiographies of better known figures are common enough – Forster, Lawrence, Sassoon and others all, in different ways, acknowledged a debt to Carpenter.[27] Recent scholarly work has revealed further sides of Carpenter's personal influence in the lives of Rupert Brooke, C.R. Ashbee, and Hugh Dalton.[28] His *mass* appeal, however, inevitably remains obscure, his popular readership anonymous, hidden from biographer and historian alike. What is certain is that it was very large over a period of twenty or thirty years, that it extended considerably beyond the frontiers of the labour movement in Britain, and that it was built around a group of issues which were not, always and everywhere, consistent with contemporary socialism, in the then conventional notation of the term.

The time has come to give some account of these issues and their resonance in the period between 1890 and the end of the First World War. No full, narrative account of the development of Carpenter's ideas and writing can be attempted here. In any case, other contributions to this volume deal in detail with various important aspects of Carpenter's *oeuvre*. What is attempted here is not so much a reconstruction of Carpenter's intellectual development, an attempt to rediscover the red thread of coherence which inhabits his work, and which commentators so far have found difficult to locate. Rather, the purpose is briefly to reveal the significance of a number of recurrent themes in terms of the broader *context*, of the seemingly inert structures of power and culture in late-Victorian and Edwardian Britain.

Carpenter's subjects as a public lecturer give a useful guide to these themes. For more than fifteen years after 1890 Carpenter lectured as many as a dozen times a month. He was in constant demand as a speaker to trades union branches, socialist societies, labour churches, ethical societies, Independent Labour Party groups, Fabian societies, Humanitarian League meetings and so on. His lectures varied enormously, ranging from matters concerning small-holdings and allotments; the possibility of a "non-governmental society," that is, a social formation without a state; the humanising of work, and the end of alienation from its product; the need to dismantle the principle of private ownership, especially of the means of production for use; attacks upon the free market and its social relations; on the stultifying manners and morality of "respectable" bourgeois society, as well as calls to free human sexuality from the corrupting restraints which it imposed; accounts of industrial pollution and the brutal relations of the factory; the futility of modern science, and a demand for an end to vivisection as a scientific practice; as well as extensive attempts to define his notion of democracy.[29]

Seldom did his argument or analysis refer in detail to matters of *agency*, to methods by which these desirable goals might be achieved. Almost never did he address the question of social and political power. References to social evolution – his theory of "exfoliation" – and general hopes for the future inscribed in a labour movement seen as "a great river fed by many streams"[30] had to do service in this respect. It is this attenuated concern for agency which, more than anything else, places Carpenter's work in a utopian frame. What he offered, in the main, was an excoriating critique of the present and a dream of a better future, without too much concern for how the journey from here to there might be made. In some respects, Carpenter's was a cast of mind well described by L. Kolakowski in his essay, "The Concept of the Left":

> By utopia I mean a state of social consciousness, a mental counter-part to the social movement striving for radical change in the world – a counterpart itself inadequate to these changes and merely reflecting them in an idealized and mystified form. It endows the real movement with the sense of realizing an ideal born in the realm of pure spirit and not in current historical experience. Utopia is, therefore, a mystified consciousness of an actual historical tendency. As long as this tendency lives only a clandestine existence without finding expression in mass social movements, it gives birth to utopias in the narrower sense, that is, to individually constructed models of the world, as it *should* be. But when utopia becomes actual social consciousness, invading the consciousness of a mass movement and constituting one of its essential driving forces, utopia, then, crosses over from the domain of theoretical and moral thought into the field of practical thinking, and itself begins to govern human action.[31]

Carpenter's "utopia" focussed on some very practical questions: the environment, and capitalism's negligent appropriation of nature; on ugliness, pollution and the brutalising quality of industrial work; on social fragmentation and alienation; on loss of community; on the philistinism of bourgeois cultural life; on the crass materialism of his own society as well as on its suffocating sexual codes and their invasion of the proper liberty of individuals. In short, it focussed on a raft of issues many of which have been re-politicised in our own times. The degree to which it meshed with the "consciousness of a mass move-ment" may be open to question, though the organisations which invited Carpenter to lecture must be some guide here. Even the contempt of some historians and others for the philosophical underpinnings of Carpenter's system in this context requires mitigation. The issues he identified and stressed throughout his life plainly contributed to the contemporary critique of capitalism. In Carpenter, the romantic tradition emphatically did not lead to reaction and nostalgia, to a self-serving, escapist utopian dream. Rather, in his hands, that tradition was made to support a utopian socialism, with strong popular under-tones, corresponding closely to that set of meanings which, in English labour history, is referred to as "ethical socialism." Moreover, besides *Towards Democracy*, Carpenter fed into this movement a stream of books directly on social questions. *England's Ideal* was the first in 1887, quickly followed by *Civilisation: its Cause and Cure* in 1889. *Love's Coming-of-Age: A Series of Papers on the Relations of the Sexes* appeared in 1896; *Prisons, Police and Punishment* in 1905. *The Healing of Nations* was published in 1915 and *Towards Industrial Freedom* two years later.

In all of them, the texture of the romantic-idealist tradition is plain enough, with attacks upon "social atomisation," on the "cash nexus" of capitalist social relations,[32] and on machine production. But Carpenter transformed the tradition, introducing notions of "democracy" in place of Coleridge's and Carlyle's calls for responsible, but very different, leadership. Not for him a future society guided by an "aristocracy" of talent and social responsibility, a "clerisy" of philosopher-kings recruited to pursue the higher interests of the nation, or to combat the excesses of the "commercial spirit." Rather Carpenter argued that the abiding virtues which should inform a new society were to be found in the "common-sense" and integrity of the daily life of the people. Only accept these and

> Government and laws and police then fall into their places – the earth gives her own laws; Democracy just begins to open her eyes ... and the rabble of unfaithful bishops, priests, generals, land-lords, capitalists, lawyers, kings, queens, patronizers and polite idlers goes scuttling down into general oblivion.
> Faithfulness emerges, self-reliance, self-help, passionate com-radeship.[33]

The working class possessed the potential for its own emancipation. It was commonly let down by its leaders, and the schismatic inclination of socialist organisations sometimes made Carpenter despair, especially late in his life,[34] but he never doubted the self-emancipatory potential of the class.[35] This belief in the popular-democratic possi-bilities inherent in the autonomous culture and commonsense of the working class meant that Carpenter never subsided into the eccentric metaphysics of the romantic-idealist position. Loyal, throughout his life, to a socialist's belief in improvement and change, he remained active in support of socialist politics and progressive causes. His hatred of his own world and its social relations, the "kid-gloved, rotten-breathed paralytic world, with miserable antics mimicking the appearance of life,"[36] fuelled the desire for fundamental change. He did not retreat into a life of elevated contemplation, the destination of romantics coruscatingly described by Byron in *Don Juan*:

> He, Juan (and not Wordsworth) so pursued
> His self-communion with his own high soul,
> Until his mighty heart, in its great mood,
> Had mitigated part, though not the whole
> Of its disease: he did the best he could
> With things not very subject to control,
> And turn'd without perceiving his condition,
> Like Coleridge, into a metaphysician. (First Canto)

Mystical and utopian perhaps, religious and diffuse possibly, Carpenter's categories – nature, democracy, intuition, ideal – were all deployed in an oppositional way as an uncomfortable assertion that what was, was not necessary, let alone desirable, and that it could and should be different. It may well be the case that his pivotal conception – democracy – was cast in extra-rational terms, that it required a prior belief in the ultimate political efficacy of human spontaneity, in a profound, natural, intuitive "feeling" for a better future. All this stood in place of a thoroughgoing analysis of capitalist production and capitalist society, and of a close consideration of organisations adequate to their overthrow or transformation. But his conception was unremittingly hostile to the co-ordinates of his own society, its brutality, philistinism, exploitation, poverty, sexual neuroses, and choking respectability. It caused him to trespass into areas of work and writing which were unwelcome in established churches and government departments – writing on homosexuality or contraception, for example, or open support for anarchist groups and publications.

Carpenter's vision of a future democracy offered, it may be supposed to thousands, a powerful, ethical, humane critique of the particular conditions of their own world. This concrete particularity alone separates Carpenter's contribution from that of other-worldly dreamers and visionaries. His utopia was firmly fixed in an aesthetic, moral, intellectual and hard-edged revulsion from the works of industrial capitalism around the turn of the century. "England!" bellowed Carpenter's democracy to all who would hear, "for good or evil it is useless to attempt to conceal yourself – I know you too well ... For who better than I should know your rottenness, your self-deceit, your delusion, your hideous grinning corpse-chattering death-in-life business at top? (and who better than I the wonderful hidden sources of your strength beneath?)."[37]

Carpenter's was a politics for a bad conjuncture: unprogrammatic, idealist, sometimes high-flown. But it resonated among his contemporary readers and lecture audiences, sometimes upwards of two thousand strong, in many industrial towns and cities in Scotland and the North of England. He may not have been the organic intellectual of a class struggling for political consciousness, and he may not even have met Kolakowski's severe definition of an "adequate" utopian, organically linked to an actual mass movement. But for thirty years, in a dozen different ways, he illuminated for a mass audience the terrible discontinuities between the structural requirements of capitalism and the world of human needs. Carpenter's "other world" was not some alternative ideal of mental or ecstatic harmony. It was this one, transformed and humanised.

KEITH NIELD

NOTES

1. Paul Eluard, quoted in Peter de Francia, *Léger's 'The Great Parade'*, 1969.
2. Sidney Webb, *Socialism in England* (London: Swan Sonnenschein, 1890), p.42.
3. George Orwell, *The Road to Wigan Pier* (1937; Harmondsworth: Penguin, 1967), p.152.
4. For example, Carpenter was approached repeatedly in 1891 and 1892 by C.E.G. Crawford, a pushy representative of an implausible organisation: the Fellowship of the Naked Trust. See MSS 386, Carpenter Collection, Sheffield City Library.
5. Gilbert Beith, ed., *Edward Carpenter: In Appreciation* (London: Allen & Unwin, 1931).
6. His piece was entitled "A Sage at Close Quarters," a title whose obvious irony reflected its content.
7. Henry Pelling, *The Origins of the Labour Party, 1880–1900* (1954; Oxford: Clarendon P., 1965), p.143.
8. G.D.H. Cole, *A History of Socialist Thought, Vol. 4: Communism and Social Democracy, 1914–1931* (1958; London: Macmillan, 1962).
9. E.P. Thompson, *William Morris: From Romantic to Revolutionary* (1955; London: Merlin P., 1977), pp.289–90.
10. See Chushichi Tsuzuki, *Edward Carpenter, 1844–1929: Prophet of Human Fellowship* (Cambridge: Cambridge U.P., 1980); Sheila Rowbotham and Jeffrey Weeks, *Socialism and the New Life: The Personal and Sexual Politics of Edward Carpenter and Havelock Ellis* (London: Pluto P., 1977); Emile Delavenay, *D.H. Lawrence and Edward Carpenter: A Study in Edwardian Transition* (London: Heinemann, 1971); Stanley Pierson, "Edward Carpenter, Prophet of a Socialist Millenium," *Victorian Studies*, 13 (1969–70), 301–18.
11. Frederic Vanson, "Edward Carpenter: The English Whitman," *Contemporary Review*, 193 (1958), 314.
12. Havelock Ellis, *My Life* (London: Heinemann, 1940), p.163.
13. See lists at the back of Edward Carpenter, *My Days and Dreams* (London: Allen & Unwin, 1916), extended in the 1918 edition, and *A Bibliography of Edward Carpenter* (Sheffield: Sheffield City Libraries, 1949).
14. Karl Federn, Letter to Edward Carpenter, Feb. 1912, MS. 270.17, Carp. Coll.
15. Edward Lewis, *Edward Carpenter: An Exposition and an Appreciation* (London: Methuen, 1915).
16. An adequate critique of the Leavisite method lies beyond my competence but see Raymond Williams, *Culture and Society 1780–1950* (London: Chatto & Windus, 1958) for a self-conscious departure from it.
17. Karl Mannheim, *Ideology and Utopia: An Introduction to the Sociology of Knowledge* (1936; London: Routledge, 1960), p.240.
18. Talcott Parsons, "The Role of Ideas in Social Action," *Essays in Sociological Theory* (1949; London: Collier-Macmillan, 1964), p.19.
19. Quentin Skinner, "The Limits of Historical Explanations," *Philosophy*, 41 (1966), 213, 215.
20. See "Postscript: 1976" in E.P. Thompson, op. cit.
21. Quintin Hoare and Geoffrey Nowell Smith, ed. and trans., *Selections from the Prison Notebooks of Antonio Gramsci* (London: Lawrence & Wishart, 1971) is the pivotal theoretical text here.
22. See Louis Althusser, "Ideology and Ideological State Apparatuses (Notes towards an Investigation)," *Lenin and Philosophy and other essays* (London: NLB, 1971), pp.121–73.
23. Gramsci, op. cit., and "Introduction" to Section I, *Problems of History and Culture*.
24. Carpenter provided £300 of the original capital which established *Justice*.
25. See Keith Nield, "Edward Carpenter (1844–1929), Socialist and Author," *Dictionary of Labour Biography, Vol. 2*, ed. Joyce M. Bellamy and John Saville (London: Macmillan, 1974), pp.85–92.
26. Symptomatic of this unexpected connection is the fact that some of Carpenter's

work was published in Germany by Eugen Diederichs, editor of *Die Tat*, and a leading protagonist publisher of the *völkisch* movement. What can be made of Carpenter's favourable quotation from Otto Weininger as the masthead of his *The Intermediate Sex* (1908) is difficult to judge. It is striking that Weininger was selected for particular attack by Günther Grass in *Dog Years*, as the author of a text incipiently fascist in style and symptomatically so in content.

27. See Delavenay, op. cit.; E.M. Forster, "Edward Carpenter," *Two Cheers for Democracy* (1951; London: Arnold, 1972), pp.205–7, and MSS 271, Correspondence, and MSS 351–86, Supplementary MSS, Carp. Coll.
28. See Paul Delany, *The Neo-Pagans: Friendship and Love in the Rupert Brooke Circle* (London: Macmillan, 1987); Alan Crawford, *C.R. Ashbee: Architect, Designer and Romantic Socialist* (London: Yale U.P., 1985); Ben Pimlott, *Hugh Dalton* (London: Cape, 1985).
29. Fragments of Carpenter's lecture notes, together with lists of places in which they were given, and newspaper notices where they attracted very large audiences, survive in Sheffield City Library's Carpenter Collection, *passim*, by date.
30. *MDD*, p.38.
31. L. Kolakowski, "The Concept of the Left," *Marxism and Beyond* (London: Paladin, 1971), pp.90–1. See also Zygmunt Bauman, *Socialism: The Active Utopia* (London: Allen & Unwin, 1976).
32. "Does It Pay?" he asked, in a widely reprinted article from *To-day*, Oct. 1886, pp.141–5.
33. *Towards Democracy*, Part I, Section XL.
34. Writing to his friend George Clemas in 1927, two years before his death, Carpenter said, "What is to be done? Though I have written on the Cure of Civilisation generally I grieve to say I have no panacea for the present mass of human ills." MS. 390.65, Carp. Coll.
35. He never entertained the possibility, as recent historians have shown, that divisions within the working class itself provided precisely the arena in which the cultural hegemony might work. This is the "labour aristocracy" thesis, in which the increasing divisions of labour required by developing capitalism at the same time fragment the class, differentiating it in terms of skill, sex, income and consumption, and laying elements of it open to "negotiated" forms of its own incorporation.
36. *Towards Democracy*, Part I, Section XV.
37. Ibid.

Identified with the One: Edward Carpenter, Henry Salt and the Ethical Socialist Philosophy of Science

E.M. Forster, who sadly but confidently predicted that Carpenter's reputation would decline to the point of invisibility, would have been surprised and delighted to see the current revival of interest in his friend's life and work.[1] There have been the two major studies by Rowbotham and Tsuzuki and the provocative if condescending earlier article by Pierson.[2] Carpenter is currently in print once more, as part of the Gay Men's Press project to produce new editions of selected works.

But this revaluation has been understandably selective, concentrating on his sexual politics, his vegetarianism and the Simple Life. The endpaper of the new anthology puts the matter thus:

> While directly involved in the labour movement, he also championed women's liberation and animal rights, and believed in a life close to nature. But above all, his socialist vision was inspired by the homogenic love of other men ...[3]

All this is true enough, but it neglects a systematic idealist philosophy which supported a critique of contemporary science and a distinctive epistemology.

Carpenter was not alone in advocating these views. To an extent, they were widespread in the ethical socialist movement of the 1880s and 1890s and articulated very clearly in the work and writing of Henry Salt. This study examines the philosophy the two men shared and shows how both a view of science and a programme of opinion-shaping were derived from it. The aim is to present a fuller view of Carpenter and to locate him within a climate of humanitarian opinion which has surprising resonances with some of today's concerns about the environment and the rights of animals.

I

Carpenter was not reticent about his philosophy or about the image of human nature derived from it. Works like *Civilisation: its Cause and Cure, Angels' Wings, The Art of Creation* and *Towards Democracy* itself presented an elaborate and totalising metaphysic which saw cohesion at the heart of the universe. Quite explicitly Carpenter refused to separate the human race from the rest of nature. Rather the whole universe was an expression of a purposive mystical entity, known variously as the Great Self, the Universal Ego or the World Soul.

Humanity's role in this scheme was both prodigal son and saviour: inside nature and yet at the same time capable of viewing it from the outside, human experience was to be the agency through which the connectedness of things was to be celebrated and the shattered wholeness of the cosmos to be re-integrated.

Human experience was a microcosm of the deep reality of things:

> ... there is in Man a Creative Thought-source continually in operation, which is shaping and giving form not only to his body, but largely to the world in which he lives. In fact, the houses, the gardens, the streets among which we live, the clothes we wear, the books we read, have been produced from this source.[4]

As below, so above: if familiar objects bore the signature of their origins in human intentions and if they were daily remade in our apprehension of them, why should not the whole of the cosmos be the expression of the thought of the cosmic subject? Nature's unity would then stem from a common origin and the myriad forms of life could be seen as a scale of being along which the creative will had expressed itself. This view gave equal dignity and status to all the manifestations of creation. Our experience of the world was not really an encounter with the Other; instead it was an epiphany between one manifestation of the Great Self and another. There was no form of life too humble to be an expression of the cosmic purpose: "Every oyster has its fads and fancies."[5]

But if every individual had a value, it was not as isolated and lonely atoms that they possessed this worth. Carpenter recorded the teaching of his own gnani (spiritual teacher or guru) with enthusiasm: one should not speak of helping others, for although the practice was praiseworthy, this form of speech encouraged the delusion that "you and they were twain."[6] Nor were the elements and processes of inorganic matter separate either. Rocks and stones and trees, plants and insects and animals all had their individuality and were made of the same mind stuff, the underlying vivifying principle of the universe. In diversity there was also unity.

These were strange views to hold in the face of the assumption of isolated individualism that characterised commonplace Victorian thinking about the person and the nature of nature. Carpenter's explanation was that we lived in fallen days. In pre-history (and in the so-called primitive societies of his own day), there had been a connectedness among mankind and a feeling of community between man and nature: "the natural life of the people was in a kind of unconscious way artistic and beautiful ... Nature and man lived friendly together" (*AW*, pp.6–7). But in an argument that recalled both Marx and Rousseau, Carpenter chronicled how this bliss had been replaced by "Civilisation," whose benefits included the development of private property, the rise of antagonistic social classes and the domination of men over women.[7]

There were corresponding changes in consciousness. Isolation and alienation arose with competitive individualism; industrialisation and an urban way of life separated us from an authentic contact with nature; modern man's disintegrated mentality meant that he was no longer at home in the world. Through its over-valuation of rationality, modern "brain-cultured" humanity was left "face to face with a dead and senseless world" (*AC*, p.58).

How could such self-estrangement come about in a universe that was so fundamentally integrated? Carpenter's answer was that Civilised man was creation's Prometheus: primitive harmony was deficient in its lack of human self-awareness. The third and final stage of the cosmic subject's teleology was to be the unification of primitive feeling and intuition with the more recently acquired faculties of rationality and self-consciousness:

> Finally, with the complete antagonism of subject and object, of "self" and "matter" ... of intellect and emotion, the individual and society, and so forth – and the terrible disruptions of life and society which ensue – comes the third stage. (*AC*, p. 59)

This last stage was of course the Democracy towards which the long and often revised eponymous poem pointed. Not only was it the "Celestial City of equals and lovers," it was also the end and the aim of history, the terminus that was the destiny of the universe. Carpenter's views of the cosmos as an integrated and organic unity striving teleologically towards an as-yet undiscovered end state hardly fitted with the assumptions of Victorian and Edwardian science. A confident if unreflective empiricism had become a powerful model through its success in biology and physics:

> It must be remembered that this was the very flood-tide of materialism, agnosticism – the mechanical theory of the Universe, the reduction of spiritual facts to physiological phenomena.[8]

This paradigm was not unduly troubled by its unconsidered auspices and assumptions, for it could rely on a vulgar ability to produce an increasing amount of accurate knowledge. Nevertheless, there existed rules which the science game had to observe if it were to be played at all:

1. The subject matter of science was naively conceptualised as being "out there," making carbon copies of itself in our minds through its action on our senses. This view, of course, traded on a kind of practical man's common-sense philosophy that had its roots in Hobbes and Locke.

2. As scientists learned more, they were adding to a body of knowledge that was unequivocally true for all times and all places. Lord Kelvin looked forward to the time when matter would hold no more mysteries.[9]

3. This cumulative model of knowledge was very often allied to an uncritical induction, where laws of universal application were derived from specific instances.

4. The obvious meta-aim of science was to provide an increasingly secure control of nature, gained through the application of technology.

5. The scientist was seen as unproblematically outside the phenomena studied. (The Fabians transferred such a doctrine to the field of social science, and Carpenter's relationship with them is discussed below.)

However widespread these assumptions, there was not one to which Carpenter would not have objected. Perhaps his most basic difference is found in the construction of the way in which human beings confronted the rest of creation. In reality, we were not observing and studying the Other: rather we were one part of an immensely complex system that was interacting with another part of that same system. There was an underlying unity between knower and known, seeming subject and seeming object, a

> countless interchange of communication between countless selves; or, if these selves are really identical, and the one Ego underlies *all* thought and knowledge, then the Subject and Object are the same, and the World, the whole Creation, is Self-revealment. (*AC*, p.44)

We were sharers in the process where the universe revealed itself to itself through human enquiry. It is as if Spinoza had met Hegel and they had come to a synoptic if surprising common point of view.[10]

Carpenter's epistemology reinforced these metaphysics. Things did not, contrary to the views of the empiricists, constitute a simple reality that was passively registered by the human mind. On the contrary, the world was deeply interfused with our knowing of it. The boundaries between the knower and the known were not clear cut and the statements we could make about the properties of objects were inextricably linked with the human senses and with human social purposes. It followed that a view of the universe as dead or senseless matter "may at once be dismissed, not only as having no meaning, but as being incapable of having meaning to us" (*AC*, p.39). We made our picture of the world through our senses and our understanding: modern science elided that active perceptual process until it came to seem that the picture was an account of the properties of the world itself:

> But it is just here that the fallacy of the ordinary scientific procedure comes in; for, forgetting that these common phenomena are mere abstractions from the real phenomena, we credit *them* with a real existence, and regard the actual phenomena as secondary results, "effects" or what-not of these "causes." (*AC*, p.69)

As science had become more abstract, it had lost sight of the constitution of its subject matter and hypostasised and reified its statements until they took on a unwarranted life of their own.

To Carpenter, science was concerned with the study of appearances, not with the reality that lay behind them. We looked at the Platonic shadows and not at the substances. Tolstoy had another metaphor: someone examining an object would not do so from distance that obliterated all surface detail and colouration, leaving only an outline shape. And yet these were the methods of science, "convenient modes of generalisation, which by no means express actual facts."[11] In the light of this criticism, science's claim to be discovering laws with atemporal and universal validity was subverted. Systems and regularities depended on our particular standpoint in time and space. Things could look thus from here, but very different from somewhere else. Spinoza too had thought that the universe would be different for minds and senses other than our own.

Time presented an even more crushing objection to the arrogance of contemporary science. By comparison with the millenia before the emergence of modern science, today's knowledge was based on the observation of at best a few centuries. It could only assume that the world had conducted itself through its long unobserved history in the way that it did now:

> What would you think of an intelligent foreigner who, coming to England to study the game of cricket, remained on the cricket field for a quarter of a minute … and … went away and wrote a volume on the laws of the game? (*CCC*, p.166)

The edifices of modern science were in fact rather flimsy confections. We should have more humility and recognise that our knowledge was provisional and temporary and, most importantly, profoundly shaped by the attitudes and assumptions of the society and times to which the scientist belonged. With an argument that would remind the modern reader of Kuhn, Carpenter showed how certain ideas in the history of science were shaped by the influence of the pre-scientific, the social and cultural.[12] Tycho Brahe's epicycles, for example, were heroic attempts to accommodate planetary movement to a geocentric universe; more bizarrely, one Conrad Gessner "began classifying animals according to the number of their horns," a victim of his culture's assumptions about what counted as an appropriate unit of study (*CCC*, p.57). And if the commonsense of everyday life permeated natural science, how much further had it penetrated the self-confident but unquestioning assumptions of Political Economy?

These arguments formed a powerful critique of contemporary science and, though Carpenter argued his position forcefully, he also implied that it was not unexpected for knowledge to take this shape in our own times. The self-estranged and deracinated consciousness of Western civilisation could hardly produce anything other:

The various theories and views of nature which we hold are merely the fugitive envelopes of the successive stages of human growth – each set of theories and views belonging organically to the emotional stage which has been reached ... (*CCC*, p. 52)

But the future held better things, forms of knowledge that were not alienated and unduly dependent on rationality alone.

This confidence was based on Carpenter's view of evolution which, in deference to Whitman, he termed "exfoliation." It was a theory that implied progress and perfectibility and which emphasised the continuities among the superficially different manifestations of creation.

Man is organic with the rest of creation; and Carpenter cannot look into the eyes of the cattle in the field without seeing the human soul gazing out therefrom.[13]

Carpenter's metaphor for exfoliation was human creativity: our actions emerged from vague and half-articulated desires which gradually hardened into motives and plans. Nature was directional in the same way. What we saw superficially was the world of appearances, that is the effects of the intentions of nature; hidden to us, but nonetheless real, were the intentions and thoughts of the animating spirit of the universe, the Great Self. This was obstinately lodged in the essence of every organic being:

A dominant Idea informs the life of the Tree; persisting, it *forms* the tree. You may snip the leaves as much as you like to a certain pattern, but they will only grow in their own shape ... (*AC*, p. 29)

If the desire of the world spirit produced this stability and persistence what would happen when that desire changed? For Carpenter, an organism changed its nature by seeking new activities: his slogan was "Desire precedes function" (*CCC*, p. 133). Organisms were the agent of the life force in a conscious if not always rational attempt to become other and more developed:

Who shall say that the lark, by the mere love of soaring and singing in the face of the sun, has not altered the shape of its wings? (*CCC*, p. 135)

The universe was therefore a chain of desire and intention, and each manifestation of life was another part of the Great Soul's teleology. An obvious and important implication was that humanity was not set apart from this process.

This was the line of thought that informed Carpenter's idea of a rational and humane science, for it must be stressed that in attacking the unreflective verities of empiricism he took care to avoid implying that the project of understanding the world was itself flawed:

But while we think that this search of Science for *uniformity* is delusive, it is clear that the instinct which underlies all this movement, the instinct of Nature's *unity* is correct enough. (*AW*, pp. 127–8)

Carpenter was calling for a science which did not separate and atomise; it was a demand for a way of seeing nature as a unity of organic relationships which included its rational and self-conscious element. Science should make human enquiry and knowledge an element of the picture of the world that it generated. We were not spectators but participants. Rather like Schelling, Carpenter believed

> Only this pre-established harmony between nature within and without my-self makes it possible not only to understand a living nature, as well as I understand my own life; it makes possible the view of nature as itself visible spirit, and of spirit as invisible nature.[14]

Such an integrated view of the practice and subject matter of science demanded an adjustment in our view of the human faculties that made such a practice possible. We had three ways of meshing into the world and understanding it. One of these was intellect, the only mode of apprehension that contemporary science endorsed. It neglected, however, our sensuous and perceptual qualities on the one hand; and similarly ignored our emotional and intuitive properties on the other. We had developed a brain-cultured science that was bound to distort for it relied too heavily on one mode of understanding, rationality, which suffered from the added disadvantage of being evolutionarily late and therefore rather superficial. A new science would incorporate emotion and intuition and thereby make reason the servant, not the master, of our deeper faculties:

> Do we not want to feel *more*, not less, in the presence of phenomena – to enter into a living relation with the blue sky, and the incense-laden air, and the plants and the animals – nay, even with poisonous and hurtful things to have a keener *sense* of their hurtfulness? (*CCC*, p. 87)

Such a science was not to be confined to the laboratory, nor should it be the exclusive preserve of professional scientists. Knowledge and experience of our universe were to be part of the texture of the everyday life of ordinary men and women, for it was through the variety of their responses to nature that the new science would arise.[15] We would experience nature's unity and diversity through a series of epiphanies of the universe and the organisms with which we shared it. Eventually, we would understand that the natural world was not an object of study so much as a pattern of communication from which we were excluded only artificially:

> The sex-life, from the most primitive forms onwards, seeks union, cohesion. Everywhere it is making signals of attraction: in plants

by the bright colours and forms of the flowers; in birds by the winning sweetness of their song ... (*AW*, p. 81).

The new science implied a different relationship between ourselves and nature within. Civilised man was almost a passenger inside his body; but the citizen of the future would experience a deeper and organic unity between the mental and the physical. In turn, this implied a new view of medicine. Instead of providing a series of palliatives for symptoms, medicine would be centrally devoted to the idea of positive health and would incorporate many of the previously neglected insights of primitive people about the right relationship with the body:

> [Health] ... consists in rendering the body, by proper habits of life, pure and healthy, till it becomes, as it were, transparent to the inner eye, and then projecting the consciousness *inward* so as to become almost as sensible of the structure and function of the various internal organs, as it usually is of the outer surface of the body. (*CCC*, p. 173)

Human health and vitality was linked with the welfare of animals, for Carpenter thought that a carnivorous diet was "inflammatory" and an addictive "stimulant" (*CCC*, p. 37 and *EI*, p. 101). Perhaps more importantly, Carpenter's view of exfoliation meant that every organism was an equally valuable expression of the cosmic purpose. They therefore had a right to sympathy and consideration from us, even though such finesse was not to be found in the predatory relationships that existed between many species in the wild. Since we were the most developed life form, we had responsibilities towards animals that they could not have towards us or to one another:

> Behold the animals. There is not one but the human soul lurks within it, fulfilling its destiny as surely as within you ...
> I saw deep in the eyes of the animals the human soul look out upon me ...
> I caught the clinging mute glance of the prisoner, and swore that I would be faithful.[16]

At least this aspect of the new science could be promoted in the here and now through campaigns for animal welfare and for vegetarianism. And in promoting socialism, reformed science and animal welfare, Carpenter had a diligent ally in Henry Salt.

II

Henry Salt came from the same sort of comfortable upper-middle-class background as Carpenter. The son of an Indian Army officer, he spent most of his early childhood at the home of his grandfather, a barrister, who lived in Shrewsbury. His youth and his life as a young man were deeply linked with Eton. As a pupil, he seems to have noted the sporty and anti-intellectual atmosphere of the place, but not to have rebelled against it. His perceptions were a little sharper when he returned as a junior master, after a respectable degree in Classics at Cambridge in 1875. By then Eton had come to seem a machine for producing conformity. Science, philosophy and humane studies all took second place to the socialisation of the next generation into respectability.

In 1879 he married Catherine, the sister of J.L. Joynes, who also taught at Eton, but who was rapidly developing an interest in Henry George's ideas about land reform and socialism, ideas that would soon render him unsuitable for his post. In 1884, the Salts left Eton and took up the Simple Life in a cottage near Tilford. Salt devoted his life to writing and to propaganda for socialist and humanitarian causes. There were books on Shelley, Thoreau, Jefferies, James Thompson, Tennyson and De Quincey. He published translations of Lucretius, Virgil and Martial. And after the turn of the century, Salt turned his attention to topics connected with natural history and devoted himself to three volumes of autobiography.

Salt's work as a publicist was principally channelled through the Humanitarian League, founded in 1895 with the central aim of improving our treatment of animals. As an administrator, Salt was diligent and imaginative: he organised sub-committees to further the separate facets of the League's work, promoting vegetarianism and opposing hunting, vivisection and the trade in fur and feathers. With an eye to publicity, Salt organised campaigns against the Royal buck-hounds and against the Eton beagles. But the League did not confine its attention to animals. There was a campaign to improve prisons and agitation against corporal punishment, which, as Salt's biographer, George Hendrick, wryly shows had some unanticipated consequences:

> [In] 1904 Salt decided to use prose satire in his attacks against inhumanity, and published one issue of the *Brutalitarian: A journal of the sane and strong* ... The paper supported imperialism, flogging, blood sports. The printers had many requests for copies ...[17]

Such was the work of the League.

Carpenter was closely associated with the League and wrote an important pamphlet on vivisection for it.[18] This collaboration with Salt emerged from a biographical link between Carpenter and Salt which was close and long-lasting, though not without its complications and disenchantments. According to Shaw, it was Carpenter's article in *England's Ideal* about the practicability of living the Simple Life on £100 a year that led to Salt's leaving his post at Eton.[19] Carpenter recalls first meeting Salt in 1884, and he became a frequent visitor to the Tilford cottage.[20]

Shaw shows us how complicated the self-styled simple life could be:

> Salt's tragedy was that his wife (born Kate Joynes, and half

German) would not consummate their marriage, calling herself
an Urning. She got it from her close friend Edward Carpenter who
taught Kate that Urnings are a chosen race. Carpenter and I used
to meet at Salt's cottage at Tilford. We all called him "The Noble
Savage," and wore the sandals he made. He and I played piano
duets with Kate ... We were "Sunday husbands" to her. Salt was
quite in the friendship.[21]

Clearly the relationship was very close and lasted three decades or
more. In 1910, Henry and Kate moved to a cottage near Carpenter's
home at Millthorpe, where it seems they became a little disillusioned
with what came to be seen as Carpenter's pretensions.[22] Salt thought
there was an element of self-conscious image projection in Carpenter's
role as a seer and prophet. He also thought that Carpenter was
"amazingly superstitious."[23]

Despite these qualifications, the two men shared many interests
and activities that stemmed from fundamentally similar philosophies,
which Salt defiantly insisted should be proclaimed from the grave itself.
His own funeral was marked by an oration which he had written himself
in anticipation of his death: "I shall die, as I have lived, a rationalist,
socialist, pacifist and humanitarian."[24] In point of fact all these epithets
depended on the informing philosophy of nature that he and Carpenter
shared. For Salt's part, the central ideas of this position had been
developed in the 1890s in the work *Animals' Rights*.

Salt's title was deeply misleading. "Have the lower animals rights?"
he asked. "Undoubtedly – if men have."[25] But the reader who expected
a discussion of human rights to follow would be deeply disappointed.
We had interests, we had a notion of our welfare. These elements were
enough for Salt to dismiss the notion of rights in two pages. We might
consider this downright shoddy, but in fairness Salt had landed himself
in the middle of a debate of extraordinary complexity. Mary Midgley
remarks:

> Rights. This is the really desperate word. As any bibliography of
> political theory will show, it was in deep trouble before animals
> were added to its worries.[26]

Salt's use of the word "rights" was in fact an appeal to the idea that the
strength of a claim to consideration was reinforced by its urgency. It was
the needs of animals that gave them rights.[27]

Salt's case did not really depend on the idea of rights and his glad-
handed use of classic and modern philosophers had more than a hint of
the undiscriminating. First of all there was Bentham: if an organism had
the capacity for suffering, then it had the right not to be abused or
killed. " 'Pain is pain,' says an honest old writer, 'whether it be inflicted
on man or on beast.' "[28] Peter Singer has recently made much the same
point:

> Bentham points to the capacity for suffering as the vital charac-

teristic that gives a being the right to equal consideration ... The capacity for suffering and enjoyment is a *prerequisite for having interests at all.*[29]

Salt was also pleased with the position that could be derived from utilitarian indifferentism: our pleasures could not be preferred to an animal's pains.

Salt's second line was to emphasise the evil effects that the ill treatment of animals had on those humans who actually perpetrated cruelty. We should be kind to animals so as not to erode our moral sensibilities towards human beings. Kant had made the point very elegantly: "He who is cruel to animals becomes hard also in his dealings with men ..."[30] Bentham of course had expressed much the same opinion.

With his case opened by the utilitarians, Salt started to present his own position. Animals were individuals. We were used to thinking of them as anonymous and almost interchangeable with each other, and our language reflected this with suitably distancing phrases, such as dumb beasts or livestock. But in reality animals were distinct personalities with a central interest in living out their lives and expressing their natures. Our control over them violated the claim to an unfettered existence that came from Salt's optimistic and revisionist reading of Schopenhauer:

> To live one's own life – to realise one's true self – is the highest moral purpose of man and animal alike; and that animals possess their due measure of individuality is scarcely open to doubt. (*AR*, p. 15)

Salt was trying to appropriate those arguments about rights which would have been vitiated by a view of animals as undifferentiated automata. Indeed, Salt went so far as to refer to the claim of the popular naturalist, the Rev. J.G. Wood, that animals had souls, a view which had given Wood's fellow clerics some difficulty.

Salt was arguing towards Carpenter's position, though in a manner that was more domestic and less grandiose. Human beings should not see themselves as separate from and apart from nature: creation was a continuum without sharp breaks between one species and another. Just as Aristotle had found slavery quite natural while the modern Bentham had abhorred it, so the circle of sympathy would further expand beyond the human race to encompass the "lower" species:

> The present condition of the more highly organized domestic animals is in many ways very analogous to that of the negro slaves of a hundred years ago: ... the same exclusion from the common pale of humanity; the same hypocritical fallacies to justify that exclusion; and, as a consequence, the same deliberate stubborn denial of their social "rights." (*AR*, p. 21)

One of the "fallacies" that stood in the way of the recognition of brotherhood between the expressions of creation was our excessive veneration of rationality. Rather later, Shaw was to call the brain evolution's "darling object," but for Salt and Carpenter it led us to neglect the intuition and emotion we shared with other species.[31] "Our true civilization, our race-progress, our *humanity*" were compromised if we did not learn to listen to those faculties inside ourselves that we shared with animals (*AR*, p.111). Salt was surely referring here to Carpenter's Democracy without its metaphysical trappings.

Indeed, this capacity to domesticate the operatic was Salt's especial forte. Carpenter's sometimes histrionic denunciation of his own times was replaced by Salt's quiet analysis of the ideas that had allowed European civilisation to become so savage to animals. A millenium and a half separated the benevolence of Pythagoras and Plato from the resurgence of the humane attitude of Voltaire and Rousseau. The Cartesian idea of animated automata was a deeply rooted attitude; Salt recognised that change would be slow and devoted the major part of *Animals' Rights* to a piecemeal programme of reform.

Salt felt we had a special duty towards domestic animals: after all, we benefited from their labour and they were entitled to "food, rest and tender usage" (*AR*, p.34). He appealed for better treatment of super-annuated horses, but interestingly enough did not call on society to abandon the horse as a form of transport altogether. This was because such a use did not violate the nature of the animal. As to wild animals, the best we could do for them was nothing. They had the right to be left alone to express their Schopenhauer-esque individuality. Wanton killing was therefore *a priori* quite wrong. Salt quoted the *Disquisitions on Several Subjects* of the eighteenth-century courtier and writer, Soame Jenyns, with approval:

> I know of no right which we have to shoot a bear on an inaccessible island of ice, or an eagle on the mountain's top, whose lives cannot injure us, nor deaths procure us any benefit. (*AR*, p.48)

But Salt was not absolutist about these rights when there was a genuine need to control them or when human survival was at stake. For example it was inexcusable for the fashions of modern society to encourage the use of fur and feather as trimmings. For the Eskimo on the other hand, the use of fur was a necessary and legitimate part of their life. Salt's ethics were historical and situational rather than atemporal. He was more interested in what was wrong for us than in some putative trans-historical morality.

It goes without saying that Salt had nothing but contempt for hunting, though he amused himself with the inconsistencies in the arguments of its defenders. How could the quarry have been cleanly despatched when boys from the Eton College pack regularly and calmly spoke of its having been "broken up" at the end of the chase? How could sportsmen claim to rid the countryside of pests when they needed to preserve or even introduce the animal they wished to hunt? Vegetarianism was similarly defended with a series of counter-arguments that demolished the meat-eaters' position. People did not need meat for health, animals were not necessarily a part of a "natural" diet and were not our legitimate prey. Carnivores were left only with the frail argument of Bishop Paley who could find no good reason for eating meat except that it had explicit scriptural authority (*AR*, p.57). Even if we were justified in killing for food, it was difficult to defend the low quality of life that this produced for farm animals. And nothing could excuse the cruelty of long journeys in appalling transport to the slaughterhouse. This became an important campaign for the League.

Salt's programme made another connection with Carpenter in his critique of Victorian science. The zoo was a symbol of all that they despised in contemporary culture. Clearly the animals themselves were miserable, a simple consequence of their confinement. Neither were they of scientific or educational value, for caged animals were unable to be themselves. They were the shells of real active animals in their proper environment, "*simulacra* of the denizens of forest and prairie" (*AR*, p.51). The zoo represented a style of alienated knowledge that was static and mechanistic. In biology the text-books were metaphoric paper zoos, where the descriptions of animals were superficial and both literally and figuratively dead.[32] The anima, the vital spirit of the beast which it could demonstrate only by living its life in its natural habitat, was suppressed. But even this stilted and deformed knowledge was preferable to the collector's cult of the specimen:

> Does a rare bird alight on our shores? It is at once slaughtered by some enterprising collector ... It is a dismal business at best, this science of the fowling-piece and the dissecting knife ... (*AR*, p.92)

"Experimental torture" and the "Scientific Inquisition" were just two of the phrases Salt applied to vivisection (*AR*, p.96). His argument made much of the suffering of laboratory animals, but he also pointed out that the pleasures and pains of a consistent utilitarian had only an equal claim to consideration with those of an experimental animal. People who really believed in the benefits of suffering should volunteer themselves as subjects, especially since the results of animal experiments were often difficult to interpret in regard to humans. Here Salt was beating a path which Carpenter was to follow later with his own paper on vivisection, which took the daring line of opposing vivisection and conceding at the same time that scientific knowledge could advance by the practice. Carpenter squared this circle by arguing that a growing capacity to treat illness produced a neglect of the circumstances that promoted positive health; medical science was not attacking the causes of disease by learning better technical methods of curing it:

There *is* the power of Health in man, which through long ages of experience he has to develop. If he is diseased it is because he has failed so far to learn or to obey the laws of his own being – it is his ignorance or his sin. Shall he then, when he has been untrue to his own nature, turn upon the animals and rend them, as an atonement?[33]

Vivisection epitomised the way that a superficially powerful science was a deformed and alienated kind of knowledge. It was based on a neglect of the right way to live and concentrated on remedies for conditions that stemmed from a life separated from nature.

Animals' Rights can fairly be called a blue-print for many aspects of Carpenter's Democracy. At the same time it provided an agenda for the work of the Humanitarian League. We may surmise that at times Salt was arguing for what he thought was possible in the short term rather than what was ultimately desirable. Nevertheless there was a consistent view of nature and science which supported and informed the specifics of reform. This was a philosophy that Salt and Carpenter shared: it was vitalist in that it saw a unifying principle in the whole of nature; and it was expressivist in that creation was involved in a process of becoming, travelling teleologically towards the Democracy that was to be the end and, paradoxically, the beginning of history.

III

What is the significance of these arguments for our understanding of British socialist thought? The most obvious answer is that this philosophy is a vital component of an oppositional way of life that has so far been de-emphasised in favour of conventionally-defined politics on the one hand and discourses about sexual radicalism and the New Life on the other. The simplest claim to make for Carpenter's and Salt's philosophy of science is that both of them self-consciously and deliberately devoted time, thought and effort to these matters and a balanced assessment of their thought demands that we take these issues as seriously as they did.

This work of revaluation raises the issue of the relevance of Carpenter and Salt to contemporary issues and concerns. This study has deliberately eschewed anachronistic praise for the extent to which this pair anticipated later views and arguments in the philosophy of science. Nevertheless, Carpenter's recognition of the provisional nature of scientific knowledge has affinities with Popper's position, where science consists of the as-yet not disproved.[34] Other aspects of Popper's thought, such as his insistence on hypothesis and falsification, would not have been attractive to Carpenter, however. Another parallel can be drawn between Carpenter and Kuhn, whose conception of the paradigm is a more rigorous and formal statement of Carpenter's recognition that science depended on essentially social assumptions before it could proceed with its ostensible subject matter.[35] Carpenter was very sensitive to the idea that science was an assembly of stories which were not palpably untrue and which worked, that is they enabled explanation and prediction.

Salt, too, has continuities with contemporary argument. Singer refers warmly to *Animals' Rights* and indeed restates many of Salt's arguments: "Animals are not the same as humans, but in important ways entitled to the same treatment and consideration."[36] Adventitiously, there is a further link between Salt and Singer: the latter must be one of the few writers to include a chapter on cookery in a technical volume of philosophy. Salt, for his part, edited the short-lived *Vegetarian Messenger* and neither he nor Carpenter disdained to include a few culinary hints in their work. This is not simply a whimsical point. They thought that it was as important to show people how to be vegetarians in practice as to persuade them towards a theoretical moral principle.

Salt's concerns have also re-surfaced in two very recent works, Regan's *Case for Animal Rights* and Clark's *Moral Status of Animals*, where no fewer than six of Salt's texts are cited.[37] Indeed Clark refers to the debate between Salt and Ritchie over animals' rights and concludes that Salt had the worst of the argument but was nonetheless correct about the issue.[38] This recrudescence of serious academic interest clearly demonstrates that the concerns of Salt and Carpenter are far from being a dead letter. Conversely it explains why we are in a position to see these elements in their work more clearly.

Having sketched the relationship between our own intellectual climate and the agenda set out by Salt and Carpenter, we could invert the time sequence and enquire about the intellectual traditions to which they adhered, which shaped them and which they re-interpreted for their own generation. The two had much in common intellectually. They were both the products of a conventional upper-middle-class education, where public school was followed by a degree at Cambridge. Neither was attracted by the heartiness and anti-intellectualism of either school or university. Both were very widely read and familiar with the canon of both modern and classical literature. Broadly speaking, both were a sort of amalgam between English romanticism and German idealism. But there were important differences of detail and emphasis between them, which can be confidently traced because both left behind detailed records of their reading.

The sources of Carpenter's thought are embarrassingly prolific and a non-exhaustive list of the writers explicitly mentioned by him would include Kant, Fichte, Hegel and Schiller; Plato, Plotinus and Eckhart; Nietzsche and Schopenhauer; Carlyle and Ruskin; Emerson, Whitman and Thoreau; the anonymous authors of Indian sacred texts; dozens of authors on anthropology and sexuality, not to mention his wide reading in English literature, philosophy and theology. But if these were the warp and the weft of Carpenter's thought, the pattern he wove was distinctively his own.

Carpenter's idealism could hardly avoid the influence of Hegel. Human history was about three moments, unself-conscious integrity, fall and then redemption: the role of mankind was to be the saviour through whose activity the cosmic subject rescued itself from self-estrangement:

> Subjectivity thus spawns two worlds, as it were, the unconscious world of nature, and the conscious one of moral action and history. Having the same foundation, these two strive to rejoin each other.[39]

But other idealists were of equal importance. In Carpenter's insistence on the need for the free expression of our intrinsic natures, there was more than a hint of Herder. And in his view of the common-place natural world (*natura naturata*) as the outward and visible manifestation of an inner and underlying principle (*natura naturans*), the influence of Schelling was also visible.[40]

Carpenter was also familiar with the ideas that had in turn influenced his own immediate influences. He referred approvingly to the mysticism of Eckhart, for example:

> God is the soul of all things ... He is the light that shines in us when the veil (of division) is rent. (*AC*, p.66)

Furthermore, Carpenter and Eckhart shared a mistrust of the intellect and a willingness to suspend the most unquestioned of basic beliefs and concepts:

> As long as a man has time and place and number and quantity and multiplicity, he is on the wrong track and God is far from him.[41]

Similar examples of influence and incorporation could be adduced, for example about Carpenter's debt both to Plato and to Plotinus or his easy but not uncritical acceptance of the esoteric mysteries of Hinduism.[42]

In short, Carpenter's thought was a rich amalgam, which can be regarded as a late derivative from the tradition that Lovejoy entitled the Chain of Being, which traced a continuity of concern from Plato to the German romantics. It was a vision of the world as orderly and purposive, a home for mankind that was somehow uniquely and especially suitable because humanity and the world shared the same ultimate origins. Things were not adventitious, but part of a pattern:

> The generation of the lower grades of being ... directly by the Soul of Nature, and ultimately by the Absolute, is, it will be seen, regarded by the Neoplatonist as a logical necessity.[43]

Lovejoy was writing about Macrobius here; Carpenter's summing up of Whitman struck exactly the same note:

> Everything, the whole earth, all its shows, men and women,

sinners and saints, the stars, insects, solar systems – all are beings envisaged in order to be identified with the One.[44]

Carpenter was thus a late descendant of a long tradition in Western thought. Ultimately it was a doctrine of comfort and reassurance: not only was there a scheme of things, but also each individual had a place in it that was not fortuitous, but part of an integrated pattern.

Salt's range of reference was almost as wide as that of Carpenter; and the titles of Salt's books are a sort of catalogue of his reading and his enthusiasm. Lucretius, De Quincey, Richard Jefferies, Thoreau and above all Shelley (seven separate volumes) all received Salt's literary attention. Lucretius is obviously no mean source of zoophilia, the doctrine that other forms of life are also special and almost sacred. But it was to Shelley (another Eton atheist) that Salt owed the most obvious and massive debt. At one level, Salt was bowled over by the sensuous aesthetic of Shelley's poetry:

> The things which I love best of all in English poetry are Milton's *Lycidas*, that gem of perfect art, so rapturously beautiful to the ear, and certain passages and lyrics in Shelley's *Prometheus Unbound*, not less beautiful to the ear and still more to the heart.[45]

But Shelley appealed to the mind also. He was the "poet-pioneer of the great democratic movement," whose interests and ideas had "increased enormously in importance ... since his death."[46]

What were the resonances that Salt found so important? They certainly had nothing to do with the savagery and bitterness with which Shelley attacked corruption and the abuse of power. Salt's typical tone was one of civility or irony, far removed from, for example, the grim figures that Shelley depicted in the murderous Castlereagh, the fraudulent Eldon and the hypocritical Sidmouth.[47] It was not at the level of overt politics that Salt found in Shelley a congenial body of thought. Rather it was Shelley's pantheism and vitalism that attracted him. There was a vision of nature as a great chain of being, progressing from the simple to the complex, but the differences between and amongst organisms were less important than their shared status as links in the chain. Nothing was insignificant in the scheme of things:

> There's not one atom of yon earth
> But once was living man;
> Nor the minutest drop of rain,
> That hangeth in its thinnest cloud,
> But flowed in human veins.[48]

Wholeness, integration and quite literally the constant circulation of the matter of the universe were the natural order of things. Humanity should have been the ornament of creation, the jewel in the crown of the cosmos. But in something very close to a secularised Christian theology, Shelley saw man as fallen: "He fabricates/ The sword which stabs his peace.'[49] The project for mankind was therefore to re-integrate itself into the cosmic scheme of things. One crucial faculty was imagination, for this allowed us to see through the superficial differences of things, through to their core of unity and wholeness. In this way we would achieve participation in "the eternal, the infinite, and the one."[50]

The present day was, however, a fallen age, where our separation from nature was most conspicuous in the decline of the imagination, the cultivation of the rational and the instrumental, the reduction of human relationships to the cash nexus and, crucially, a carnivorous diet. Keith Thomas notes the millenial aspects of early nineteenth-century vegetarianism; Shelley certainly believed that human conduct would be transformed by a meatless diet.[51] He promised greater vitality, a heightened aesthetic sensibility and of course an honesty in our dealing with other animals. Vegetarianism was both an earnest of our sympathy towards the whole of the cosmos and the source of a more intense life of the emotions and the imagination.

These ideas explain why Salt's socialism had so little to do with what was conventionally regarded as politics. He looked forward to the death of civilisation and to its replacement by a society of free and equal members. Property would not be the mindless accumulation of things, but would become those goods which Ruskin had seen as being proper to a person. Human life would be in sympathy with nature. We would not oppress and dominate the rest of the natural order. Humanity would be the rational part of the whole, not some foreign element trying to coerce and colonise the environment. Salt and Shelley shared a secular chiliasm:

> the future race will be both natural and civilized – civilized in its retention and enjoyment of the self-knowledge which its intellectual culture can alone bestow, and natural in its still greater regard for the sacredness and healthfulness of unsophisti-cated instinct.[52]

From sources and influences that were different in detail but similar in their broad outlines, Carpenter and Salt had constructed a view of the world that was ultimately religious. There was a deity in the shape of the cosmos itself. There was an ultimate goal, for this cosmos was mysteriously but deeply purposeful. Human life was placed in the scheme of things and in the triptych of past innocence, present fall and future redemption, there was a latitudinarian doctrine to which a wide spectrum of opinion and feeling could adhere.

Recognising this religious sensibility permits a further insight into the role of Salt and Carpenter's nature philosophy, for it is part of the explanation of the popularity and influence that they enjoyed. Quite simply there was a constituency eager for ideas that would develop and extend its understanding of socialism. The Labour Church move-ment, for example, was an institution that neatly demonstrated the appetite of the 1880s and 1890s for a politics spiced with spirituality. Pierson goes so far as to see the ethical socialist movement as a transitional response of a generation which could no longer accept the specifics of Nonconformity but which found a secular socialism alien to its emotions.[53] Certainly there was a suggestive chronological coincidence: Sam Hobson noted that the popularity of the Independent Labour Party did not depend on its intellectual content

> for of that the ILP speakers were innocent. They always spoke of the appeal to the heart ... the ILP had appeared at a moment when Yorkshire Nonconformity was in a process of disruption ...
> The ILP accordingly set out to capture the soul of Nonconformity and Yorkshire was the battleground.[54]

Carpenter was a frequent speaker at Labour Church meetings, by no means all of them in Yorkshire. He often crossed the Pennines to Bolton, where in addition to the Labour Church there was a flourishing group of Whitmanites.[55] So close was the identity of interest between the Labour Church communities and the issues which concerned Salt and Carpenter, that John Trevor, the Church movement's founder, feared that its doctrine and programme might become obscured:

> the Labour Church pulpits were becoming catch-alls for most of the reforming impulses in England during the nineties. Appeals on behalf of "anti-vivisection," "theosophy," "ethical culture," "Tolstoyism," "vegetarianism," "esperanto," "cooperative dress making," and against the "tactics of Scotland Yard" were only a few of those which confronted Labour Church audiences.[56]

There is no doubt that a significant if small community, defined by the ILP and the Clarion Clubs as well as the Labour Church, was eagerly receptive to the religious tenor of Carpenter's philosophy. Not only did it provide life with an ultimate meaning and purpose, but it also legitimated the idea of living and making socialism in the here and now through the celebration of community and comradeship. And not least it rescued science from the dominion of empiricists and sceptics: indeed it promised its adherents a science better than the science of their day. Moreover, it enabled them to reject the latent accusation that they were simply anti-scientific obscurantists.

Furthermore, it showed the way to live. Salt was happy to refer to himself as a "faddist" when he spoke of vegetarianism. But the word is self-deprecating to the point of being misleading, for the diversity of advanced causes that had alarmed Trevor was anything but haphazard and whimsical. They were conspicuous issues, true enough, but organically related to each other by the web of ideas that Carpenter and Salt helped to weave. There was socialism in the making of dresses as well as in the making of demonstration; and ethical culture was as important as electioneering. The *Notebooks* of Alf Mattison show clearly how effortlessly this integration was achieved:

> March 13 (1899). A meeting of the N.A.C. of the I.L.P. was held
> in Leeds … In the evening we had a social and dance.
> March 14. At the Grand Theatre …
> March 19. Sunday. Took early morning train to Sheffield & on to
> Millthorpe. Carpenter had asked me over. …[57]

Comradeship, culture and politics were hardly distinguishable; this
organic sort of life and consciousness was made possible precisely by
ideas that refused to separate one category of experience and activity
from another.

If the ILP and the Labour Churches were enthusiastic Carpenterites,
other groupings within the socialist movement were less enchanted.
Although Carpenter was a member of the Fabian Society, he found his
ideas variously scorned or ignored by some of its core members.
True enough, there was no acrimony, but the difference between
Carpenter's philosophy of science and the assumptions and procedures
of the Webbs, for example, could hardly have been greater.

It was Beatrice who expressed most explicitly the epistemology of
mainstream Fabianism. In an argument which revealed the lasting
influence of her childhood mentor, Herbert Spencer, she wrote:

> We have always claimed that the study of the structure and
> function of society was … a science … and ought to be pursued by
> scientific methods used in other *organic sciences*.[58]

These were of course just such methods as Carpenter had criticised
as a deformation of true knowledge and deep experience. Beatrice's
methods were also a symptom of the gulf between her and Carpenter.
She and Sidney pursued their investigations by the indefatigable
collection of notes, each of which was written on a separate piece of
paper. These could be ordered and re-combined in a variety of ways,
reducing a complex totality to its constituent parts and allowing comparison and contrast. This procedure had a similar function to that of
the "blow-pipe and test-tube in chemistry": it enabled the student to
arrange material

> in new and experimental groupings in order to discover which
> coexistences and sequences of events have an invariable and,
> therefore, possibly a causal significance.[59]

Such a reduction of a whole to its parts was anathema to Carpenter. Not
only were Sidney and Beatrice murdering to dissect, they were also
claiming a special status for what was merely a new way of categorising
the shadows on the wall of the Platonic cave.

This biologism and conceptual atomism allowed Beatrice to fuse the
role of scientist with that of propagandist. If social processes were other
and separate from the disinterested and self-effacing observer, social
policy based on these auspices could bask in the reflected glory of
science. Simey comments:

when the Webbs sought to explain their motivations in carrying out their researches ... they expressed themselves as attempting something that was a blend of, or half way between, the life of the natural scientists and that of the public administrator or politician aware of his responsibilities to his fellow citizens.[60]

If anything this judgement errs towards the charitable. The Webbs could (and did) use this position as part of an ideology of expertise which was sometimes openly contemptuous towards the non-Fabian non-academic majority. Beatrice had "little faith in the 'average sensual man [sic]',"[61] while in a letter to Wells, Sidney wrote that "all experience shows that men need organising as much as machines, or rather, more so."[62] Such an alienating scientism could not have been further from the generous, inclusive and democratic instincts of Carpenter's philosophy.

Forster wittily pointed out Carpenter's differences with the main-stream of the Labour movement. It had not gone back to the land and the simple life, but instead had lost its way by attempting to manage the unnecessary complexities of urban industrial life. It

advanced by committee meetings and statistics towards a State-owned factory attached to State-supervised recreation-grounds. Edward's heart beat no warmer at such joys. He felt no enthusiasm over municipal baths and municipally provided bathing-drawers.[63]

Forster had hit on an important and significant disagreement and it is hardly surprising that thus separated at a very basic level, the paths of Carpenter and Salt diverged dramatically from those of mainstream Fabianism.

This contrast raises a further question as to why Carpenter stayed in the Society when it was moving so far away from his own views. The answer, perhaps surprisingly, is also related to his philosophy of science. Carpenter believed that the doctrine of exfoliation would eventually achieve the full and finished state of Democracy. Quite consistently, therefore, Carpenter refused to endorse any one road to socialism at the expense of others. In fact, he was willing to give his blessing to tendencies that were in their own terms opposed, such as anarchism and parliamentarianism. This was analogous to Hegel's cunning of history. Humanity had to work through conflicting forms of society and social change in order to discover its identity with and in the Absolute. The most unpropitious beginnings were thus not really unpropitious:

I saw a new life arise.
Slowly out of the ruins of the past – like a young fern-frond uncurling out of its own brown litter –
Out of the litter of a decaying society, out of the confused mass of broken down creeds, customs, ideals, ... (*TD*, p.260)

The logic was the same as he had deployed in his critique of science. Empiricism was misguided but necessary. It was a stage through which we had to go in order to see its deficiencies and understand the need for Carpenter's rational and humane science. The same argument explains what some have seen as vagueness and imprecision in Carpenter's socialism. But if all roads eventually led to Democracy, it was important not to close off any path prematurely.

Salt's position was similar, but because he was more concerned with individual issues, seeming inconsistencies in his thought are by no means so obvious. The "Creed of Kinship" to which he touchingly referred in his funeral oration was eventually bound to establish itself through a process very similar to exfoliation. Many years earlier he had expressed the same confidence about the role of diet reform as part of the transition from barbarous Civilisation to a better future:

> Vegetarianism is no more and no less than an essential part in the highly complex engine which is to shape the fabric of a new social structure, an engine which will not work if a single screw be missing.[64]

This was Carpenter's position expressed through a different metaphor. Independently of our intentions and through combinations of events that might seem unlikely, the future would achieve itself.

The thought of Salt and Carpenter was much more systematic than it might seem. There was a coherent view of the universe, which integrated a series of rich resources from European philosophy with a defensible view of science and an optimistic and undogmatic socialism. These concerns are not incidental to their lives and work but an organic and informing influence which found a ready response from the ethical socialist movement. Consequently questions about their philosophy of science can help us see the rest of their achievement more clearly, providing a fuller matrix of understanding within which their more salient ideas can be located.

CHRISTOPHER E. SHAW

NOTES

1. See Forster's memoir in Gilbert Beith, ed., *Edward Carpenter: In Appreciation* (London: Allen & Unwin, 1931), p.80.
2. See Sheila Rowbotham and Jeffrey Weeks, *Socialism and the New Life: The Personal and Sexual Politics of Edward Carpenter and Havelock Ellis* (London: Pluto P., 1977), Chushichi Tsuzuki, *Edward Carpenter 1844–1929: Prophet of Human Fellowship* (Cambridge: Cambridge U.P., 1980) and Stanley Pierson, "Edward Carpenter, Prophet of a Socialist Millenium," *Victorian Studies*, 13 (1969–70), 301–18. There are also Ph.D. theses from D.K. Barua (Sheffield, 1966) and Terry Eagleton (Cambridge, 1968).

3. Edward Carpenter, *Selected Writings: 1. Sex*, ed. Noël Greig and David Fernbach (London: G.M.P., 1984), endpaper.
4. Edward Carpenter, *The Art of Creation* (1904; rpt. London: Allen & Unwin, 1919), pp.24–5. Further references are incorporated into the text.
5. Edward Carpenter, *Angels' Wings* (London: Swan Sonnenschein, 1898), p.127. Further references are incorporated into the text.
6. Edward Carpenter, *From Adam's Peak to Elephanta* (London: Swan Sonnenschein, 1892), p.177. Further references are incorporated into the text.
7. Edward Carpenter, *Civilisation: its Cause and Cure* (1889; rpt. ed., London: Allen & Unwin, 1917), pp.25–6. Further references are incorporated into the text.
8. Frederic W.H. Myers, *Fragments of Inner Life* (London: The Society for Psychical Research, 1916), p.15.
9. Sir William Thomson (Baron Kelvin), *Popular Lectures and Addresses*, 3 vols. (London: Nature Series, 1891–4), vol. 2, p.177.
10. Sprigge's comment on Spinoza invites close comparison with Carpenter's thought: "a physical universe which is conscious of itself through and through is so different from so much mere matter, as we usually think of it, that this conception raises our conception of matter rather than lowers our conception of God," T.L.S. Sprigge, *Theories of Existence* (Harmondsworth: Penguin Books, 1984), p.157.
11. Leo Tolstoy, "Modern Science," *New Age*, 31 March 1898, 413.
12. Thomas S. Kuhn, "The Structure of Scientific Revolutions," *International Encyclopaedia of Unified Science*, 2, 2 (Chicago: Chicago U.P., 1970).
13. Edward Lewis, *Edward Carpenter: An Exposition and an Appreciation* (London: Methuen, 1915), p.69.
14. George G. Seidel, *Activity and Ground: Fichte, Schelling and Hegel* (Hildesheim: Georg Olms Verlag, 1976), p.104.
15. This fusion of the scientific and the experiential became very important to D.H. Lawrence. For example the catkins in the classroom scene in *Women in Love* become charged with a deep emotional significance; the "red pistillate flowers" are "little red flames" with a "mystic-passionate attraction" for Ursula. See D.H. Lawrence, *Women in Love* (1921; Harmondsworth: Penguin Books, 1960), p.41.
16. Edward Carpenter, *Towards Democracy* (1883; rpt. London: Allen & Unwin, 1931), p.175. Further references are incorporated into the text.
17. George Hendrick, *Henry Salt: Humanitarian reformer and man of letters* (Urbana: Illinois U.P., 1977), p.82.
18. Edward Carpenter, *Vivisection* (1893; rept. London: Reeves and Bonner, 1899).
19. G. Bernard Shaw, "Preface" to Stephen Winsten, *Salt and his Circle* (London: Hutchinson, 1951), p.9.
20. Edward Carpenter, *My Days and Dreams: Being Autobiographical Notes* (London: Allen & Unwin, 1916), p.235. Further references are incorporated into the text.
21. G. Bernard Shaw, "Preface" to Winsten, *Salt*, pp.9–10.
22. Hendrick, *Henry Salt*, p.160. This disenchantment might have been reciprocal: Carpenter's comments on Salt in *MDD* are very cool considering the duration of their friendship.
23. Winsten, *Salt*, p.198.
24. Ibid., p.1.
25. Henry Salt, *Animals' Rights Considered in Relation to Social Progress* (London: George Bell, 1892), p.1.
26. Mary Midgley, *Animals and Why They Matter* (Harmondsworth: Penguin Books, 1983), p.61.
27. Many of Salt's fellow Fabians found this formulation unsatisfactory. D.G. Ritchie read a paper on "Natural Rights" to the Society in 1891, when he came very close to the judgement of "nonsense on stilts." *Natural Rights* (London: Swan Sonnenschein, 1903) followed with some trenchant criticisms of Salt and Carpenter: they were anti-rationalistic mystics. See pp.64–5.
28. Salt, *Animals' Rights*, p.24. (Hereafter references are incorporated into the text abbreviated as *AR*). He quoted from Humphrey Primatt, *A Dissertation on the*

Duty of Mercy and Sin of Cruelty to Brute Animals (1776).

29. Peter Singer, *Animal Liberation: A new ethics for our treatment of animals* (London: Cape, 1976), pp.8–9.

30. Immanuel Kant, *Lectures on Ethics*, trans. Louis Infield (London: Methuen, 1930), p.239.

31. G. Bernard Shaw, *Man and Superman* (1903). See *Collected Plays* (London: Odhams Press, 1934), p.379.

32. There is rather a surprising comparison here with Foucault's views. In a quite different vocabulary he makes a similar point: "the locus of this history is a non-temporal rectangle in which, stripped of all commentary, of all enveloping language, creatures present themselves one beside the other, their surfaces visible, grouped according to their common features, and thus already virtually analysed, and bearers of nothing but their own individual names" (Michel Foucault, *The Order of Things* (London: Tavistock, 1970), p.131).

33. Carpenter, *Vivisection*, pp.14–15.

34. See Karl Popper, *Conjectures and Refutations* (London: Routledge & Kegan Paul, 1963).

35. Kuhn, *Scientific Revolutions*. "Scientific knowledge, like language, is intrinsically the common property of a group or else nothing at all. To understand it we shall need to know the special characteristics of the groups that create and use it" (p.210).

36. Singer, *Animal Liberation*, p.5.

37. See Tim Regan, *The Case for Animal Rights* (London: Routledge & Kegan Paul, 1984) and S.R.L. Clark, *The Moral Status of Animals* (Oxford: Oxford U.P., 1984).

38. Clark, *Status of Animals*, pp.209–10 and p.11.

39. Charles Taylor, *Hegel* (Cambridge: Cambridge U.P., 1975), p.42.

40. We can even trace the probable route by which Carpenter first came to Schelling. His father was an avid reader of "broad Church mysticism," including works of German philosophy (*MDD*, p.38). Further, his father had met Coleridge several times (Tsuzuki, *Carpenter*, p.8); in turn Coleridge had found a "genial coincidence" between his own views and those of Schelling (Frederic Copleston, *A History of Philosophy: VII: i, Fichte to Hegel* (New York: Image Books, 1965), p.181).

41. Meister Eckhart, *Selected Treatises and Sermons*, trans. J.M. Clark and J.V. Skinner (London: Faber, 1958), p.202.

42. Edward Carpenter, *A Visit to a Gnani* (London: Allen & Unwin, 1911).

43. E.O. Lovejoy, *The Great Chain of Being* (Cambridge, Mass: Harvard U.P., 1961), p.63.

44. Edward Carpenter, *Days with Walt Whitman* (London: George Allen, 1906), p.86.

45. Henry Salt, *Company I Have Kept* (London: Allen & Unwin, 1930), p.42.

46. Henry Salt, *Percy Bysshe Shelley, Poet and Pioneer: A Biographical Study* (London: Reeves and Turner, 1896), p.5. Carpenter was also a Shelley enthusiast. For example, on Easter Sunday 1897 he gave a lecture on "Shelley and the modern democratic movement" to a Sheffield audience. It was a "much appreciated address, Ed. C. clearly demonstrating how the poet had anticipated many of our present day Reform movements." Notebooks of Alf Mattison, Brotherton Collection, University of Leeds, pp.41–2.

47. P.B. Shelley, "The Mask of Anarchy". See Edward Aveling and Eleanor Marx, *Shelley's Socialism* (1888; London: Journeyman P., 1979), p.41. Marx and Aveling were anxious to recruit Shelley: he was "in harmony with modern socialistic thought" (p.38). But they did not ignore his pantheistic nature philosophy, "the doctrine of the eternity of matter and the eternity of motion, of the infinite transformations of the different forms of matter into each other, of different forms of motion into each other, without any destruction or creation of either matter or motion" (p.20).

48. P.B. Shelley, "Queen Mab," II, ll. 211/15. See *Poetical Works*, ed. T. Hutchinson (London: Oxford U.P., 1967), p.760.

49. Ibid., III, 199–200 (Hutchinson, p.812).

50. P.B. Shelley, "A Defence of Poetry". See *Shelley's Prose or the Trumpet of a Prophecy*, ed. D.L. Clark (Albuquerque: New Mexico U.P., 1966), p.279.
51. See Keith Thomas, *Man and the Natural World* (London: Allen Lane, 1983), p.296.
52. Henry Salt, *Richard Jefferies: A study* (London: Swan Sonnenschein, Lowery, 1893), p.73.
53. Stanley Pierson, "John Trevor and the Labor Church Movement in England 1891–1900," *Church History*, 29 (1970), 463–478. For a more inclusive view of the role of the Labour Church within the culture of ethical socialism, see Stephen Yeo, "A New Life: The Religion of Socialism in Britain, 1883–1896," *History Workshop Journal*, No. 4 (1977), 5–56.
54. Sam Hobson, *Pilgrim to the Left* (London: Arnold, 1938), p.116.
55. Paul Salveson, *Loving Comrades: Lancashire's Links to Walt Whitman* (Bolton: Salveson/W.E.A., 1984), p.8. Most appropriately, in 1891 Carpenter met R.M. Bucke, author of *Cosmic Consciousness*, through this connection.
56. Pierson, "Labor Church," pp.469–70.
57. Mattison Notebook, p.85.
58. Beatrice Webb, *The Diary of Beatrice Webb, vol. 2, 1892–1905*, ed. Norman and Jeanne MacKenzie (London: Virago and L.S.E., 1983), p.170. The emphasis is mine.
59. Beatrice Webb, *Our Partnership*, ed. Barbara Drake and Margaret Cole (1948; Cambridge: Cambridge U.P., 1975), pp.154–5.
60. T.S. Simey, *Social Science and Social Purpose* (London: Constable, 1968), p.31.
61. Beatrice Webb, *Partnership*, p.120 (from her diary of 2/2/1908).
62. Webb, Letter to H.G. Wells, 8 December 1901. See Sidney and Beatrice Webb, *The Letters of Sidney and Beatrice Webb, vol. 2, 1892–1913*, ed. Norman MacKenzie (Cambridge and London: Cambridge U.P. and L.S.E., 1978), p.144.
63. E.M. Forster in Beith, op. cit., p.78.
64. Henry Salt, *The Logic of Vegetarianism* (London: Ideal Publishing Union, 1899), p.11.

"Non-governmental Society":
Edward Carpenter's Position in the
British Socialist Movement

Edward Carpenter's fame during his lifetime was largely as an important figure in the British socialist movement. It cannot be denied that on the whole he was a militant for the socialist cause and defended most of its ideals, as is testified by the long list of the lectures he gave throughout Great Britain.[1] Since he always remained in contact with the various organisations associated with the movement, from his joining William Morris's Socialist League in 1886 to his death in 1929 – the very year of the world's greatest economic crisis – his longevity made him an exceptional witness of the socialist movement.

The essential ideas developed by Carpenter, expressed on numerous occasions in his lectures and frequently taken up again in his writings, are of particular interest as regards the history of British socialism. The first thing worth noting is that the general tenor of his writings never much changed. He simply adapted them to the immediate context or to his audience, perhaps adding some new illustration suggested by current events. Carpenter was not averse to repetition, a device used commonly by teachers and preachers to convince their audience, for indeed Carpenter's aim was always to persuade. It was with this intention that several of his articles and a number of his lectures were re-used over the years, then collected in book form. "Transitions to Freedom," for example, was first published in 1897 in *Forecasts of the Coming Century*. It was re-published in 1905, with the new title "Non-governmental Society," in *Prisons, Police and Punishment*, and again, in 1917, in *Towards Industrial Freedom*.[2] The variants of this text are of considerable interest because they allow the reader to trace the development of their author's thought regarding the problem of the organisation of future society. From the analysis of this essay, and of a number of others, the present discussion will open out into a consideration of Carpenter's position in the socialist movement as a whole.

For any socialist, changing society for the common good implies removing the monopoly of the land, as well as the monopoly of the country's capital, from the hands of the owners. This demand was first made in 1886, in the Sheffield Socialists' first Manifesto which stated that:

> (1) the Monopoly of Land must be done away ... The land must belong and be used for the benefit of the People – to be let to genuine occupiers – the rents going to national, local or municipal purposes.

    (2) the Monopoly of Capital must be done away ... Gradually the larger industries must be taken over into the hands of the People.[3]

It was repeated in the two later Manifestos of 1890 and 1899.[4] Using different terms, these three texts set out as a priority the appropriation by the people of the means of production. That Carpenter strongly supported this demand is clear in what he wrote in *England's Ideal*, at an early stage of his links with the movement:

> The people are demanding, and will with rapidly increasing loudness demand, that the land of this country and the machinery of industrial production shall be put into the hands of the producers. Under various names, as Nationalisation of the Land, Nationalisation of Capital, Cooperation, Socialism, etc. ... they will practically demand one thing – namely, that the workers shall directly inherit the fruits of their work.[5]

The various arguments put forward by Carpenter in favour of the acquisition of the means of production by the State and/or the municipalities are also seen in a number of later lectures. In "The Future of Labour," a lecture which he first gave in 1892 and repeated many times afterwards, he develops the theme in detail, and sees in it the direction which society must take:

> This indicates, of course, in a general way, the direction in which we have to go. It indicates the acquirement by the public bodies – either by the State or the municipalities – of the means of industry and the carrying on of these industries to some extent by those bodies. It means the nationalisation of the land.[6]

Here Carpenter is simply reiterating the points of view of most of the socialist organisations who put forward the same demands, and hoped, for the most part, that industrialised societies would evolve towards collectivism. In 1897, he himself remarked in "Transitions to Freedom," the first version of the article with which we will be particularly concerned, that "they all agree that we are approaching a Collectivist stage in which industrial arrangement will be largely handled or regulated by governmental agency."[7]

In Carpenter's view, State control is one of the ways in which to restore a sick organisation to health, and on a number of occasions he gives examples of the benefits which society gains from public administration. In his lecture "Socialism and State-Interference" (1908), he explains, with statistics to support his argument, all the advantages which the British economy has drawn from the various Factory Acts passed in recent years: far from seeing her commerce collapse, Great Britain now has an increasingly healthy external balance. Likewise, the State's having taken over the Postal Service has helped increase the Postal Service's profits, "in contrast with the state of things which would prevail if twenty or thirty companies were competing for the business." To summarise, he states that "state-interference was natural and had, so far, been beneficial."[8]

But even more than its financial advantages, Carpenter sees the extension of the public sector as having a moral influence on society. For Carpenter was not only concerned with profit, as the importance he always attached to individual life clearly shows. This constant concern emerges from various lectures, including, for example, the following passage from "The Transformation of our Industrial System" where he demonstrates how the damage done by capitalism can be mitigated, if not eradicated, by public administration:

> Public administration allays the evil of excessive Competition, and the cut-throat warfare and waste which goes on still in the outside trades. ... Public administration practically puts an end to the evil of Adulteration; it curbs an enormous amount of Fraud and Waste. Under it, Fluctuations of employment, which we have seen to be a great curse, are much more easily controlled; Hours can be shortened at need, and sections of unemployed so absorbed; Wages and conditions made much more equable and favorable or just to the worker; and in general the Robbery of the poor by the rich minimised and gradually extinguished. (*TIF*, pp.4–5)

We might be tempted to conclude from passages like this that Carpenter is completely in favour of nationalisation and the development of the public sector. But his position is in fact much more finely shaded, partly because of his concern that each individual should remain able to express his or her personality freely, even though, at the same time, Carpenter is striving to establish the "common life." Given this double objective, Carpenter's thought constantly oscillates between the two poles: preserving individual freedom and organising a socialist society. Furthermore, Carpenter's stance differs according to the degree of his relation at a particular point in time to the organised socialist movement. In this respect, a comparison of the different versions of certain texts is particularly revealing.

This is the case with the text from which we have just quoted, "The Transformation of our Industrial System," an earlier version of which was published in 1910 with the title "The Wreck of Modern Industry and its Reorganisation." Here, Carpenter continues the passage quoted above with the following words:

> The only probable danger will be the growth of officialism and red tape – and this is no doubt a danger which *will* have to be guarded against. ... No Socialist (that I know of at any rate) is such a fool as to want to make a cast-iron system to regulate every detail of daily labour. And it is obvious that there will always remain a large fringe of independent workers – from village joiners and shoe-

makers to decorative artists and dramatists – to embody and illustrate the individualistic principle in Society.[9]

He concludes by expressing his conviction that

> the Socialist population of the future will be amply able to decide on the proper balance between the individualist and communist principles in social life – when the time grows ripe for that decision to be made.[10]

Seven years later, however, in the final version of the essay, as it appears in *Towards Industrial Freedom*, Carpenter, who had been forced to recognise the evidence of the evil he had feared, modifies his text, replacing the passage just quoted with the following:

> But – and this is a most important "but" – it brings with it the very great danger of the growth of officialism, bureaucracy, red-tape, than which, if allowed free sway, few things can be more fatal to the real life of a nation. The multiplication of officials ... strangles the spontaneous vitality of the people; it creates a vast body of parasites, as bad as the dividend-drawing parasites of Commercialism; and betrays the public into the power of a class hostile to change and to progress. (*TIF*, p.45)

The ill of parasitism, so strongly decried, had reappeared, and Carpenter had apparently not foreseen such an eventuality. His new conclusion to the essay, in which moderate hope ("we may ... hope") replaces absolute certainty ("I do not doubt"), confirms the fears the writer now has regarding the possible benefits of nationalisation:

> Thus we see that while we plead in many departments for more public administration of Industry, it will be necessary at the same time to guard against the great danger of officialism and Bureaucracy. We may of course hope that a new alertness in the masses and a far more thorough education in Citizenship will in the future come to our aid; but we see that to guard against these dangers *will* require all our alertness. (*TIF*, p.47)

The textual variations of "The Wreck of Modern Industry" just underlined undoubtedly owe something to the special economic circumstances arising from the First World War. But what is striking in them is the urgency which one can feel in Carpenter's tone in the 1917 version, and which appears for instance through the repetitions of the word "alertness" or of the expression "we see." As the years went by, Carpenter was more and more aware of the dangers of bureaucracy and of the necessity to make the workers themselves more vigilant.

The variants found in "Transitions to Freedom" (1897) and its two later versions, published as "Non-governmental Society" (in 1905 and 1917) are also worth examining. After expressing the wish to see the attraction of the "Common Life" spread, Carpenter continues in the 1897 text with:

> We must acknowledge that – in order to foster new ideas and new habits – an intermediate stage of Collectivism will be quite necessary. Formulae like the "nationalisation of the land and all the instruments of production", though they be vague and indeed impossible of *rigorous* application will serve as centres for the growth of the sentiment.[11]

In 1905, the word "Collectivism" disappears, to be replaced by "definite industrial organisations," and in the final version of 1917, the last sentence has been deleted. Again Carpenter's reservations with regard to collectivism, particularly after the turn of the century, would seem to be apparent.

A little further on in "Transitions to Freedom," we read:

> It is this general rise in well-being due to the next few years of collectivist development which will I believe play the part of the good fairy in the transformation-scene of modern society. With the dying-out of fear and grinding anxiety and the undoing of the frightful tension which today characterises all our lives Society will spring back nearer to its normal form of mutual help.[12]

In the 1905 version of "Non-governmental Society," the beginning of the passage reads, "It is possible that some such general rise in well-being, due to a few years of wise and generous organisation of labour, may play the part of the good fairy, etc." (*PPP*, pp. 199–200). Two phrases here suggest uncertainty ("it is possible" and "may"), underlining the writer's reservations concerning what is no longer a collectivist development, but rather a "wise and generous organisation of work." In the 1917 version, this paragraph no longer appears at all. Carpenter has apparently ceased to believe in the good fairy of collectivism!

A few more lines also disappear from the final version of "Non-governmental Society," lines in which he had wished to reassure and to express the hope that a *voluntary* form of socialism, and not one imposed by the State, would later emerge. The 1897 and 1905 versions read:

> we need not fear that State-organisation will run to the bitter end so often prophesied – nor is there any danger of poetry and ginger beer being converted into government monopolies. But it may perhaps be hoped that it will go far enough to form the nucleus of immense growths of *voluntary* Socialism.[13]

It is interesting to note that if there is no more reference to State organisation, the term "voluntary" is, however, used again in 1917, Carpenter indicating that we are moving towards a "perfectly voluntary" society (*TIF*, p. 94). By 1917, Carpenter is no longer so optimistic and he has to convince his readers that the voluntary participation of individuals in shaping the society to come is extremely important, if not essential. In his opinion, it is the only effective way to prevent municipal or national government from having too great a control over the economic and social life of the country. He is thus led to develop the idea of what he calls a "double collectivism." By this, he understands the coexistence of a state collectivism, leading to the socialisation of the land and industry, with a "voluntary" collectivism, the beginnings of which he sees in the action of the trade-unions and cooperative societies:

> The Trade-Unions and Cooperative Societies ... are creating a society in which enormous wealth is produced and handled not for the profit of the few but for the use of the many; a *voluntary* collectivism working within and parallel with the official collectivism of the State.[14]

It is within this paradoxical concept that Carpenter sees the solution to the problem he has raised. He tries to reconcile the two poles and find the right balance between State control of the organisation of industry and commerce (which he thinks necessary) and freedom, which is indispensable, for without it, according to him, "Common Life" is but an empty phrase.

The stand taken by Carpenter against State control in 1917, in the middle of the First World War, throws light on the three Manifestos of the Sheffield Socialists – in the writing of which Carpenter undoubtedly had a hand – in which explicit references are made to the appropriation of the means of production by "the People" rather than by the State. It shows the continuity of Carpenter's thought since from the very start he inclined towards the individual as opposed to the State. It helps us to understand why Carpenter, in several places, declares that he is in favour of what today we would call workers' control. If such a form of organisation appeals to him, this is because it has a significant educational effect, "for the management of their own concerns is after all the chief and most important item of a people's education,"[15] and also because in his opinion "the management of industries by the workers themselves today lies in the direct line of progress."[16] At this stage of his evolution, that is, after the turn of the century, Carpenter is convinced that the danger of collectivism is almost as great as that of capitalism, if it does not give people responsibility. In Carpenter's conception, the ideal future society must allow each individual the freedom to develop and give him/her the possibility of fulfilment. He sees in the workers' taking over and managing of the companies a means of counteracting too important a state role in production, and an advance on a strictly collectivist form of organisation, such as that put forward by the socialists:

> Until lately, the Socialist State, with its dangers of bureaucracy and over-government, seemed to be the only way out of our present evils ...; the fact that the workers generally are tumbling

to the idea that they, after all, are the proper people to manage industrial production, or at least that they should be the chief people to be consulted in its management – this mere fact is encouraging and promising.[17]

The solidarity found between members of the working class seems to Carpenter to be the best guarantee of a form of administration which would serve the community, and State intervention would be necessary only in a few specific areas:

> The central government will still remain to watch the total interests of the nation, to harmonise the claims of the various trades, and to reserve a certain public right in such things as the land, the railways, the mines, docks, and other national property.[18]

In other words, Carpenter would be happy to see a nationalised sector, though a limited one, with the rest of industry being subject to workers' control. In relation with the two quotations just given above, Carpenter's support for syndicalism – as opposed to trade unionism – which developed in the early 1910s, at the time of "Labour Unrest," must be underlined. Carpenter could not but welcome a movement which aimed at giving the workers more independence and a greater sense of solidarity, and put the stress on the necessity of freedom. Syndicalism more than trade unionism suited his anarchistic tendencies.

Edward Carpenter's stance as regards the organisation of industry, then, squares perfectly with his idea of future society, the free nature of which is, in his view, imperative.

The great importance Carpenter always attached to freedom can be traced in all his writings. It is the opening word of his poem "Towards Democracy," which, according to Tom Swan, is "a paean to man emancipated."[19] It is also one of the fundamental themes of the complete work bearing the same title. The vision which he offers is one of a free society:

> The dream goes by, touches men's hearts, and floats and fades again –
> Far on the hills, away from this nightmare of modern cheap-jack life:
> The finished free Society.[20]

"The free Society," this is mankind's long-term goal. If Carpenter does not envisage its immediate realisation, this is because

> The dregs and scum of the old society exist, and will exist yet for a long period, and somehow or other they will have to be dealt with and disposed of during the time that a new and freer society is shaping itself. There will necessarily be a long and difficult period of transition. (*PPP*, pp.46–7)

Yet the fact that a free society should be seen as belonging to a distant future does not diminish Carpenter's conviction that progress towards this society is possible, and so he invites the reader to take in the short term all the measures which might help toward its realisation:

> Of the *possibility* of a free communal society, there can really, I take it, be no doubt. The question that more definitely presses on us now is one of transition – by what steps shall we, or can we, pass to that land of freedom? ("Non-governmental Society," *TIF*, p.93)

Carpenter does not, then, exclude the notion of freedom going hand in hand with a communal organisation of society, and the manner in which he resolves this apparent contradiction leaves no doubt as to his final aim of a perfectly free society:

> If any one will only think for a minute of his own inner nature he will see that the only society which would ever really satisfy him would be one in which he was perfectly free, and yet bound by ties of deepest trust to the other members; and if he will think for another minute he will see that the only condition on which he could be perfectly free (to do as he liked) would be that he *should* trust and care for his neighbour as well as for himself. (*TIF*, p.92)

This passage, from "Non-governmental Society," illustrates the fundamental importance of this text in Carpenter's written works.

While Carpenter constantly underlines the necessity of each individual's voluntary participation in creating the new society, the emphasis he puts on spontaneity should also be stressed. He considers that "in fact a spontaneous and free production of goods would spring up, followed by a spontaneous and free exchange" and that "people relieved from care do spontaneously set themselves to work" (*TIF*, p.83). He concludes by saying that

> it appears to be at least *conceivable* that a people not hounded on by compulsion nor kept in subjection by sheer authority, would set itself spontaneously to produce the things which it prized. (*TIF*, p.84)

Spontaneity should be encouraged in work and production, as well as in the organisation of society, which Carpenter sees as "a perfectly spontaneous arrangement" (*TIF*, p.87), and in the relationship between men and women, which must be "the spontaneous expression of their attachment to each other."[21]

There would be no place in this future society for laws imposed from the outside, on whatever level. From this point of view, the essay included in *Love's Coming-of-Age*, whose title is in fact "The Free Society," sheds further light on the particular type of free society to which Carpenter aspired, and towards the construction of which he worked. He writes:

> No doubt the Freedom of Society in this sense, and the possibility
> of a human life which shall be the fluid and ever-responsive
> embodiment of true Love in all its variety of manifestation, goes
> with the Freedom of Society in the economic sense. (*LCA*, p. 121)

As Tom Swan summarises, the author's message is that "outward
liberty is as essential to the well-being and the happiness of society as
inward liberty is to the well-being of the individual."[22] In the words of
Emile Delavenay, the free society of the future will, as far as the
individual is concerned, be one in which he will be "free to follow the
law of his own being."[23] As far as institutions are concerned, the society
will represent "a non-governmental (or Anarchist) stage in which
authoritative regulation will fall off, leaving such arrangements largely
to custom and spontaneous initiative."[24]

To bring about a free society in which men and women will be free of
all hindrances means first to get rid of capitalism and to put an end to the
oppression of the workers by the rich and idle classes. But, according to
Carpenter, no real free society can ever exist if it is controlled by a
strong centralised State.

It is in this context that Carpenter's relation to anarchism may be
considered, for in any evaluation of his socialism, the character and
quality of his relations with the anarchists, and the links he had with
Kropotkin, must not be overlooked. Although William Morris, despite
definite libertarian tendencies, finally took up a clear position against
the anarchists, Carpenter never tried to hide the attraction anarchism
held for him. He gives evidence of this both in *My Days and Dreams* and
in his lecture "The Way Out," in the notes to which we find the
following words: "Self I hold to Anarchist Ideal – Spontaneous free
Society."[25]

Carpenter's stance with regard to anarchism must, however, be
more clearly defined. This is all the more necessary because British
anarchism during the 1890s, when this lecture was delivered several
times, was slightly different from what is usually understood by the
term. In 1893, Sidney Webb defined this difference as follows:

> The English Anarchists, unlike many of the American and some
> of the Continental claimants of that misleading appellation, are
> advocates of a free and voluntary communism. ... Some of them
> admit that a free communism is only a remote ideal, to be reached
> only after a considerable development of collectivism, but their
> practical tendency is usually against further advances of collective
> activity.[26]

Many points in this definition fit Carpenter. His idealistic character, his
doubts regarding collectivism, his conviction that the final stage in the
evolution of socialism will be a "non-governmental (or anarchist)
stage,"[27] all suggest a similar attitude to the one described by Webb. But
Carpenter never approved of the Anarchists' violent activity, as he

clearly stated during the anarchist Fred Charles's trial in 1892, when he spoke as a character witness on behalf of Charles.[28] As to his support of revolutionary syndicalism, the main reason for this was his mistrust of State control and the activities of traditional unions.

The extent of Carpenter's anarchism can also be seen from his relationship with Kropotkin. To say that the émigré Russian prince was his master would clearly be to put the matter too strongly. Carpenter never concealed the reservations he felt with regard to the stances taken by this particular anarchist. But those of Kropotkin's ideas of which he most probably approved, even if he did not adopt them, are suggested by the following quotation, an extract from Carpenter's tribute to Kropotkin on the occasion of the latter's seventieth birthday in 1912:

> You have taught us to rely in social life on that most important force, the voluntary principle ... which is now among the modern societies taking its place as the leading factor in their development – in contra-distinction to the merely regulative and governmental principle, and which in the form of over-legislation certainly tends to render a people deficient in originality and initiative.[29]

Like Kropotkin, Carpenter wished to see the establishment of a society without government, based on the freedom of the individual and free association, but he differed from Kropotkin in refusing to consider the very existence of a government as the sole cause of all social ills.

This no doubt explains why his attitude concerning the role of the State in society fluctuated. While in the essay from which I have already quoted, "Non-governmental Society" – whose title is quite unambiguous – Carpenter advocates the abolition of such forms of authority as laws, the police and government, in his lecture entitled "State Interference with Industry" (1910) he insists on *"the absolute necessity of Interference,"*[30] at least in the first stage of development, and in a number of places he expresses his satisfaction with certain social improvements brought about by the new legislation.

The development of Carpenter's career reflects his hesitations. There is no doubting that he gave his support to movements with an anarchist tendency, such as guild socialism and revolutionary syndicalism. But he never totally rejected or broke with those organisa-tions, such as the Fabian Society, which were in favour of significant state intervention in society, and he gave his support to the Labour Party from its creation.

In fact, Carpenter's form of anarchism does not concern solely the political and institutional domains, but is the logical outcome of a philosophical position which gives particular importance to the individual. It is also a sign of his faith in the individual's potential for personal fulfilment. Politically speaking, it is the means of allowing self-expression. This is indispensable, in Carpenter's view, as the counterbalance to the "Common Life" to which socialism must lead. In this sense, Carpenter's anarchism is not in contradiction to his personal conception of "socialism" nor does it distort it. Rather it has a humanising influence and serves as a guard against the possible dangers of excessive state control and collectivism.

The particular problem of the role to be given to the State in future society, and Carpenter's predilection for a "non-governmental society," account for the difficulties we face in trying to define Carpenter's place within the British socialist movement. Furthermore, the notion of socialism itself presents a problem. In Carpenter's time, in Great Britain, the term was not without ambiguity and vagueness for it encompassed a great variety of political currents. During the period concerned at least, Hyndman and the S.D.F.'s brand of Marxism, the Fabians' reformism, William Morris' utopianism and Kropotkin's anarchism were all often referred to, whether by their followers or in the press, as socialist movements.

Carpenter himself was well aware of this, noting that many organisations, of varying size and influence, belonged to the socialist movement, without any individual organisation predominating or being able to claim exclusive rights on the ideology. But far from deploring the fact, he rejoiced in it, stating:

> If the movement had been pocketed by any one man or section it would have been inevitably narrowed down. As it is, it has taken on something of an oceanic character; and if by its very lack of narrowness it has lost a little in immediate results, its ultimate success we may think is all the more assured.[31]

In this way, he justifies having embraced the cause of socialism in the most comprehensive way possible, and he sheds light on his position within the movement. The diversity of the various socialist organisations and their different approaches to socialism explain, moreover, why Carpenter was, in his time, regarded as one of the intellectual leaders of socialism and one of its inspiring forces, as numerous articles in the press testify. For he always found a group of militants who recognised their own ideas in his, or vice versa. The range of issues which he engaged in reflects to some extent the plurality of the British movement.

It is possible, nonetheless, to point to a number of positions held in common by most of the different groups and parties concerned. To consider, along with A.R. Orage, editor of the magazine *The New Age*, that the only thing on which the members of the various socialist groups agreed was the idea that property was the root cause of poverty,[32] would be an over-simplification, for there were several other points of convergence. The denunciation of profit-making exercises, of the exploitation of the working class, of a class division of society, the need to change the system of production and the organisation of society, to transfer property as well as control of capital, land and industry to the state, the wish to see competition make way for cooperation, and the

common good take precedence over individual interests are all fundamental principles, largely agreed upon within the socialist movement.

If we look at Carpenter's particular form of socialism from this point
of view, then his adherence to the movement is without question. His
denunciation of private property and competition, his support for a
cooperative organisation of society, and his desire to see a new form of
communal life can easily be fitted into such a general scheme as the one
defined above. It is when we come to the means of bringing about these
general aims, when it is a question of proposing a new shape for society,
that divergences and differences of attitude emerge.

Carpenter cannot be placed alongside either those socialists of
Marxist inspiration, such as the members of Hyndman's S.D.F., or the
Fabian reformists. His links with these two groups are of a personal
nature, on the level of friendship, more than on an ideological plane.
He knew several members of these groups well, and although he
addressed meetings of both organisations, this did not necessarily
mean that he adhered to their positions and methods.

Little trace of Marxism remains to be seen in Carpenter. It coloured
mainly his first publications and interventions in the cause of socialism.
In *England's Ideal* (1887) and *Civilisation, its Cause and Cure* (1889),
the influence of Marx can be felt, and Marx's name, along with that of
Engels, appears several times. In later works, however, there are
hardly any references to these two thinkers. Moreover, Carpenter
never laid any particular stress on the economic aspect of the problems
he discussed. We know he had reservations about Marx's theory of
surplus-value, reservations expounded in Carpenter's article "The
Value of the Value-Theory," written in 1889.[33] On the level of his
criticism of the socio-economic aspects of society, Carpenter was to
retain throughout his works an approach indebted to Marxism, and
until the end of his days he spoke out against class divisions, the
parasitism of the rich, and the crises brought on by over-production.
But Carpenter's position was never limited to this.

Although Carpenter was also close to the Fellowship of the New Life
from which the Fabian Society developed, it is apparent that he never
allied himself closely with the Society. While he had friends amongst
the Fabians, he was also strongly criticised by some of them, notably
G.B. Shaw.[34] The violent reactions of some Fabians to the ideas
expressed by Carpenter in his lecture "Civilisation: its Cause and
Cure," when given at one of their meetings in 1889, demonstrate the
hostility of the Fabians to certain of Carpenter's positions.[35] Carpenter
did not believe in systematised action at municipal or even national
level, and he had at times his reservations concerning official legal
measures which aimed to improve, temporarily and in any case
inadequately, the condition of the workers. Nor did he ever show much
enthusiasm for isolated reforms, limited in scope.

Carpenter is much closer, ideologically, to William Morris. Both
wished to see the rise of new relationships between people. Both

conceived of a future society which would allow each individual to live fully and in complete freedom. The idealism seen here, and their belief that society was already evolving in a way which corresponded to the one they wanted, colours their socialism with a shared utopianism. Morris and Carpenter are both visionaries and dreamers who do not hesitate to give their dreams the weight of reality. Carpenter never drew up a model of his ideal society as complete and well-structured as Morris' in *News from Nowhere*. However, if we leave aside the more visionary descriptions to be found in *Towards Democracy*, Carpenter's essay "Non-governmental Society" can to some extent be considered as expressing his socialist utopia. The essay, whose importance in Carpenter's "political" works cannot be over-emphasised, is marked with the undeniable stamp of Morris' influence, and, moreover, Carpenter pays tribute to Morris in this work.

The proposals put forward by Carpenter for the organisation of future society are similar to those found in Morris' political writings, of which *News from Nowhere* is a fictional illustration. From this point of view, "Non-governmental Society" is to be set beside such texts as "The Society of the Future," "The Beauty of Life"[36] or "How we Live and How we Might Live," in which Morris sets out the measures needed if each individual is to enjoy a better life. Health, education, leisure time, work as something useful and as a source of joy, a healthy and simple lifestyle, the beauty of the environment, and a communal organisation of society are all concerns shared by the two writers. For both Carpenter and Morris, the aim of socialism must be to put an end to the gnawing fear and sense of alienation felt by men and women, and thereby allow them to find fulfilment and freedom. A free society, from which authoritarian power is absent, is, in their eyes, the only one which would allow the fulfilment of the individual. Socialism is thought of as an essentially liberating movement.

The particular form of social organisation towards which they aspire is tinged with anarchism, which for Morris as for Carpenter goes hand in hand with utopianism. This same anarchism leads them both to show some mistrust, Morris for the "socialist machine," and Carpenter for state collectivism and bureaucracy. Their choice of the word "communism" and their use of it to designate a communal future society, is itself significant, for it points to a conception of socialism in which there is an element of utopianism. In the classic, and no doubt out-moded, opposition of scientific socialism and utopian socialism, Carpenter's position is similar to Morris'. He quite clearly rejected " 'Scientific Socialisms' and other blunderbusses"[37] and chose equally clearly to place himself in the utopian tradition. In an article of 1921, having noted that "there have been many speculations in the past, in Communism," he mentions first Plato, then Campanella and Thomas More,[38] seeing a foreshadowing of a possible form of communism in More's *Utopia*.

The comparison just made between Carpenter and Morris should not, however, lead one to conclude that Carpenter was merely a second Morris, and even less a second-rate one. Both belong to that strand of socialism which emphasises the moral transformation of man, a concern with the quality of life, and with individual fulfilment, and does not concern itself primarily with purely material and economic matters. But their paths diverge at various points, notably in the mystical dimension of Carpenter's thought, and his integration of sexual problems into his criticism of society. Nor must we forget that Carpenter outlived Morris by more than thirty years, during which time the socialist movement underwent many changes and had to confront many problems.

However famous Edward Carpenter may have been in the British socialist movement and whatever influence he may have had on it, it cannot be denied that he never became one of its national leaders and never played any concrete political part in it. One of the reasons for this may be found in his individualism, a dominant characteristic of his personality, which he found difficult to overcome. This no doubt explains why he felt he had found the answer in a form of socialism strongly coloured by anarchism. If we look at Carpenter's career, we see that he always chose to side with those socialists who attached the highest price to the freedom of the individual. Despite his association with Hyndman, he was closer to William Morris' Socialist League than to the S.D.F.; he felt more akin to revolutionary syndicalism than to official trade unionism or the Labour Party, and he gave his support to guild socialism, a movement which was born from an opposition to the state control advocated by Labour, and continued to develop in this direction. Paradoxically, however, despite his remaining on the fringes, Carpenter is nonetheless a fairly typical representative of what was called "ethical socialism" in Britain at the time, and which disappeared with the development and official recognition of the Labour Party, for which political action and national material issues took precedence over moral problems and individual self-realisation.

After the First World War, though the name "Carpenter" remained famous and was still associated with the socialist movement, the ideas which he stood for were no longer of interest to those ready to take over the government of Great Britain. From this date onwards, it was the man rather than his thought and works which attracted tributes, for Carpenter lived according to his ideas, and this is not the least of his merits. At his death, a number of his friends, moreover, expressed the opinion that his life, more than his writings and reflections, was exemplary and worthy of attention. It is, furthermore, true that his fame is in large part due to the breadth of his personal experience, to the example he set, and to his lifelong role as wise man, inspirer and model.

Thus, once the man had disappeared, and with him the extraordinary charisma which had contributed to his fame during his lifetime, Great Britain let fall into oblivion the man who had criticised so strongly the society he lived in. And so E. M. Forster's prediction "He will not figure in history"[39] in part came true. But if Carpenter does not figure in history books, he remains nevertheless an important witness and mirror of the history of British socialism, and the travelling companion of the movement in which he never ceased to see, above all, the hope of new human relations and a better life.

MARIE-FRANÇOISE CACHIN

NOTES

1. See Marie-Françoise Cachin, "Edward Carpenter (1844–1929), compagnon de route du mouvement socialiste britannique." Diss. Paris 1985. Annexe III, pp.649–60, gives a chronological listing of Carpenter's lectures. A copy of the thesis is in the Carpenter Collection, Sheffield City Library.
2. Edward Carpenter, ed., *Forecasts of the Coming Century* (Manchester and London: Labour Press and the Clarion Office, 1897); Edward Carpenter, *Prisons, Police and Punishment* (London: Fifield, 1905) and *Towards Industrial Freedom* (London: Allen & Unwin, 1917). Further references are to these editions and are included in the text.
3. *Manifesto of the Sheffield Socialists*, 1886. A copy is in the Carpenter Collection.
4. *Manifesto of the Sheffield Socialists*, 1890, MS.37.2, Carp. Coll.; *Sheffield Socialist Society*, 1899, copy in the Brotherton Collection, University of Leeds.
5. *England's Ideal, and other papers on social subjects* (London: Swan Sonnenschein, 1887), p.39. Further references are to this edition and are included in the text.
6. Report of Carpenter's lecture in *Sheffield Daily Telegraph*, 25 Nov. 1907. Copy in the collection of newspaper cuttings in the Carpenter Collection.
7. "Transitions to Freedom" in *Forecasts of the Coming Century*, p.174.
8. "Socialism and State Interference – E. Carpenter's Lecture at Chesterfield" (Oct. 1908). Unidentified newspaper cutting in the Carpenter Collection.
9. *The Wreck of Modern Industry and its Re-organisation* (Manchester: National Labour Press, [1910]), p.15.
10. Ibid.
11. "Transitions to Freedom" in *Forecasts of the Coming Century*, p.187.
12. Ibid., p.189.
13. Ibid., p.190, and *PPP*, p.111.
14. *FCC*, p.188; *PPP*, p.108; *TIF*, p.94.
15. *My Days and Dreams* (London: Allen & Unwin, 1916), p.290.
16. "Counsel from Edward Carpenter," *Amalgamated Engineers' Journal*, April 1905. Copy in the collection of newspaper cuttings in the Carpenter Collection.
17. "Cooperation and Syndicalism," *The Cooperative News*, 29 June 1912. Copy in the collection of newspaper cuttings in the Carpenter Collection.
18. Ibid.
19. Tom Swan, *Edward Carpenter: the Man and his Message* (Manchester: Swan Sonnenschein, 1902), p.31.
20. *Towards Democracy* (London: Swan Sonnenschein, 1905), Part IV, "The Dream Goes By," p.387.
21. *Love's Coming-of-Age* (Manchester: The Labour Press, 1896), p.117. Further references are to this edition and are included in the text.
22. Tom Swan, p.31.
23. Emile Delavenay, *D.H. Lawrence and Edward Carpenter: A Study in Edwardian Transition* (London: Heinemann, 1971), p.154.
24. "Transitions to Freedom" in *Forecasts of the Coming Century*, p.175.
25. "The Way Out" (November 1893), MS. 58, Carp. Coll.

26. Sidney Webb, *Socialism in England* (London: Swan Sonnenschein, 1893), p.55.
27. "Transitions to Freedom" in *Forecasts of the Coming Century*, p.175.
28. *Times*, 4 April 1892.
29. "To Peter Kropotkin," MS. 181.26, Carp. Coll.
30. "State Interference with Industry" (11 Nov. 1910), MS. 159, Carp. Coll.
31. *MDD*, p.126.
32. Philip Mairet, *A.R. Orage, A Memoir* (London: Dent, 1936), p.44.
33. "The Value of the Value-Theory," *To-day*, June 1889, 179–82.
34. Shaw in a letter to Henry Salt, 19 Aug. 1903, spoke of Carpenter as "that ultra-civilized impostor, the ex-clergyman of Millthorpe." See G. Bernard Shaw, *Collected Letters, 1898–1910*, ed. Dan H. Laurence (London: Max Reinhardt, 1972), p.348.
35. Chushichi Tsuzuki, *Edward Carpenter, 1844–1929: Prophet of Human Fellowship* (Cambridge: Cambridge U.P., 1980), pp.79–80. It is perhaps because of this lecture that Carpenter was nicknamed the "Noble Savage."
36. Carpenter gave a lecture bearing a similar title several times in the 1910s.
37. "The Value of the Value-Theory." See note 33.
38. "Free Bread for All," *Daily News*, 17 Aug. 1921.
39. E.M. Forster, "Some Memories," in *Edward Carpenter: In Appreciation*, ed. Gilbert Beith (London: Allen & Unwin, 1931), p.80.

Robert Blatchford, The Clarion Movement, and the Crucial Years of British Socialism, 1891–1900

I

In 1895 Tom Mann, the secretary of the Independent Labour Party (ILP) endorsed the Social Democratic Federation (SDF) maxim of "revolution by any means," but stated: "I agree with those who contend that the most available means for us are political." He went on to point out that if the parliamentary course seemed to be closed at a later date, the SDF one would again prove attractive.[1] Mann's thinking here was not as perceptive as it could have been. Although the parliamentary movement did not qualitatively advance the revolution that he envisaged, the concentration upon this method was to close the door on the more directly revolutionary ideas of the SDF. Moreover, the implementation of a parliamentary strategy also had a considerable effect upon the ideology and vision of the movement. Socialists like Edward Carpenter and Robert Blatchford, who concerned themselves chiefly with a quest for "the new life," were to find themselves out of harmony with the growing parliamentary movement and its more limited aims. By the first decade of the new century the frames of reference of the movement had become labourist as opposed to socialist. The aim of this paper is to attempt to provide an insight into some of the mechanics of change within a living movement which, for a period, exhibited millenial hopes and aspirations but eventually found itself filling the role of a "respectable alternative."

II

On 12 December 1891 a new weekly newspaper, edited by Robert Blatchford and called *The Clarion*, was sold on the streets of Manchester. Over the next decade it was to reach average circulations of 40,000 readers per week. Although not exclusively concerning itself with labour-related questions (wide coverage was given to theatrical, literary and sporting matters, for example), its socialistic stance was an integral part of its character. From the very beginning the paper exhibited a distinct antipathy towards the two political parties of the status quo, for example in an address to "Hodge" the country labourer:

> I know two parties fair to see
> Who can both false and friendly be;
> Trust them not they are fooling thee.[2]

Alongside this, Mont Blong, otherwise Montague Blatchford, the editor's brother, wrote, quoting Dickens, "the first strong necessity is to rouse the people up," and continued "it will be the duty of the blowers of the Clarion to accomplish that 'first strong necessity,' or bust themselves in the attempt."

In the end the blowers were to bust themselves, but while it lasted the attempt seemed well calculated and, at times, spectacularly successful. Often bitterly satirical articles exposed the swindles and wrongdoings of the plutocracy, while a stream of articles about the lives of different sections of a widely defined labour force, from policemen to seamstresses, aimed to bring the workers together through a knowledge of one another. This aim was expressed most dramatically in the *Clarion*-backed Labour Day demonstrations, first held in Alexandra Park, Manchester, on 1 May 1892, of which Blatchford wrote:

> The people will meet – that is the main thing. We shall see each other face to face, feel each other shoulder to shoulder, hear each other voice to voice, trust each other soul to soul, and we shall go away open eyed and conscious of a change.[3]

The paper also covered debates within the socialist movement and published accessible expositions of socialist arguments, of which Blatchford's *Merrie England* was only the most famous. This propaganda, however, was always combined with a mixture of short stories and pieces of general interest which attempted to show that there was more to socialism than "rebels without a pause." At the time the paper was very conscious of itself as "a new departure in journalism"[4] and, since, Margaret Cole has written of it in the following terms:

> There never was a paper like it; it was not in the least the preconceived idea of a socialist journal. It was not solemn; it was not highbrow; it did not deal in theoretical discussion, or inculcate dreary isms. It was full of stories, jokes and verses – sometimes pretty bad verses and pretty bad jokes – as well as articles. It was written in language that anyone could understand, 'with no middle class unction' ... it believed that anyone whatever his condition or education, who could read plain English could be made into a socialist, and that socialism was not a difficult dogma, but a way of living and thinking which could make all men behave like brothers in the ordinary pursuits of life.[5]

Although, in reality, a joint effort, *The Clarion* was chiefly associated with the name of its prolific editor Robert Blatchford, or pseudonymously "Nunquam." After jumping his apprenticeship as a brushmaker's assistant for a seven-year career in the army (which he thoroughly enjoyed), Blatchford entered journalism in 1885 as a writer for Edward Hulton's sporting paper *Bell's Life in London*, and in 1887 he began writing for Hulton's Manchester-based *Sunday Chronicle*, a widely-circulated paper catering for the new mass literacy. It was in his period with the *Chronicle* that Nunquam first began to attract attention among northern working-class readers. An early reading of Dickens and Carlyle and a later reading of Henry George, the Fabian tracts, and Morris and Hyndman's *A Summary of the Principles of Socialism*, combined with the awful revelation of the Manchester slums and the influence of members of the Manchester SDF, were converting him rapidly to socialism in this period. Indeed, by May 1889 he was writing a series of articles in the *Chronicle* about the slums, and in August 1889 he began writing a series of letters *Re. the Affairs of John Smith and Co.* which advocated trade unions for every branch of labour and an organisation of working-class voting power, and inspired Cunninghame Graham, MP for North-West Lanark and president of the Scottish Labour Party, to suggest their writer's candidature for Labour in the by-election at Carlisle. Around the turn of the decade Blatchford's reputation was steadily growing; his writing had been read by, and influenced, the striking Scottish railwaymen in January 1890 and the striking Manningham Mills wool operatives in Bradford in 1891, out of which dispute arose the Bradford and District Labour Union, an organisation before which he was to make his oratorical debut as a somewhat reluctant prospective parliamentary candidate for East Bradford. During this time he had met John Burns and Keir Hardie and had been urged in vain by the London Fabian, W.S. De Mattos, to take the lead in forming a national party. After an argument with Hulton, Blatchford left the *Sunday Chronicle* in October 1891, and after a brief spell with Joseph Burgess's *Workman's Times*, during which he became involved in John Trevor's newly-formed Labour Church in Manchester, he founded *The Clarion* with some colleagues from the *Chronicle*.[6]

Certainly, the new paper was given something of a headstart considering that the pseudonyms used by its writers were those under which they had gained popularity with the *Chronicle*. But from the foundation of *The Clarion*, their popularity, and especially Blatchford's, reached new heights. Holbrook Jackson saw him as being, in the years between 1893 and 1910, "the greatest living danger to the existing social system."[7] Indeed, there is plenty of evidence to support Stanley Pierson's statement that "through the nineties, Robert Blatchford ... was by far the most effective recruiter for socialism in England":[8] in March 1892 Hyndman stated that Blatchford had given socialism "a tremendous push forward in the North of England," and went on, "I find his converts in every direction,"[9] while a correspondent wrote to *The Clarion* in 1892 stating that Blatchford's reputation was "high indeed among the workers."[10] In 1894 *The Clarion* quoted a *Justice* leader, "Perhaps no-one since William Cobbett has ever had so direct an influence over the minds of working class readers,"[11] and by February 1893 *The Clarion* was attracting enough attention to be taken in the House of Commons' reading room.[12]

If Blatchford was gaining popularity from his days with the *Chronicle*, however, it was what he called "his gift to the socialist movement," *Merrie England*, which made him. A simple and concise exposition of the principles of socialism (Ramsay Macdonald was to say "*Merrie England* is like a man fully explaining a motor car by describing a wheelbarrow"),[13] it was first published as a series of letters to workmen in *The Clarion* in 1892–3. When the letters were collected into one volume, priced at a shilling, the first edition of 25,000 rapidly sold out. The following penny edition, published in 1894 (at an inevitable loss, due to the trades union rates paid to the printers) sold over 700,000 copies in a matter of months without any outlay on advertising at all. Indeed, a further edition at threepence raised the sales to 1,000,000, and they were eventually to top 2,000,000. This brilliant popularisation caused nothing short of a sensation. "Merrie England classes" became a widespread phenomenon, and for a time "Merrie England" entered the vocabulary of the movement as shorthand for the New Jerusalem to come.[14] A.M. Thompson wrote in the preface to Blatchford's autobiography,

> A year before its issue there were not 500 Socialists in Lancashire; twelve months after there were 50,000. A census taken at the time in a North of England Labour Club showed that 49 members out of 50 had been converted by *Merrie England*. As the *Manchester Guardian* lately said, "for every convert made by *Das Capital*, there were a hundred made by *Merrie England*."[15]

Indeed, there are a number of reasons why historians of the labour movement should give *The Clarion* adequate consideration as a source. First, its mass circulation makes it important. It was the first socialistic newspaper since the Chartist *Northern Star* to pay its own way. Certainly some caution is needed here: we must not assume that every reader followed or agreed with *Clarion* policy; but on the other hand, we may conjecture that *The Clarion* reached more than this number of readers through the process of lending.

Second, it is clear from the letters pages, and reports and advertisements of meetings, that *The Clarion*'s appeal was not simply a sectional one. Blatchford himself was a founding member of the ILP, but was also in the SDF, and, despite his fierce opposition to permeation – which he once called "a hopeless, spiritless unclean abortion"[16] – was also a Fabian. This ecumenical approach was also exhibited by other members of the staff and, judging from correspondence, many of the readers. It is also exhibited in the range of contributions to the paper, which covered virtually the whole breadth of the socialist, and at times the anarchist, movement. Even at the height of the Boer War, for example, which Blatchford supported, contributions were received and printed from pro-Boers as vehement as Karl Liebknecht.

The paper's real importance, however, becomes apparent when we acknowledge that we are dealing with something more than a newspaper when we look at *The Clarion*. We are, in fact, dealing with a movement. Besides a relentless stream of propaganda, the paper took under its wing a range of other activities, many of which cannot be termed directly political. Clarion cycling clubs, social clubs, Cinderella clubs for the enjoyment of slum children, vocal unions, holiday camps, field clubs, fellowships and Clarion Scouts to spread the socialist message were among these. Indeed, the appeal of *The Clarion* ranged into many areas of life; the paper's message was that self-improvement was synonymous with social salvation – the great change would only come when the workers learnt to value the higher things in life, such as art, beauty, fellowship and the countryside. This religious, self-salvationary, aspect of socialism, characterised by the Labour Churches with which *The Clarion* was closely connected, has been well-documented by historians such as Stephen Yeo.[17] The Clarion Movement constituted an important part of this impulse, and to see it simply as another faction within the movement as a whole would probably be underestimating its appeal. Members of both the ILP and the SDF and many more unaligned socialists were happier as members of the less ideologically-restrictive Clarion Movement. Indeed, at the end of *Merrie England*, Blatchford wrote: "The fact is, John, I wish you to be a Clarionette as well as a socialist."[18]

III

At this point we need to return to the process of transformation mentioned in the introduction, that from socialism to labourism. *The Clarion* played a crucial role in this process, but this role cannot be understood unless it is placed within the context of a wider infrastructure of practicalities and ideologies, within which the newspaper was an important nodal point. On a practical level, this involved, for example, the advertisement and reports of meetings and socialist literature, and the raising of funds for striking workers and socialist parliamentary candidates. On the ideological level, it involved the liberal airing of differing views and conceptions of "the cause" with which the rest of this paper will chiefly concern itself. Before these are examined, however, the nature of this infrastructure, which existed on both the ephemeral level (the propaganda van or the political meeting or lecture, for example) and on a more permanent level (the political tract or newspaper, for example), must be made clear. The important point to make here is that the infrastructure as a whole was held together by an ethical basis common to almost all forms of socialism and supported by a belief in the imminent success of "the cause" and the impending collapse of capitalism. To examine this ethical basis is not really within the scope of this paper, but it may be observed as it was portrayed by Walter Crane in his "Garland dedicated to the Workers" (Figure 1) on May Day 1895. Here we see a synthesis of practical and ideal aims held together easily by Crane's striking feminine image of "the cause."

No. 177.

PRICE ONE PENNY.

·A·GARLAND·FOR·MAY·DAY·1895·
DEDICATED·TO·THE·WORKERS·BY·WALTER·CRANE

Fig. 1

If this ethical foundation made for the overall cohesion of the movement's ideology in these years, however, the reality was that within the infrastructure there existed a diversity of both practical and theoretical tensions which, under the pressure of short-term electoral failure and intense opposition from the system it was working against, were to fragment the movement and make the comprehensive attainment of its ideals impossible. *The Clarion* provides a good vantage point from which the historian can see these tensions, which are reflected not only in its relationships with other points of the matrix – *The Clarion* and Keir Hardie's *Labour Leader* never quite saw eye to eye, for example[19] – but also within its own stances and ideological complexion.

One of the most striking of these is the tension between the fading revolutionary pulse of the SDF and the parliamentary tactics advocated by the ILP and (in a less coherent fashion) by *The Clarion*. In assessing these tensions, it is important to remember that the ILP and *The Clarion* were themselves the result, at least in part, of the propaganda work carried out by the earlier and more revolutionary Social Democrats. Many Clarionettes were themselves members of the Federation, and many ILP members may well have had revolutionary sentiments similar to those professed by the SDF, at a time when what party a particular person joined depended, to no small degree, on what party happened to be most active in his or her immediate neighbourhood.

The position of *The Clarion* on the question of violent revolution seems clear enough at first impression. In January 1892, Montague Blatchford wrote:

> The law has provided us with a sufficiently powerful weapon – namely, a vote – with which we shall be able to work the harmless wonders we dream of, as soon as we have persuaded a majority of our peaceful fellow-citizens to use their reasoning faculties ...[20]

while the editorial of the same issue stated, in reaction to the discovery of the Walsall Anarchist conspiracy:

> England has at this time of day only loathing and scorn for schemes of violent revolution. The need for armed uprisings is long since past. ... reform can be won steadily by education and constitutional means .... The people have the power, if they have the will, to bring about by peaceful means the emancipation of the people.

Indeed, the movement was to be so peaceful that on the first May Day Labour demonstrations in 1892 Blatchford wrote, "Our Army of God does not break windows nor throw pebbles," and an appeal for "the most complete order" was published in *The Clarion* along with a request to pay "great attention to the shrubs and flower beds" and an acknowledgement of cordial co-operation from the police and town corporation.[21]

In its outward appearance and intentions, then, *The Clarion* rejected outright the ideas of violent revolution. A closer look at the movement, however, reveals lingering revolutionary sentiments and stances. The Clarion Scout Movement, formed to spread propaganda, provides some index of the nature of this feeling. In 1894 a scout wrote a piece for *The Clarion* entitled "Active Service." It describes how

> six of us ... set out, armed with "Merrie Englands", to raid a southern suburb of Huddersfield. It was a hostile country, garrisoned by working class conservatives and liberals. We made our wills, kissed our wives, waved our lily white hands, and stepped it. ... We told off two of our bravest and best, and bid them storm first the Liberal Club. Our reception was mild, they didn't even kick us. And we sold six of our "Merrie England" bombs to the members.

The whole article is full of words and images of a military nature: "attack," "parley," "close our ranks in case of an ambush," "the soldier and his steel," etc.[22]

It would, perhaps, be wrong to read too much into this evidence. Military modes of organisation were not uncommon in this period – the Salvation Army being the obvious example – and if Robert Tressell's description of the violent reception of the scouts in *The Ragged Trousered Philanthropists*[23] is to be trusted, even in part, such modes are an understandable response. Nevertheless these accounts reveal that the scouts saw themselves very much as an advance vanguard working for a change which, they expected, would be sudden once they had done the basic work of mass conversion. We may see the Clarion Scout movement as a working out of the revolutionary energy engendered by the vision of socialism as presented in the utopias of Morris's *News From Nowhere* or Blatchford's *Merrie England*. Fred Brocklehurst's statement of 1895 that "they are thirsting for new worlds to conquer"[24] brings out the nature of this energy well. Rather than the bomb, the tool of revolution was argument and conversion.

It was clear from the early days of the movement, in fact, that revolution was never really a viable option for British Socialism in this period, and this was made more apparent when workers faced the system in head-on confrontations like that at Trafalgar Square in 1887. The only real option left open was, in Morris's phrase, to "educate, agitate and organise"[25] and wait for history to do its stuff. Indeed, the myth, provided by Marx, that capitalism was destined to collapse under the weight of its own contradictions, helped on its way by the invisible hand of history, served an important psychological need for many socialists at a time when an open declaration of allegiance ran the risk of losing one's livelihood. It meant, however, that socialist theorists often failed to make important links between their educational activities and the final takeover of power. Blatchford's maxim "Make socialists and you will get socialism,"[26] although very catchy, failed to fill important theoretical gaps which arose when it became clear that the time-scales he worked with (in 1894, he set the minimum time-scale at six to seven years[27]) were unrealistic. Indeed, in moments of depression he despaired of the success of the cause altogether, leading him to periodic withdrawals from politics, and, apparently, bouts of whisky drinking.[28]

If the "making socialists" option was an unrealistic one, it was clear, especially as isolated socialists found their way to parliamentary seats, that some form of makeshift basis for political activity needed to be devised to fill in the gap between Babylon and the New Jerusalem. Out of this need arose the concept of "Practical Socialism." Blatchford, himself, was coming to terms with this paradox as early as 1892 when he drew a distinction between what he called ideal and practical socialism. The former he saw as a system of social organisation based on co-operation and mutual aid, in fact a system that we would understand better as anarchism. The latter he saw as a series of reforms, like nationalisation of the means of production and the eight-hour day.[29] In *Merrie England* he synthesised the two ideas:

> Really they are only part of one whole; practical socialism being a kind of preliminary step towards ideal socialism, so that we might with more reason call them elementary and advanced socialism.[30]

Another manifestation of this fundamental division is shown in an article by E.D. Girdlestone, written in 1895, entitled "The Two Socialisms." Girdlestone made the distinction between internal socialism, that is "a socialistic disposition on the individual's part to be influenced by education" and "external socialism," as demonstrated in socialist legislation and institutions. He stated:

> It is, in fact, the absence from many Socialist ideals of the internal element that, I submit, gives rise to, or permits of, those 'dissents, prejudices, and egotisms' both of parties and individuals ..., the presence of which sometimes makes me almost despair of Socialism.

The synthesis that he aimed for was one of "true socialism"; "a just economy with corresponding individual motives."[31]

If these fundamental divisions between different conceptions of socialism could be harmonised in theory, however, practice often led to more difficult divisions. In the 1890s, after the formation of the ILP, they were reflected in differing self-perceptions and ideas about the tactical and practical roles of the party.

Indeed, from the first conference of the party in January 1893 such tensions surfaced in the debate over the so called "Manchester Fourth Clause." This clause had been written into the constitution of the Manchester ILP by Blatchford at its formation in May 1892. It proposed that socialists should abstain from voting in the absence of

Labour or socialist candidates. Although the Manchester branch of 700 members endorsed the clause, a report in *The Clarion* of the debate over its adoption was to foreshadow later arguments over the advisability of such a policy. It reads:

> Some criticism of the Fourth Clause was offered by Messrs. Leonard Hall (Navvies Union) and A. Howarth (N.E. Manchester Labour Electoral Association), who, although averse to permeation, were in favour of using the vote to gain strategical advantages, as was done in the Home Rule struggles by the Irish Party. There was, however, an overwhelming preponderance of feeling in favour of the fourth clause as it stood, the bulk of the audience evidently understanding that the moral effect of the fourth clause would quite atone for any temporary or minor loss of influence.[32]

At the first ILP conference in Bradford in January 1893 the Fourth Clause, which by then was gaining notoriety within the movement, was defeated after the "longest and sharpest discussion" of the conference.[33] Blatchford accepted this defeat, stating: "The Fourth Clause is very dear to me. I believe it to be imperatively necessary to the maintenance of the independence of the party." But, he went on, "The majority are our General. If our General issues an order we must obey it. ... I will not be an example of disruption."[34] Nevertheless, he invited Keir Hardie, an opponent of the clause, to take up the matter in the columns of *The Clarion* and the debate was to drag on through further conferences. Although at the foundation of the ILP Blatchford had held very high hopes for its success, its rejection of the principle of complete independence, as embodied in the clause, was to mean that his attitude towards the party could be no more than ambivalent from then on. The party had taken up the course of political action which he favoured and he always advised Clarionettes to vote for ILP candidates when they stood (as he advised them to vote for *any* socialist candidates irrespective of party), but the party's political field of vision was out of harmony with Blatchford's wider approach to the problem of socialising the nation. An array of tactical arguments against the clause were produced, upon which the influence of the Irish Nationalist success in playing off one part of the political system against another should not be underestimated. For Blatchford, however, the idea of working within an unchanged political system for piecemeal change, for any other reason than a propagandist one, was anathema. If the rejection of outright revolutionism was as much a tactical as a moral matter, the agitation for Fourth Clause style independence was as much moral as tactical.[35] How could the ILP become the political expression of what was basically a moral crusade (for Blatchford, at least), underpinned by the assumption that the New Era was about to arrive, when it insisted upon a political interchange with what had already been damned? The differences which arose over the Fourth

Clause are really symptomatic of a far deeper ideological cleavage within the socialist movement in this period. As early as July 1892 Blatchford complained about Labour representatives "still clinging to the rotten plank of intrigue; still reluctant to forego the privilege of bidding for the worthless, jerry-made 'promises' which Whig and Tory cheapjacks put up for auction." He went on:

> of all the labour forces in the country the only uncompromising, incorruptible, and thoroughly earnest party is the maligned and discredited party of the Social Democrats. ... If there is ever to be a real Independent Labour Party it must be based upon the wise and honest lines which the Social Democrats have so clearly laid down and so bravely and consistently defended.[36]

In August 1893 Blatchford dropped his official links with the ILP by resigning as president of the Manchester branch, and by December of that year he had publicly proclaimed his membership of the SDF.

In practice, then, Blatchford could not work with the ILP without coming into confrontation with a series of compromises upon which rested its electoral survival. These compromises were only permissible given the assumption that electoral survival was the most important objective of the movement. From the *Clarion* viewpoint this was not the case; representation rested, necessarily, upon a bedrock of feeling that could only be created by a large-scale and wide-ranging propaganda effort undertaken by an honest and morally sound party (that is one which refused dealings with the old order).

The difference of emphasis between the parliamentary and the propagandist-based strategies is reflected in the artwork of the movement. We have already looked at Walter Crane's feminine image of socialist ideology; figures 2 and 3 provide further examples of such imagery, as drawn by the *Clarion* staff artist William Palmer. This, however, was not the only image of socialism to be drawn in the period; an equally striking masculine image was also created (see figures 4 and 5, also by Palmer). The difference between these two images illustrates well the underlying contradictions in socialist tactics in these years. On the one hand the masculine image may be interpreted as a representation of the political fighting force of socialism. It is significant that the ILP champion has socialism as a shield, or a detachable appendage. On the other hand we may interpret the feminine image as a representation of the ethical appeal of the movement (noting that the cartoonist was male). The feminine character in this artwork is always socialism embodied rather than a representation of a party with socialism as an appendix. It was one aim of the *Clarion* movement to synthesise these two aspects of socialism. For a brief while in the mid-1890s Blatchford gave support to Andrew Reid's New Party and National Union of Socialists, a movement which forlornly attempted to bring together the divided socialist ranks into one party. Indeed, Walter Crane's frontispiece (figure 6) to the book, edited by Reid,

HESITATION.

CAPITALIST EMPLOYER (*To unemployed workman*): "Come, my man, we've
   done well together on the whole, and I'm sure you're too hard-headed to
   take any notice of that soft-spoken hussey, who means to rob you—and me
   too."
*John is at present wondering how she is going to do it—as he has nothing to
be robbed of.*

Fig. 2

which described the New Party,[37] harmonised the two images of
socialism. The feminine image of ideology and creativity symbolised by
the distaff around which the words "social progress" are wrapped
seems to be leading the more business-like male image of practicalities
and necessities symbolised by the axe of "social reconstruction."
Ideology and party are mythically synthesised and heading off towards
the New Era hand in hand.

Reid's movement was short-lived, however, and *The Clarion*'s own
agitation for "One Socialist Party" was ultimately to be unsuccessful,
within its own frames of reference. The fundamental point of division
was that of the planned appeal of such a party. The calculation of this

BASHFUL ADVANCES.

LORD TWEEDMOUTH WOOING THE NEW PARTY.

"Whether in or out of office, the Liberals are bound to tackle the great problems which are before them, must take up the working class views, and join them in a great alliance to achieve their desires."—*Eighty Club Speech.*

Fig. 3

appeal was dependent upon which way socialists viewed a central problem concerning the movement in these years: that of human nature. If human nature was basically good or unselfish, socialism could appeal to the country as a whole to reconstitute itself into a "co-operative commonwealth"; if it was selfish, the appeal would be limited to a class-based one. *The Clarion* had, from its very first issue, attempted to propagate a non-sectionalised appeal based on an attainment of the co-operative commonwealth which would, circumstantially, materially benefit the workers more than any other section of society because they were the most ill-treated. The editorial of issue number 1 read: "The policy of *The Clarion* is a policy of humanity; a policy not of party, sect, or creed; but of justice, of reason and mercy."[38]

THE TWO CHAMPIONS

"It is for us, the Unionist Party, to maintain the Institutions, and to resist those Socialistic schemes, which I fear, not because I think they could ever be carried out—for they are impossible—but because they will destroy that security which is the basis of our commercial supremacy, and which gives bread-and-butter to our millions."–*Mr. Balfour before the Primrose League.*

Fig. 4

The electoral reverses of 1895, however, brought this appeal into question, and led to a series of exchanges between Blatchford and the New Unionist Leonard Hall in *The Clarion* in 1896, which prove illuminating.

In an article entitled "Altruism, Self-Interest and Land," Hall argued, first, that propaganda methods based on what he called "mesopotamias and sentimentalism" were characterised by inutility and weakness, second, that "human fellowship and kindness are flowers that will flourish only when grounded in justice," by which he meant economic justice, and third, that economic reform must precede what he called the "altruistic millennium." He went on to state, in a reply to a list of reforms which Blatchford claimed were the result of

FACE TO FACE

THE NEW CHAMPION: Now, then, you hoary old fraud, there isn't room in one world for both of us. Which is to survive?

Fig. 5

altruism, "every one of the reforms you mention as examples of 'pity and mercy' were actually carried upon waves of self interest (tinctured by fear), of which the ingredients of pity and mercy formed only the sunlit ripples." Bearing this in mind, he advocated a policy of land nationalisation as the basis for a socialist appeal, a policy, he argued, which reached the roots of monopoly and among other things "appeals to the best self interest of all in useful occupations."[39]

Blatchford's arguments in the debate took the opposite line.[40] He argued that the check at the polls was irrelevant and socialism would continue on its march even if all socialist organisations ceased to exist, first because socialism "was just and reasonable in itself," and second "because socialism has behind it the strongest sentiment of modern times – the sentiment of human love and mercy called Altruism." Blatchford firmly put sentiment before facts and figures and protested

Fig. 6

that Hall's argument that the future of socialism must be built upon the "selfishness of the mob" would pain many Clarionettes. He went on:

> Sever the socialist movement from the Altruistic 'sentiment' and it is a lost cause ... Stripped of all its sentiment and poetry, deprived of the warmth and colour which it takes from Altruism, socialism means nothing but the substitution of collective owner-ship for the private ownership now in vogue.

Without altruism socialism would become "a bloodless, soulless, inhuman creed ... a body without a soul." The thing for *Clarion* socialists to do was to

> fan the divine embers of love into a flame, to aid by every means in our power the spread of Altruistic sentiment among the people ... To make Altruists firstly, and secondly to convert those Altruists into socialists, that is our true line of action.[41]

In another article, Blatchford defined the major difference between his view and that of Hall's:

> To put this difference simply and plainly I shall say that while Leonard believes that the many are selfish and the few unselfish, I believe that the many are unselfish and the few selfish.[42]

He drew a distinction between the way people acted in public life when selfishness was forced upon them and in private life when they were allowed to act naturally with unselfishness. The only way to change the system was to liberate the spirit of humanity within people which capitalism forced beneath the surface. It was important, however, that this was done in the right order, starting at the human end. He stated: "economics are to Altruistic sentiment as the bullet to the powder. You'll win no battles with blank cartridges, nor will it avail you anything to double shot your guns if they will not go off."[43]

Here we see, then, two mutually incompatible approaches to the problem of how the new era was to be ushered in. When the socialist movement failed comprehensively to fan the embers of altruism into a flame, an appeal to self-interest was the only route left for it to take. For Blatchford this failure resulted in a bitter frustration which was often vented upon his readers; for example in a piece titled "To the Average Man," he wrote:

> You are an excellent good fellow, honest, sensible and kindly; but the sight of you fills me with bitterness. The thought of you makes my soul sad. You are on the wrong road; you are one of the greatest obstacles to the emancipation of the people; you are a perpetual thorn in the side of earnest reformers. Oh! my friend; God make incision in thee; thou art raw ... You cannot think ... you cannot see ...[44]

Nevertheless, to shift his appeal towards self-interest would have destroyed the very basis of his socialism.

Given fundamental disagreements such as these, it is not surprising that practical attempts at unity proved difficult. Andrew Reid's New Party and National Union of Socialists, to which Blatchford gave his support briefly in the mid-1890s, has already been mentioned. Alongside this Blatchford ran his own campaign for unity which gained momentum from 1894 onwards, especially when William Morris came out in support of the proposals in October 1894. Indeed, the original aim in forming the Manchester ILP was, to quote *The Clarion*, to "band together in one strong federation all the various forces of the Labour army in Manchester and Salford."[45] In fact Blatchford's initial vision of the ILP was very different from the reality of the party which ultimately emerged. He originally conceived it as

> something more than a mere Labour electoral club. It is something more than a mere socialist society. It is an organisation formed to rouse, to educate, and to unite the vast inert masses of the workers, and to give the strength of sympathy and cohesion to the scattered companies and isolated forlorn hopes of social reformers. It will do more than bring out Labour candidates. It will constitute itself into a great machine for the spreading of knowledge, for the destruction of falsehoods, for the investigation of all national and local administrative affairs.[46]

As it became clear that the ILP did not fit Blatchford's dream, but was just another socialist faction, he attempted to use *The Clarion* to create a party more in line with his ideals. The theme which runs throughout this agitation is that the move for unity needed to come from the rank and file and not the leadership. Indeed, features like "Notes From The Front" are full of reports of joint action, say by SDF and ILP groups, at the grass-roots level, and advertisements for meetings often show them to have been organised as co-operative ventures. In one of his optimistic moods Blatchford wrote:

> Let our friends be patient and confident. These people will come together. It is not a question of who shall unite them; no man can long keep them divided,[47]

while a *Clarion* referendum in 1898 recorded 7,897 votes for a united party and only 280 against.[48]

This grass-roots co-operation encouraged by the all-encompassing nature of *Clarion*-style socialism, was, however, contrasted by an inability among the labour leaders to come to terms; Ben Tillett, Tom Mann and Keir Hardie all wrote against unity, for example, and the *Labour Leader* did not hesitate to lampoon those, like John Burns, who remained outside their party. This contrast came to its climax in April 1896 at the ILP conference in Nottingham. Joseph Burgess reported the conference in *The Clarion* and wrote:

The proposal [for one socialist party] was hopeless from the moment the correspondence which in November and December of last year passed between the NAC of the ILP and the Executive council of the SDF was laid before the conference. ... If it had been the funeral of the one socialist party the circumstances could not have been more depressing.[49]

Although the SDF was still an important force at this time and was attractive to many socialists who did not like the compromise involved in joining a party without a specifically socialist title, the overtures which the ILP was making to the largely non-socialist trade unions made fusion an impossibility, and successive attempts at conference were to prove equally unsuccessful. Blatchford was to realise this and between 1897 and 1900 he largely ignored the problem of SDF–ILP relations, leaving the political stance of *The Clarion* largely under the control of A.M. Thompson, and directing his efforts towards P.J. King's trades federation scheme.

IV

This paper has mainly focused upon the way in which tensions within the infrastructure of British socialism in the 1890s were exhibited at one of its nodal points, in the columns of one of its literary organs. Before concluding we may examine the nature of these tensions further through a brief study of the relationship between Blatchford and a socialist not so directly connected with the Clarion movement, Edward Carpenter.

First, it is important to stress the amount of common ground between the two writers. Both shared the same ecumenical vision of "the Cause"; we have seen how this operated in Blatchford's case, while Carpenter, in his autobiography, was to celebrate the "oceanic" wideness of the socialist movement,[50] and in a piece he wrote for *The Clarion* in 1894 he stressed, in very Blatchfordian style:

A larger heart we want towards each other all through the Labour Movement. Such a big thing it is – and is going to be – such innumerable work to be done, and of all sorts and kinds. Burns at his kind, Keir Hardie at his, Nunquam at another, Morris or Kropotkin at another, and the unknown equally important workers each at theirs. Criticise each other's work by all means, but don't make the mistake of thinking that because the other man is working at a different part of the same building from you, that therefore he is working in opposition to you. Don't go and kick the hodman's ladder down because you individually are not going to use the bricks which he is bringing up.[51]

Moreover, the ideological content of both Blatchford's and Carpenter's socialism was easily harmonised, springing, as it did, from a common heritage; the influence of writers like Ruskin, Morris and Whitman was acknowledged in both cases, and the primacy of self-salvationary and fellowship-type strategies within the theoretical framework of both men allowed plenty of scope for mutual agreement and understanding.[52] On a practical level too, the sort of activity which Carpenter was involved with in Sheffield was very similar to the Clarion model of local activism.[53]

Given this basis of agreement, it is not surprising that we find Carpenter writing for *The Clarion* on several occasions during this period[54] and, indeed, maintaining good relations generally with Blatchford and his movement. Despite this unity of cause and vision, however, agreement on matters of concrete politics proved more illusive, as it did throughout the Labour movement. One difference, that over attitudes to political violence, may be highlighted with reference to the divergent reactions of *The Clarion* and Carpenter to the Walsall Anarchist case of 1892.

We have already looked at the response of *The Clarion* to this incident. The paper, in fact, barely covered the trial and sentences of the alleged conspirators, except in so far as to dissociate itself from acts of violence. In the same issue in which the editorial dismissed the participants as "misguided or weak minded fanatics ... [who] have no following, and are not taken seriously," "Boggs," the staff poet, stressed the distinction between socialists and "these Anarchists from foreign shores," lamenting that

> ... when the law has puzzled out
> A plot to kill or maim;
> The socialists – without a doubt –
> Are sure to get the blame.[55]

At the time of the trial and sentences of the conspirators Blatchford wrote a longer article expressing his views more fully, in response to "two or three letters" objecting to his treatment of the subject. Entitled "Reason or Revolution?", the article specifically rejected any concept of a "class war" and damned the "physical force men" as "the worst enemies of true socialism, and the worst enemies of the people."[56]

Carpenter, on the other hand, took a very different line on the incident. He appeared in court to testify on behalf of the defence, and worked alongside David Nicoll, the editor of *Commonweal*, in an effort to get the sentences reduced.[57] The clearest expression of his views was published in the Anarchist monthly, *Freedom*. Asserting that the defence of "our Walsall friends" should not rest too heavily upon the spurious nature of the charges, he went on:

> What more serious indictment of existing society and institutions could we have than this? When society drives its best men to such extremity, how rotten indeed must it be! ... if society's explanation is that the men have gone mad, then Society cannot

but also see that on it lies the responsibility of having driven them mad.

He rested his case upon the assertion that "the very circumstances of the case prove that society itself is the criminal and that on it lies the chief blame ..."[58]

We may observe, then, a fundamental divergence of opinion between Carpenter and Blatchford over this incident; although Carpenter was not prepared overtly to condone the use of violent methods, he refused to share Blatchford's anxiety to distance himself from the alleged conspirators. Nevertheless, at the same time Blatchford was still prepared to praise Carpenter in *The Clarion* as a "great poet, a great thinker, a great scholar, and a great man."[59]

The same pattern of conciliation and disagreement may be observed in a debate between Carpenter and the Blatchford brothers which was precipitated by disagreements within the Halifax Labour Union, over the alleged dealings of some of its members with the Liberal Party, late in 1894. Blatchford's condemnation of the members in question had moved Carpenter to protest and, in an article he wrote for *The Clarion*, he raised the general problem of the role of the delegate within the socialist movement.[60] Noting a "spirit of distrust and suspicion" within the movement, he objected to what he called "the dancing doll delegate theory" favoured by Blatchford. Instead, he advocated giving delegates more scope for personal initiative:

> ... fix your man on the fundamental points; be sure that he is fair and square on these ..., and then, for goodness' sake, leave him free to exercise some judgement and manhood in the minor details ... our men must take their heads along with them, and not be decapitated before they go.[61]

Carpenter's article produced replies from both Robert and Montague Blatchford in the next edition of *The Clarion*, Montague dealing with the specific details of the Halifax case, and Robert meeting Carpenter on the wider issue of democracy within the movement. Championing the will of the majority against the rights of the delegate, Blatchford used his normal line of reasoning:

> What I demand is the recognition of the principle that the elected representatives of the people represent the people and not represent themselves ...
>
> ... our working people are too modest, and submit too much to the airs and patronage of their inferiors; ... many, if not most, of the men with great reputations for intellect are very second rate men indeed, and that amongst the ranks of the "uneducated" workers there are large numbers of men of sterling honesty and great capacity.[62]

He went on to express a hope that "Democracy shall not contract the baneful habit of leaning upon its leaders." If there was a clear disagreement between Blatchford and Carpenter over this matter, however, it was only within the context of a more general mutual sympathy; Blatchford, anxious not to be too abrasive, wrote, in the same article: "In this matter of Democracy Carpenter and I are very much nearer in accord than he seems to suppose," and identified himself with Carpenter (and William Morris) as a man "with no axe to grind." Carpenter too, in a reply to *The Clarion,* despite complaining that he had been "deliberately scalped by you [Blatchford] and Mont Blong between you," conceded that "on some of the main subjects of my letter Nunquam and I are agreed."[63]

Finally, during the 1890s, we find Blatchford and Carpenter in disagreement over a central part of Carpenter's own thought, the question of sexual relations. Blatchford set out his position clearly in a letter to Carpenter, who had written to him raising the subject and giving his opinion that socialists should discuss it in the open. "In short," replied Blatchford, "I think the time is not ripe for Socialists as Socialists, to meddle with the sexual question." Although expressing a belief that "the sexual relations are all wrong now," he proposed that "the economic and industrial change" must come first and would be retarded if it were too closely identified with a campaign for such changes. "Perhaps I am a prejudiced old Tory," he admitted, "but the whole subject is 'nasty' to me. Be charitable. I can't help it."[64]

Blatchford's position on this issue is illuminating. Not only does it raise questions as to the "largeness" of his own socialism, or reveal inconsistencies within his general stance (especially when contrasted with his stand against religion in the early 1900s), but it also goes further to demonstrate the nature of the relationship between the two writers that we have observed already, a relationship that allowed for disagreement over specific items of policy or strategy, but only within the context of a wider, if less defined, sphere of agreement and mutual identification. The same letter that outlined Blatchford's position of distance from the sexual debate ended with a request for articles for *The Clarion* and the statement that "... I wish you were one of *The Clarion* "Board" ... You are a better man than I am".

The relationship between Carpenter and Blatchford in the 1890s illustrates well the nature of relations within the Labour movement as a whole during this period. An infrastructure flawed by a series of internal contradictions but held together by a set of common aspirations and a condemnation of the status quo could (and did) achieve results in terms of propaganda work, and has achieved a sort of mythical unity in the currency of historians. When an earnest attempt to achieve power was made, however, the pressure upon the infrastructure was increased and the tensions were made more obvious. Edward Carpenter, in one of his *Clarion* articles, showed his awareness of the problem:

As long as you are standing at a street corner doing propaganda, you shape society according to your ideal. That is right enough. But as soon as you come into your legislative or executive body, you find society won't be shaped, nor will the other members of your council be shaped, to your ideal![65]

V

On 27 February 1900, while most of the country had its eyes on the news of Cronje's surrender in South Africa, the Labour Representation Committee, which R.B. Suthers described at the time as "A little cloud, no bigger than a man's hand which may grow into a united Labour Party,"[66] was formed, with the aim of providing a united organisation working for labour representation in parliament. When the meeting had disbanded it had agreed on a policy, if it could be called that, not based upon Socialism, but on this single plank. The effect of this, especially as the Taff Vale decision and the Osborne judgement drove the trade unions into the movement, was to further fragment the ideology of socialism into a number of different pieces. The Social Democratic Federation left the conference, complaining, with specific reference to the debate on the class war, that it had simply "afforded the chiefs of the ILP an opportunity for a display of that treachery to which we have, unfortunately, by this time become accustomed."[67] Within a year it was to withdraw from the LRC altogether. At the same time the ILP and the Clarion movement had reached loggerheads over Blatchford's attitude to the Boer War, which had led to an ILP boycott of all Clarion publications and a statement from Blatchford that "from natural causes *The Clarion* and the ILP have drifted asunder ... we can do without them far better than they can do without us."[68]

These splits were to institutionalise themselves as the machinery of the new party developed along with its tactics. Keir Hardie wrote in 1903, with inferred reference to *The Clarion*, "for a time in England the fibre of the Socialist movement was almost totally destroyed by a spirit of irresponsible levity, the effects of which remain to this day."[69] The past tense of this statement is instructive. Hardie was writing here very much from dry ground after his own "serious" policies had been justified in the creation of the committee, while *The Clarion* remained in the uninstitutionalised wilderness.

The electoral success of the LRC in 1906 and the subsequent formation of the Labour Party, which still refused an open declaration of socialism, made this break between institution and ideology irreparable. Indeed in 1908 we find *The Clarion* raising funds and supporting the dissident socialist Victor Grayson in the Colne Valley by-election, and in 1909–10 Grayson was allowed to use *The Clarion* to organise the British Socialist Party.[70]

The process of change then from millennialism to institutionalism, or socialism to labourism, was pushed along by a fracture which we may tentatively date at 1900, the causative tensions of which had been evident throughout the 1890s.

It is important to remember, however, that the LRC was only one of a number of fragments. The reason why it got on so well was that it was prepared to compromise and work within the ideological and institutional channels set up for it by the system many socialists wanted to see washed away completely (as MacDonald's readiness to come to terms over electoral arrangements with Herbert Gladstone testifies[71]). Bearing this in mind, we should not forget the other fragments, which may become obscured by the fact that we are so used to seeing the Parliamentary Labour Party as the only mainstream expression of Socialism today. *The Clarion's* readership, in fact, rose to around the 80,000 mark in the 1900s, while perhaps the most important socialist propagandist of the twentieth century, Robert Tressell, was a member of the SDF and exhibits in *The Ragged Trousered Philanthropists* many of the hallmarks of Blatchford's influence. Half a century later we see the same traditions re-emerging in the stance of the socialist writer George Orwell, whose position as a writer, outside the narrow boundaries of party dogma, is not too dissimilar to that of Blatchford, and whose appeals to truth and justice are basically those of pre-Labour Party politics.

Blatchford wrote at the beginning of his career with *The Clarion*: "I am an incorrigible dreamer, and walk almost incessantly with my head in the clouds, so that it is not to be wondered at if I often bang my shins against obstacles that were easily avoided."[72] The failure of the Labour Party to accommodate such incorrigible dreamers may say much about the fact that when the New Jerusalem did arrive in 1945, its chief architects were both life-long liberals.

MARTIN WRIGHT

NOTES

1. *The Clarion*, 26 Jan. 1895.
2. *The Clarion*, 12 Dec. 1891.
3. *The Clarion*, 30 April 1892.
4. *The Clarion*, 26 Dec. 1891.
5. Margaret Cole, *Makers of the Labour Movement* (London: Longmans Green, 1948), p.195.
6. For an account of Blatchford's early career in Manchester see Judith Fincher, "The Clarion Movement: A Study of a Socialist Attempt to Implement the Co-operative Commonwealth in England, 1891–1914," M.A. diss. Manchester, 1971, pp.9–76, and Laurence Thompson, *Robert Blatchford, Portrait Of An Englishman* (London: Gollancz, 1955), pp.1–85.
7. Quoted in L. Thompson, op. cit., p.9.
8. Stanley Pierson, *Marxism and the Origins of British Socialism* (Ithaca and London: Cornell U.P., 1973), p.149.
9. *The Clarion*, 5 March 1892.

10. *The Clarion*, 14 May 1892.
11. *The Clarion*, 18 August 1894.
12. *The Clarion*, 18 Feb. 1893.
13. Circa 1909, quoted in L. Thompson, op. cit., p.96.
14. Even such an anti-Blatchfordite as Hardie wrote, as late as July 1914, "I would have England a 'merrie England'." Emrys Hughes, ed., *Keir Hardie's Speeches and Writings* (Glasgow, 1928), p.162.
15. Quoted in Preface to Robert Blatchford, *My Eighty Years* (London: Cassell, 1931), p.xiii.
16. *The Clarion*, 2 July 1892.
17. Stephen Yeo, "A New Life: The Religion of Socialism in Britain, 1883–1896," *History Workshop Journal*, No. 4 (1977), pp.5–56.
18. Robert Blatchford, *Merrie England* (1893; London: Journeyman P., 1977), p.99.
19. For example, see Blatchford's comments to Carpenter on the launching of the *Labour Leader*, Letter to Edward Carpenter, 17 April 1894, MS.386.49, Carp. Coll. Thanks to Tony Brown for this and other references from the Carpenter Collection.
20. *The Clarion*, 16 Jan. 1892.
21. *The Clarion*, 30 April 1892.
22. *The Clarion*, 27 Oct. 1894. For further evidence of this feeling see the sister paper to *The Clarion*, *The Scout: A Journal For Socialist Workers*, launched in March 1895.
23. Robert Tressell, *The Ragged Trousered Philanthropists* (1914; London: Grafton, 1965), pp.425–30.
24. *The Clarion*, 23 March 1895.
25. See Morris' design for the membership card of the Democratic Federation, reproduced in Henry Pelling, *Origins of the Labour Party* (Oxford: Oxford U.P., 1965), p.32.
26. See *Merrie England*, pp.46–7, for Blatchford's reasoning.
27. See letter to A.M. Thompson, quoted in L. Thompson, op. cit., p.124.
28. See, e.g., *The Clarion*, 1 Sept. 1894: Blatchford, "No. I cannot write about the Labour Movement this week. I am full to the lips. The Labour Movement is a battle of factions. I have no heart for it." Also see Blatchford, Letter to Carpenter, 27 Dec. 1893: "I grind my bones to make Socialist bread. It is hard and tasteless work, and I am so weary of it." MS.386.45, Carp. Coll.
29. *The Clarion*, 6 Feb. 1892.
30. Robert Blatchford, *Merrie England*, p.44.
31. *The Clarion*, 13 April 1895.
32. *The Clarion*, 21 May 1892.
33. *The Clarion*, 21 Jan. 1893.
34. Ibid.
35. The tactical argument for the clause projected the fragmentation of the Liberal Party under the pressure of a growing socialist vote created by Clarion-style propaganda. See the three columns devoted by Blatchford to the matter in *The Clarion*, 11 Feb. 1893.
36. *The Clarion*, 2 July 1892.
37. Andrew Reid, *The New Party* (London: Hodder Bros., 1895).
38. *The Clarion*, 12 Dec. 1891.
39. *The Clarion*, 23 May 1896.
40. They are reprinted in full as *Clarion Pamphlet no. 22*, "Altruism: Christ's Gospel of Love Against Man's Dismal Science of Greed" (London: Clarion Press, 1898).
41. *The Clarion*, 18 April 1896.
42. *The Clarion*, 30 May 1896.
43. *The Clarion*, 25 April 1896.
44. *The Clarion*, 16 May 1896.
45. *The Clarion*, 14 May 1892.
46. *The Clarion*, 28 May 1892.
47. *The Clarion*, 20 Oct. 1894.

48. *The Clarion*, 3 Dec. 1898. As an index to the representativeness of these figures in regard to the movement as a whole, note that at the Labour Representation Committee Conference in 1900, about 23,000 socialists (as opposed to trade unionists) were represented (*The Clarion*, 3 March 1900). The referendum was a favoured *Clarion* expedient, e.g. see A.M. Thompson, "The Referendum and Initiative in Practice," *Clarion Pamphlet no. 31* (London: Clarion Press, 1899).

49. *The Clarion*, 11 April 1896.

50. Edward Carpenter, *My Days and Dreams* (London: Allen & Unwin, 1916), p.126.

51. *The Clarion*, 24 Nov. 1894.

52. This led to similarities in their work. See e.g. Blatchford advocating Carpenter-style simplification of life in *Merrie England*, pp.16–17, or Carpenter's Blatchford-like synthesis of the ideal and the practical in *My Days and Dreams*, p.127, and his use of *Clarion*-style logic in "The Smoke Dragon and How to Destroy it" (part 2), *The Clarion*, 5 May 1894.

53. See Sheila Rowbotham and Jeffrey Weeks, *Socialism and the New Life: The Personal and Sexual Politics of Edward Carpenter and Havelock Ellis* (London: Pluto P., 1977), pp.47–75.

54. Apart from a small number of letters and pieces of verse, Carpenter's work for *The Clarion* in this period included "Saved by a Nose," Christmas edition 1892; "The Smoke Dragon and How to Destroy it" (in weekly parts), 28 April–2 June 1894; "Democracy and the Delegate Theory," 24 Nov. 1894; "Democracy: an answer to Nunquam," 1 Dec. 1894 and "Vivisection," 1 Dec. 1894.

55. *The Clarion*, 16 Jan. 1892.

56. *The Clarion*, 16 April 1892.

57. For Carpenter and the Walsall episode see Chushichi Tsuzuki, *Edward Carpenter, Prophet of Human Fellowship* (Cambridge: Cambridge U.P., 1980), pp.98–102, and Rowbotham and Weeks, op. cit., p.62.

58. *Freedom*, Dec. 1892.

59. *The Clarion*, 16 April 1892. Also see *The Clarion*, 9 April 1892, for further praise of Carpenter.

60. See "Democracy and the Delegate Theory," *The Clarion*, 24 Nov. 1894.

61. Ibid.

62. *The Clarion*, 1 Dec. 1894.

63. *The Clarion*, 15 Dec. 1894.

64. Blatchford, Letter to Carpenter, 11 Jan. 1894, MS.386.46, Carp. Coll.

65. *The Clarion*, 24 Nov. 1894.

66. *The Clarion*, 10 March 1900.

67. *Justice*, 3 March 1900.

68. *The Clarion*, 28 April 1900.

69. *Labour Leader*, 24 Jan. 1903.

70. For Grayson see Reg Groves, *The Strange Case of Victor Grayson* (London: Pluto P., 1975).

71. In September 1903 Macdonald and Gladstone came to a secret agreement whereby the LRC was allowed a free hand in 30 constituencies in return for a "demonstration of friendliness" to the Liberals in constituencies where it had influence. See Frank Bealey and Henry Pelling, *Labour and Politics 1900–1906* (London: Macmillan, 1958), pp.125–60.

72. *The Clarion*, 19 Dec. 1891.

Coming-of-Age: Edward Carpenter on Sex and Reproduction

In Britain, two texts bracketed the late-nineteenth-century socialist debate on the woman question: Harriet Adams Walther's translation of August Bebel's *Woman in the Past, Present and Future* (1886) and Edward Carpenter's *Love's Coming-of-Age* (1896). Both were popular, but the latter was unique because as well as documenting the material conditions of women under capitalism, it mapped the inner life of struggle and personal transformation involved in realising the "new life" under socialism. It did so, moreover, during a period when mainstream socialist groups in Britain were becoming increasingly pragmatic and intolerant of "diversions": "when the movement which carried the connection between personal change and socialist revolution was beginning to wane."[1] At that time, as Carpenter recorded in his autobiography, "sex-questions ... were generally tabooed and practically not discussed at all, though they now have become almost an obsession of the public mind."[2] In January 1894, for example, when Carpenter first canvassed his idea of a pamphlet series on the subject, he was advised by Robert Blatchford, editor of *The Clarion*, to "let it alone." "Perhaps I'm a prejudiced old Tory," Blatchford wrote, "but the whole subject is 'nasty' to me."[3] Blatchford went on to underscore his reluctance by arguing that such topics "seriously retarded" the socialist programme: reform of "sexual relations must *follow* the economic and industrial change" and socialists' energies should not be diverted from the main task which "will need all our energy and consume all the years we are likely to live."[4]

Carpenter, however, had personal reasons for being interested in sex questions. He was a homosexual in a homophobic and emotionally reserved society, and his sensitivity to the sexual tensions in the late Victorian period combined with his sympathy for women's struggles to inspire a series of four pamphlets on the emotional and sexual dimensions of personal life. *Sex-Love, and Its Place in a Free Society, Woman, and Her Place in a Free Society* and *Marriage in Free Society* were all published in 1894. The fourth pamphlet, *Homogenic Love, and Its Place in a Free Society*, was printed for private circulation in the following year. The first three pamphlets were combined with some additional material to produce *Love's Coming-of-Age*, which was accepted for publication by Fisher Unwin in June 1895. Two months earlier Oscar Wilde had been arrested and his subsequent trial produced "a sheer panic ... over *all* questions of sex, and especially of course questions of the Intermediate Sex."[5] So, although Carpenter had no intention of including the fourth pamphlet in the book, Fisher Unwin took fright, cancelled his agreement with Carpenter and even refused to publish and sell earlier works like *Towards Democracy*. Approaches to other publishers met with no success so Carpenter turned to the Labour Press, a small Manchester company in which he had both a financial and managerial interest, and which stood him in good stead when the taboo on sex questions caused such publishing difficulties.[6] The book was finally published in 1896.

Once published the pamphlets, and later the book, received mixed reviews. In the conventional press, they were both praised for their openness and condemned for ignoring "the claims of reticence that his readers have a right to impose" as well as their "dangerous conclusions."[7] Amongst socialists, the works were generally well received and even Robert Blatchford approved.[8] *Justice* felt "bound to agree" with most of the book but (in keeping with the prejudices of its editors) regretted that Carpenter "accepted unquestioningly the vulgar view of the present subject position of woman."[9] Socialist women were uniformly appreciative: Lily Bell, in her regular column for *The Labour Leader*, praised the book for its lack of pretence;[10] Olive Schreiner thought his work on marriage was "splendid"[11] and wrote of the many letters of praise she had received from women friends;[12] and Isabella Ford declared that Carpenter must have "been a woman in some other 'incarnation.' "[13]

The enthusiasm for the book displayed by socialist women is a measure of the poor standard of debate about the woman question elsewhere in socialist writing. Not only were questions of sex and sexuality marginalised, they were thoroughly conflated with discussions about women's reproductive role. Carpenter, in contrast, conceptually separated sex and reproduction; indeed, where his colleagues[14] were preoccupied with women's reproductive capacity, Carpenter was almost disinclined to give reproduction any weight at all. That he so turns conventional wisdom on its head was greatly appreciated by socialist women at the time,[15] yet I am intrigued that he paid so little attention to the likely reproductive consequences of sexual relations for women, and this sets the focus for my discussion of *Love's Coming-of-Age*.

In this paper, I will be leaving aside Carpenter's description of women's position in capitalist society, and what he hoped would be "her place in a free society." Instead, I wish to contrast his treatment of sex with the account of reproduction implicit in his discussions of sex, woman and marriage. In the next two sections I begin with an analysis of Carpenter's theory on sex-love and end with a discussion of his assumptions about reproduction. Two specific sites – his description of the "new woman" and his account of contraception – are then used to explore the *interplay* between his concepts of sexuality and of reproduction. In my concluding section, I argue that Carpenter, in examining the sex questions of his time, constituted a particular ideal

Woman, one which undercut Carpenter's undoubted commitment to, and limits the possibilities for, women's emancipation.

I. SEXUAL DISCOURSES:
ANIMAL DESIRE AND TRANSCENDENTAL LOVE

In the first of the free society pamphlets, *Sex-Love*, Carpenter stated the premise on which his sexual radicalism depended:

> I think it may fairly be said that the prime object of Sex is *union*, the physical union as the allegory and expression of the real union, and that generation is a secondary object or result of this union. If ... we go to the very highest expression of Sex, in the sentiment of Love, we find the latter takes the form chiefly and before all else of a desire for union, and only in lesser degree of a desire for race propagation.[16]

In contradicting the widely held Victorian belief that the main purpose of sex was procreation, Carpenter placed sexuality in the spotlight, but did so *at the expense of reproduction*. Procreation, for Carpenter, was simply the biological/physical analogue of the more important potential of sexual desire to express Love, and it was the transmutation of physical sexual desire into its "highest" form – the sentiment of Love – which concerned him. It is this preoccupation with the relationship between sex and Love, rather than sex and reproduction, which frames Carpenter's account of women's sexuality.

Carpenter's concept of sex drive anticipated Freud: Carpenter saw sex as a universal drive, generally repressed in modern civilised societies but particularly so in women. He described it as a "titanic, instinctive and sub-conscious" drive which conflicted with "his [*sic*] later developed, more especially human and moral self" (*Sex-Love*, pp. 6–7). Nonetheless, it was a drive capable of transformation:

> In the human body [there are] sensual, emotional, spiritual, and other elements of which it may be said that their death on one plane means their transformation and new birth on other planes ... There are grounds for believing in the transmutability of the various forms of the passion, and grounds for thinking that the sacrifice of a lower phase may sometimes be the only condition on which a higher and more durable phase can be attained. (*Sex-Love*, p. 9)

The assumption that union and not procreation was the prime object of sex was made in support of this "law of transmutation." It makes, as Carpenter said, "a good deal of difference in our estimate of Sex whether the one function or the other is considered primary" (*Sex-Love*, p. 23). The choice between union and procreation was undefended at this time,[17] but it did allow Carpenter to affirm the importance of sexuality.

In addition to rescuing sexuality from the pedestrian purposes of procreation, Carpenter rescues "sex-love" from the gutter. He was sharply critical of the Mrs Grundyism of Victorian society and argued that "the regeneration of our social ideas" entailed a refusal to conceive "of Sex as a thing covert and to be ashamed of, marketable and unclean" (*Sex-Love*, p.20). Here, however, Carpenter's argument fell foul of his own "law of transmutation" because while sex was beneficial, "the allegory of Love in the physical world" (*Sex-Love*, p.21), it was still an *animal* instinct in contrast to "the *human* element in Love" (*Sex-Love*, p.12).

Carpenter envisaged an almost inevitable conflict between sex and Love. Sexual intercourse so easily became the satisfaction of individual desire rather than a concern for the "welfare and happiness of the beloved one" (*Sex-Love*, p.14); the satisfaction of mere sexual drives compelled the objectification of the loved one, whereas Love required a consciousness of equality with the other;[18] and the "law of trans-mutation" itself entailed an opposition between sex and Love since the latter was achieved at the expense of the former through conscious control and self-restraint. Given this model of sexuality, it is not surprising to find the *Clarion* reviewer of *Sex-Love* baulking at the idea of Love as anything less than platonic:

> Edward Carpenter will have sex-love a dual thing, part body and part soul, and gives the soul the mastery, that it may triumph and rise superior to the body, as the butterfly from the caterpillar, or the lily from the bulb ... Here, then, is our point of divergence with our author. He will couple love with desire; and hope for some final compromise or evolution. We will divorce the two ideas, and say that love has no more to do with desire than it has to do with drunkenness. That is to say, we look upon sex-love as a spiritual thing, having no relation whatever to any physical instinct, and not belonging in any way to the function of the perpetuation of the species.[19]

Thus, on the one hand, Carpenter would not discount *physical* sexual activity but would seek a balance in which "both the satisfaction of the passion and the non-satisfaction of it are desirable and beautiful" (*Sex-Love*, p.8) and, on the other hand, his evaluation of Love as transcendent and sex as animal lent credence to the puritanical attitudes he abhorred. The apparent contradiction has much to do with Carpenter's views on the difference between male and female sexuality.

Although most of the descriptive account of an individual's experience of the sex-drive was given in normative terms (*he* finds that the satisfaction of *his* imperious impulses conflicts with the welfare of *her* he loves (*Sex-Love*, p.6)), the repression of female sexuality was a central part of Carpenter's critique of Victorian sexual practices. His view that sexual passion was natural, that "every adult at some time or other" needed to experience sexual intercourse for their general well-being, was counterposed to "the state of enforced celibacy in which vast numbers of women live to-day" (*Sex-Love*, pp.4–5). Where he was clear about the existence of female sexuality, he was less so about its *nature* and this has to be reconstructed from comments scattered throughout the essays on *Woman* and *Marriage*. It was there, in his comparative account of the nature of male and female sexuality, that the pattern of essential differences between the sexes, and the agenda for sexual freedom, began to be defined.

Man was, by "nature and needs, polygamous," even though in his higher emotions he tended towards monogamy. Woman, however, "cannot be said to be by her physical nature polyandrous."[20] Man's needs were greater, woman's more limited (*Marriage*, p.31); his were stronger and less well controlled (*LCA*, pp.26–7) while hers were more diffuse and "less specially sexual; ... it dwells longer in caresses and embraces, and determines itself more slowly towards the reproductive system" (*Marriage*, pp.10–11). "Speaking broadly," Carpenter contended that

> *all* the passions and powers, the intellect and affections and emotions and all, are really profounder and vaster in Man than in Woman – are more varied, root deeper, and have wider scope; but then the woman has this advantage, that her powers are more co-ordinated, are in harmony with each other, where his are disjointed or in conflict. (*LCA*, p.27)

In Carpenter's account, woman's greater harmony and control over sexual passion was evidence of her affectional and emotional superiority. Woman had a "more clinging affectional nature" which "perhaps accentuates her capacity of absorption in the one" (*Marriage*, p.31); for her, sex was "a deep and sacred instinct, carrying with it a sense of natural purity" which discouraged that separation of "the sentiment of Love and the physical passion which is so common with men."[21] Indeed the connection between Love and sex was so strong for women that one of the "natural tragedies lies ... in the fact that the man to whom she first surrenders her body often acquires for her ... so profound and inalienable a claim upon her heart" (*Marriage*, p.46n). Women, in Carpenter's view, found it easier to see Love as their goal and to direct their passion to this end; what in man was "an unorganised passion, an individual need or impetus" was in woman a "constructive instinct" (*Woman*, p.32).

The affectional superiority of women, and the capacity of the sex desire to be transmuted into the higher and more durable form of Love, took on particular significance in the context of evolutionary change. For Carpenter, essential sexual differences not only suggested an explanation for contemporary social relations, they also, and more importantly, indicated the direction of future change. They posited "a deep and in some sense eternal relation between man and woman

which must inevitably assert itself again" (*Woman*, p. 8; also p. 10).
Women were the agents of change in this scenario, because women's
sexuality was closer to the ideal of transcendent Love towards which
Carpenter hoped the race was developing.

Carpenter's ideas about evolution were based on works by Havelock
Ellis, especially his *Westminster Review* article, "The Changing Status
of Women" (1887), and *Man and Woman* (1894), published in the same
year as Carpenter's three pamphlets on sex, woman and marriage.[22] In
Love's Coming-of-Age Carpenter quotes extensively from *Man and
Woman*, and in a lengthy footnote summarises Ellis' findings on the
essential differences between the sexes. These listed differences
in brain characteristics, stamina, motor skills, affectability and the
nervous system (women had a greater preponderance of more primitive and fundamental nerve centres and were, therefore, prone to
hysteria, suggestibility and excitability) (*LCA*, p. 159n). Carpenter also
agreed with Ellis about the natural, sexual differences in intellectual
and psychological capacity: women were more emotional and intuitive,
deficient in logic, more empathetic but unable to grasp abstract and
general ideas such as justice and truth (*Woman*, p. 21). Morally, "Man
has developed the more active, and Woman the more passive virtues"
and here too, these differences were based on "the very nature of their
respective sexual functions" (*Woman*, p. 22).

Carpenter accepted Ellis' judgements on the implications of these
differences with one exception, the question of how invariable and
durable such sexual differences would be. Carpenter's concept of
evolution left room for plasticity: essential differences were not themselves "*absolutely* permanent" (*Woman*, p. 10) and in the long term
it was never certain what evolution was preparing (*LCA*, p. 67).
Nonetheless, the consequence of assuming some degree of sexual
differentiation was a concept of sexual equality which necessarily took
the form of complementarity. Thus, while it was desirable for social
change to bring the two sexes closer together across the gulf that
contemporary society had constructed, Carpenter thought the sexes
would remain differentiated, not "quite so *much* differentiated as now,
but only to a degree which will enhance and adorn, instead of destroy,
their sense of mutual sympathy" (*Marriage*, p. 19).

Finally, Carpenter and Ellis were agreed on woman's primary role in
evolution, but whereas Ellis was thinking of women's reproductive role
and the advantages to be gained if the reproducers took the lead in
selecting a mate, Carpenter was concerned with the transmutation of
sex into Love. Women should be the "interpreters of Love to man ...
his guide in sexual matters" (*Woman*, p. 9) because their sexuality more
readily lent itself to an appreciation of the purpose of sex, and to the
exercise of restraint which was the means to that end:

> He is indeed a master of life who accepting the grosser desires as
> they come to his body, and not refusing them, knows how to

transform them at will into the most rare and fragrant flowers of human emotion. (*Sex-Love*, p. 10)

Carpenter thought such "mastery" came more naturally to women and, in effect, the purpose of *Love's Coming-of-Age* was to convince men of the advantage of what he thought women already practised: "Restraint (which is absolutely necessary at times) *has* its compensations" (*Sex-Love*, p. 9) or, as one of Carpenter's reviewers put it, "a judicious lust is the best stairway to the higher love."[23]

The hidden agenda in Carpenter's account of sex-love was a defence of homosexuality. The main elements of his analysis – the idealisation of sentimental Love over and above physical sensuality, the presumption that restraint and denial were the mechanisms for transcending the grosser desires and gaining access to the higher human emotions, and the assumption of essential differences – were all necessary elements of Carpenter's justification of the morality of homosexuality. His first concerted defence of homosexuality came in *Homogenic Love*, the fourth of the free society pamphlets, published in January 1895.[24] It was later rewritten as a chapter on "The Homogenic Attachment" for *The Intermediate Sex* (1908).[25]

Informing his defence of homosexuality, albeit in a complex way, was Carpenter's experience of confusion, loneliness, misunderstanding and lack of guidance as a youth struggling to define his sexual identity, and later as an adult faced with the difficulties of living a homosexual life in a homophobic society (*IS*, p. 193). In his autobiography, Carpenter described his personal emotional turmoil as:

> an open wound continually bleeding. I felt starved and unfed, and unable to rest in the chilling contacts of ordinary life. As to the usual attractions set before the eyes of middle-class youth, the hopeless, helpless young ladyisms, or the bolder beauties of the gutter, they were both a detestable boredom to me.[26]

At times he felt this turmoil "threatened to paralyse [his] mental and physical faculties" so it was "with a great leap of joy"[27] that he read, at the age of 25, Walt Whitman's *Leaves of Grass* (1855) and *Democratic Vistas* (1871). There he found a description of comradely love to match his own sentiments. He had been given, he said in a letter to Whitman,

> a ground for the love of men ... For you have made men to be not ashamed of the noblest instincts of their nature. Women are beautiful but to some, there is that which passes the love of women.[28]

The practical difficulties of living a homosexual life also informed Carpenter's analysis. In both *Homogenic Love* and *The Intermediate Sex*, Carpenter suggested that physical sexual relations among homosexuals were more difficult because of "the very nature of the case," and the homosexual temperament. It is worth pointing out here that Carpenter was 47 before he met George Merrill and that his previous three or four homosexual relationships were difficult and unhappy.[29] It is also worth remembering that Carpenter was 54 before George was able to move into Millthorpe and that was in 1898, four years after Carpenter wrote *Homogenic Love*.

While neither "denying that sexual intimacies do exist" nor wanting to "condemn special acts or familiarities between lovers," Carpenter suggested that in many cases homosexuality was "not distinctively sexual at all" and only physical to the extent of "embrace and endearment" (*Homogenic Love*, pp. 14–15). His account of his own sexual feelings, in the case history he prepared for Havelock Ellis, did not deny passion but placed it secondary to love:

> I have never had to do with actual paederasty, so-called. My chief desire in love is bodily nearness or contact, as to sleep naked with a naked friend; the specially sexual, though urgent enough, seems a secondary matter ... I think that for a perfect relationship the actual sex gratifications (whatever they may be) probably hold a less important place in this [homosexual] love than in the other [heterosexual].[30]

The view of homosexuality as more spiritual than sensual would appear to be a product of experience.

The thesis put forward in *Sex-Love* was central to Carpenter's defence of homosexuality in several ways. First, the distinction between Love and sexual passion exonerated homosexuality from the charge of licentiousness:

> It would be a great mistake to suppose that their attachments are necessarily sexual, or connected with sexual acts. On the contrary (as abundant evidence shows), they are often purely emotional in their character; and to confuse Uranians (as is so often done) with libertines having no law but curiosity in self-indulgence is to do them a great wrong. (*IS*, pp. 193–4. Cf. *Homogenic Love*, p. 15)

Second, the "law of transmutation" was used to argue the greater moral rectitude of homosexual love:

> It would seem probable that the attachment of [the male homosexual] is of a tender and profound character; indeed, it is possible that in this class of men we have the love sentiment in one of its most perfect forms – a form in which from the necessities of the situation the sensuous element, though present, is exquisitely subordinated to the spiritual. (*IS*, p. 198)

The attachments formed by the "normal" homosexual male constituted an ideal type of sexual relation, especially in contrast to the more usual sensual pleasures of masculine society; homosexuality inspired greater heroism, greater romance and sentiment (*Homogenic Love*,

p. 37). This was so clearly the model of transcendent Love presented in *Sex-Love* that it seems obvious Carpenter's defence of homosexuality inspired his analysis of heterosexual relations rather than the reverse. Indeed what was offered as an hypothesis in *Sex-Love* had, in *Homogenic Love*, all the force of "law" (*Homogenic Love*, p. 36; Cf. *Sex-Love*, p. 8).

The most significant aspect of Carpenter's defence of homosexuality was his claim that it was "in a vast number of cases quite instinctive and congenital, mentally and physically, and therefore twined in the very roots of individual life and practically ineradicable" (*Homogenic Love*, p. 18). Carpenter played an important part in promoting a medical model of homosexual behaviour which was, as Weeks has argued, crucial in the emergence of "the homosexual" as an identifiable individual.[31] In Carpenter's view the homosexual was born not made, and if some of his reviewers read that as diseased and not morally degenerate, they at least agreed with Carpenter that legal repression was an inappropriate response to homosexuality.[32] Carpenter himself was much more positive. Not only was repression pointless – "no amount of compulsion can ever change the homogenic instinct in a person where it is innate" – it was socially disadvantageous because of the harm it did to a "respectable and valuable class" of citizens (*Homogenic Love*, p. 51).

The argument that homosexuals were an asset to society depended on another biological assumption: that the homosexual combined the qualities of male and female. Carpenter's extreme types of homosexual and lesbian were parodies of gender stereotypes. The male homosexual was "something of a chatterbox, skilful at the needle and in woman's work" while the lesbian, "a rather markedly aggressive person," decorated her room "with sporting-scenes, pistols, etc, and not without a suspicion of the fragrant weed in the atmosphere" (*IS*, p. 196). By contrast, the more "normal" type of Uranian combined the body of their own sex with the soul-nature of the opposite. So, the male homosexual was muscular and well built but emotionally "extremely complex, tender, sensitive, pitiful and loving ... the logical faculty may or may not, in their case, be well-developed, but intuition is always strong" (*IS*, p. 197), and the lesbian was

> a type in which the body is thoroughly feminine and gracious ... but in which the inner nature is to a great extent masculine; a temperament active, brave, originative, somewhat decisive, not too emotional ... good at organisation ... sometimes indeed making an excellent and generous leader. (*IS*, p. 199)

Edith Ellis, for example, was described by Carpenter as having "a temperament of varied composition, including great contrasts – democratic yet dominating, combative yet sympathetic, hasty yet tenacious, practical and imaginative, logical and intuitive, feminine and masculine, all in one."[33]

When placed in an evolutionary context, this meant that the characteristics of the homosexual male (tender, emotional, intuitive and caring) pointed to an advance in human evolution: a new sexual type, intermediate between the normal male and female. Thus Carpenter, despite thinking that *"Love's Coming-of-Age* ought ... to have been written by a woman,"[34] nonetheless felt justified in speaking on a topic about which he believed women had greater expertise. As a homosexual he was closer in spirit and practice to progressive female sexuality:

> Though naturally not inclined to "fall in love" [with women], such men are by their nature drawn rather near to women, and it would seem that they often feel a singular appreciation and understanding of the emotional needs and destinies of the other sex. (*IS*, p. 198)

Carpenter the homosexual can mediate between men and women because the specialised function of the intermediate sex was to act as the "reconcilers and interpreters of the two sexes to each other" (*IS*, p. 188).

This may have provided a legitimate role for the homosexual, but the assumption that sexual behaviour was grounded in biology prevented Carpenter from seeing sexual stereotypes as malleable and socially constructed. The potential for revealing the *social* construction of gender was blocked by the assumption that masculinity and femininity were fixed, and the androgynous intermediate sex became just another fixed stereotype, albeit some mixture of the two extremes. There was little strategic value in this other than enabling a specific class of identified people the freedom to express their (apparently) biologically given propensities.

While a legitimate expression of Carpenter's own homosexual concerns, this biological determinism is also the first hint of the limits his homosexual agenda places on his analysis of women's position. Not only could heterosexual men and women *not* question the social construction of their own personalities or opportunities but, as Rowbotham has pointed out, Carpenter's theory "appears to go wrong when it is applied to women in practice."[35] Lesbian women were especially poorly treated and Rowbotham offers, by way of explanation, the implicitness and inarticulateness of lesbianism during this period (a lesbian identity not emerging until the First World War).[36] More than this, however, the actual *logic* of Carpenter's argument reflects badly on lesbian women. Not only did he stereotype lesbians as masculine, in mind if not also in body, but he had to conclude from this that their sexuality did not measure up. Unlike his claims for the male homosexual, Carpenter made no positive claim about lesbian sexuality – the normal lesbian was characterised by a "powerful passion" (*IS*, p. 199) which in the extreme type was *"sensuous rather than sentimental in love"* (*IS*, p. 196. My emphasis). This is damning. Lesbians, for all they might be an intermediate type, were closer to the undesirable model of conventional male sexuality.

When you place this analysis of homosexuality in the wider context of Carpenter's sympathy for women and his criticism of conventional sexual relations, it becomes clear that lesbian women are anomalies. They were not part of the social dialogue which Carpenter hoped would transform contemporary sexual relations. The real argument in Carpenter's work was between men – heterosexual (masculinist) men and homosexuals (male bodies and female minds). Similarly the real alliance to be forged was between homosexual men and heterosexual women who most closely approximated the type of sexuality which a free society needed and which evolution favoured.

If lesbian sexuality was poorly treated by Carpenter's analysis, what of heterosexual women? Clearly, as Weeks notes, this rethinking of sexual conventions, particularly "his willingness to separate sex from procreation," should have "important implications for women as well as homosexuals."[37] Not least, it made it possible to talk about pleasurable and non-procreative sex. To this extent, Carpenter challenged the nexus between women, sex and reproduction, but in looking at the implications of this for women both sides of the equation have to be examined. After all, the impact of reproduction on male lives was not of the same order as its impact on the lives of women, and Carpenter's initial assumption that sex was separate from procreation was most self-evident in the context of homosexuality and least apparent in the experience of heterosexual women.

II. REPRODUCTIVE DISCOURSES: ROMANTIC MOTHERHOOD

By making *union* the prime object of sex, Carpenter was taking a stand against public opinion which, he argued, was strongly influenced "by the arbitrary notion that the function of love is limited to child bearing; and that any love not concerned in the propagation of the race must necessarily be of dubious character."[38] It was no easy matter for Carpenter to turn conventional wisdom on its head. He was confronted not only with the strength of public opinion on women's reproductive function but also with a scientific pragmatism which found the natural and evolutionary reason for sexual intercourse self-evident. Even Carpenter's most sympathetic reviewer argued:

> Surely the prime "object" from Nature's standpoint is procreation. I fancy the wish is father to the thought and that the conclusion is a child of Carpenter's ideality ... he is surely ... confusing the issue. Nature knows none of these distinctions in desire. Sensual pleasure is her method, race-propagation her aim. She, at least, is not an idealist.[39]

It is hardly surprising then, given the polarisation of views,

that Carpenter's answer to the eclipsing of sexuality in conventional
ideology should be the eclipsing of reproduction in his own.

Throughout *Love's Coming-of-Age*, and the pamphlets that preceded it, the only context in which Carpenter discusses reproduction is
as part of nature, as a necessary biological condition and function.
Beginning with *Sex-Love*, the separation of sex and procreation was
accomplished by leaving reproduction in the natural world from which
sexuality was more or less rescued. When Carpenter opposed animal
sex to human Love, he made a similar opposition between reproduction and spiritual union: procreation expressed union on a physical
plane, the "real union" occurring on the spiritual plane through Love.
The status of reproduction was quite clear:

> In the animal and lower human world – and wherever the creature
> is incapable of realising the perfect love ... Nature in the purely
> physical instincts does the next best thing, that is, she effects a
> corporeal union and so generates another creature who by the
> very process of his [*sic*!] generation shall be one step nearer to the
> universal soul and the realisation of the desired end. (*Sex-Love*,
> p. 22)

Once real Love was realised, "natural sexual love has to fall into
a secondary place" (*Sex-Love*, p. 22) and with it, presumably, the
reproductive consequences of corporeal union. Thus, for example,
Carpenter borrowed the mind/body distinction from Plato's *Symposium* to argue that,

> just as the ordinary sex-love has a special function in the propaga-
> tion of the race, so the other love should have its special function
> in social and heroic work, and in the generation – not of bodily
> children – but of those children of the mind, the philosophical
> conceptions and ideals which transform our lives and those of
> society. (*Homogenic Love*, pp. 42–3)

The problem with depriving reproduction of any truly human or
creative significance is that Carpenter quite uncritically adopted conventional assumptions about women's reproductive capacity, and this
clearly had implications for women's emancipation.

The closest Carpenter got to acknowledging the social context of
reproduction was when he described child-bearing and -rearing as a
burden which fell specifically on women. He always discussed it,
however, in sentimental and romantic terms: few men "ever understand the depth and sacredness of the mother-feeling in woman – its
joys and hopes, nor its leaden weight of cares and anxieties" (*Woman*,
p. 6). He spoke of the costs and self-absorption of pregnancy; the
woman's willingness to die if only the child might be safe (he made no
mention of the *fear* of pregnancy or of dying in childbed); the constant
labour to care for and rear the child; the self-effacement and sacrifice of
personal growth; the confinement to the narrow domestic sphere; the

years of unacknowledged service and the final heartache when children grow up and leave to make their own way in the world. Similarly, when discussing social reform, Carpenter considers the conditions under which women labour to give birth and rear children, but mainly because, as such an important and incomparable function, reproduction was clearly social labour and "a sane maternity is the indispensable condition of her [and society's] future advance." Women, therefore, must be fit and able "to bear children, to guard them, to teach them, to turn them out strong and healthy citizens of the great world" (*Woman*, pp. 24–5). In a free society, women must be physically fit; educated about their reproductive function; trained to be mothers; and supported economically by the state during pregnancy and child-rearing.

In *Love's Coming-of-Age*, the impact of reproduction on the lives of real women was missing. While Carpenter seemed to have listened to the sexual dilemmas of middle-class women, he did not appear to have heard anything from women on the dilemmas of fertility, pregnancy or motherhood. Part of the reason for this must be that none of his close women friends had children. Edith Lees and possibly Kate Salt were lesbians, Isabella and Bessie Ford were single, and Olive Schreiner, who alone of this circle had given birth (to a child who died shortly afterwards), does not seem to have confided any of this to Carpenter.[40] Not that Carpenter had no experience of children. His brother had children ("dear little things" he had briefly helped care for after their mother died[41]) as did both the working-class couples he lived with at Millthorpe. Yet the women's experiences of pregnancy and motherhood were spoken of casually and almost without interest by Carpenter and the men in his circle. News of Lucy Adams' miscarriage was passed off by George Hukin, a close friend and one-time lover, with "anyway the threatened addition to the family is averted."[42]

Only George Merrill seems to have had close contact with working-class women and they were, according to Carpenter, "constantly telling him all sorts of things about themselves – about their love affairs, and coming babies and so forth."[43] The experience of these women, however, was never the subject of analysis. As Rowbotham noted:

> The extraordinary record he has left us of the inner relationships within the socialist movement becomes blurred where his perception faltered at the class and sex divide. Consequently we have no means of knowing what working-class women in his circle thought and felt. For all his closeness of observation he wrote about women's oppression from the outside. He could listen to his friends like Kate Salt, Edith Lees and Olive Schreiner but perhaps not to Lucy Adams and Fannie Hukin.[44]

Carpenter's inability to "overcome the divisions of class and sex together"[45] isolated him from the most likely source of information on women's experiences of reproduction and left him not only ignorant of a major facet of women's lives but largely uncritical of it as well.

In place of an informed and critical analysis, Carpenter's account of reproduction was inconsistent and ambivalent. On the one hand he offered little to women except a maternal mystique: Motherhood was Woman's "great and sacred burden," a "priceless and inviolable trust" (*Woman*, p.7) invested in her by Nature and, despite her oppression by man, borne willingly for the sake of the race. She was

> the ark and cradle of the Race down the ages ... the fulfilment of sex is a relief and a condensation to the Man. He goes his way, and, so to speak, thinks no more about it. But to the Woman it is the culmination of her life, her profound and secret mission to humanity, of incomparable import and delicacy. (*Woman*, p.6)

Thus, like other socialists, he did not see motherhood as a burden except under capitalist social relations and, like other Victorian feminists, he argued for the social recognition and elevation of motherhood as a strategy for women's emancipation.

On the other hand, however, Carpenter's discussion of women's position was framed by a dialectic between sexuality and reproduction, and his treatment of their reproductive choices was affected by his agenda for sexual liberation. Unlike other radicals then, and despite his own romantic vision of motherhood, Carpenter would not limit women's sexual choices to reproductive choices:

> Even more than man should woman be "free" to work out the problem of her sex-relations as may commend itself best to her – hampered as little as possible by legal, conventional, or economic considerations, and relying chiefly on her own native sense and tact in the matter. Once thus free ... would she not indeed choose her career (whether that of wife and mother, or that of free companion, or one of single blessedness) far better for herself than it is chosen *for* her to-day. (*Woman*, pp.32–3)

Because Carpenter's conceptual separation of sex and reproduction opened up the possibility of non-reproductive sex, it had the potential of opening up alternatives to women's primary representation as reproductive beings. But the interplay between his new concept of sexuality and his uncritical view of reproduction was not a simple one, and his treatment of those women who made non-reproductive choices undercut his claim that womanhood is not reducible to motherhood.

III. INTERSECTING DISCOURSES:
EXCEPTIONS AND CONTRACEPTIONS

Carpenter restricted his exploration of possible non-reproductive choices to the "Modern Woman" whom he unfortunately stereotypes "in ways that are indistinguishable from heterosexual male fantasies of commanding women.'[46] His caricatures of feminists were underpinned by the assumptions he made about sexuality and reproduction. Indeed, his only discussion of a "maternal instinct" occurs in a redrafted passage in *Love's Coming-of-Age*, where he used the variation in sexual and maternal instincts to typecast feminists:

> The women of the new movement are naturally largely drawn from those in whom the maternal instinct is not especially strong; also from those in whom the sexual instinct is not preponderant. Such women do not altogether represent their sex; some are rather mannish in temperament; some are "homogenic", that is, inclined to attachments to their own, rather than to the opposite, sex; some are ultra-rationalising and brain-cultured; to many, children are more or less a bore; to others, man's sex-passion is a mere impertinence, which they do not understand, and whose place they consequently misjudge. (*LCA*, pp.66–7)

Now, whatever the truth of the connection between lesbianism and feminism, that between lesbianism and a rejection of motherhood was of quite a different order. Imputing sexual preference from the presence or absence of a maternal instinct reduces a range of social choices to a function of biology. Later, Carpenter invoked the "law of transmutation" to explain the rise of the women's movement, and in a similar way undercut the potential radicalism of his new concept of sexuality. Looking back in the late 1920s he wrote:

> when (not without much suffering and tribulation) the young women of fifty years ago found themselves debarred from their *natural* outlet in family life and *normal* sexuality ... the compensation came in the form of a great outgrowth of political activity [my emphasis].[47]

This may "excuse" feminism but it does so without challenging normative assumptions about women and reproduction.

In *Love's Coming-of-Age*, the biological explanation for this "deficiency in maternal instinct" is offered as comfort to those disturbed by the possibility that some women were uninterested in children. Carpenter observed that such women did not represent their sex and were a minority of women active in the movement. Further, he argued, even if they should seem to be drone-like, "not adapted for child-bearing, but with a marvellous and perfect instinct of social service," their efforts on women's behalf would still advance the interests of "their more commonplace sisters" (*LCA*, p.67):

> If it should turn out that a certain fraction of the feminine sex should for one reason or another not devote itself to the work of maternity, still the influence of this section would react on the others to render their notion of motherhood far more dignified than before. There is not much doubt that in the future this most

important of human labours will be carried on with a degree of conscious intelligence hitherto unknown, and which will raise it from the fulfilment of a mere instinct to the completion of a splendid social purpose. To save the souls of children as well as their bodies, to raise heroic as well as prosperous citizens, will surely be the desire and work of the mothers of our race. (*LCA*, pp. 67–8)

Within the context of Carpenter's account of women and mother-hood his sexual stereotypes simply meant that the exception proved the rule: Carpenter could, without contradiction, affirm mother-hood as women's greatest social contribution and acknowledge the existence of women who had no interest in motherhood. He could explain the exceptions as biological inverts of the normal type, coincidentally reinforcing the presumption that reproduction and women's mothering skills and mothering experiences were also derived from biology. In this way the challenge posed by some women not wanting to be mothers was defused and the questions they and "normal" women might raise about the experience of mothering remained unexamined.

One final place where we can examine the interplay between Carpenter's concepts of sexuality and reproduction is his views on contraception, a somewhat necessary precondition to sexual libera-tion. Birth control lies at the point of intersection between the two discourses of sexuality and reproduction, and is of primary importance to the experience of *women*. It was here that Carpenter was most clearly confronted by the material consequences of sexual activity and, in the absence of any means by which women could materially separate sex and reproduction, the conceptual separation Carpenter accomp-lished does not seem particularly advantageous.

Jeffrey Weeks[48] sees Carpenter's support for birth control as a *feminist* stance, and given the unanimity with which it was opposed by many socialists during this period he is, in some senses, correct. It should be remembered, however, that until the 1920s middle-class feminism was also opposed to birth control and equally suspicious of sexual radicalism.[49] In addition, Carpenter's reasons for supporting birth control were peculiar to himself and he largely missed its signifi-cance as a strategy for women's emancipation.

Until 1920,[50] his only published discussion of birth control was contained in a brief appendix to *Love's Coming-of-Age*, "On Pre-ventative Checks to Population." His justification began by firmly naming contraception an act of culture: it was human control over a rampant Nature which was "perfectly lavish" in ensuring the repro-duction of the race and "careless of the waste of seed and life that may ensue" (*LCA*, p. 149).[51] Carpenter said such waste was repugnant to "Man" who, apparently motivated by a desire for efficiency and order, seeks to control Nature's largesse. Significantly it was *men* who objected to such waste and who were the agents of culture in this context; women's concerns were less cultural, more self-interested:

> And not only Man (the male) objects to lower Nature's method of producing superfluous individuals only to kill them off again in the struggle for existence; but Woman objects to being a mere machine for perpetual reproduction. (*LCA*, pp. 149–50)

In the early editions of *Love's Coming-of-Age* this was the *only* comment Carpenter made about the impact of reproduction on women's lives. Not until 1906, by which time he had read a book on birth control by his American publisher, Alice Stockham, did he speak for the first time of "the overhanging dread of undesired childbirth, which so oppresses the life of many a young mother."[52]

In part this "oversight" might simply be explained by the inadequacies of contraceptive methods available in the early 1890s and, as we shall see, it was only with Stockham's *Karezza* that Carpenter thought he had found a sure method of contraception. I think, however, that the real reason for Carpenter's disregard of women's experience of reproduction is that the prevention of pregnancy and the freeing of women from unwanted motherhood was *not* the principal focus of Carpenter's assessment of contraceptive methods. The framework of assumptions he operated within, particularly his preoccupation with transmuting sex into Love, subverted the possibility of his seeing the need to free women from the tyranny of reproduction.

In the pre-1906 editions of *Love's Coming-of-Age*, alternative methods of contraception were assessed in such a way that preventing conception was merely a useful byproduct of larger concerns. Carpenter identified two alternatives – artificial preventatives and abstinence. Artificial methods of birth control were deemed to be unsatisfactory and, while his reluctance to endorse them reflects popular attitudes at that time, his stated reasons reveal a complex array of concerns ranging from masculinist to feminist. On the one hand, he argued, artificial checks hindered spontaneity by "their desperate matter-of-factness, so fatal to real feeling"; on the other hand they were uncertain, probably dangerous and one-sided since "the man's satisfaction is largely at the cost of the woman" (*LCA*, p. 150).

Self-control was to Carpenter a far more attractive contraceptive method than artificial checks, and he specifically recommended some form of rhythm method which exploited the periodicity of women's fertility to select "safe" times for intercourse. The advantages, as Carpenter saw them, were that it was natural, it did not make impossible demands in terms of complete abstinence and, while it was not an "absolutely certain" method of birth control, it "is perhaps sufficiently nearly so for the general purpose of regulating the family" (*LCA*, p. 150). This is revealing. Whereas lack of spontaneity was a problem with artificial checks, here it was not a consideration, and whereas the uncertainty of artificial checks negated their usefulness,

1ere it became an acceptable risk, a risk, moreover, which did not
address the demands women might make of a contraceptive method.
Women were still faced with uncertainty about the outcome of intercourse, fear of pregnancy and lack of control over the spacing of
pregnancies. They gained, over a long period of time, some hope of
limiting family size. This was, and Carpenter acknowledged it, no
solution at all if children were *not* wanted, but he side-stepped this
possibility by deploring both total abstinence and artificial methods:

> It is in the direction of self-control rather than in the direction of
> "unlimited checks" that we should look for the future; and ... if
> some effort were made towards a wise choice of the periods of
> congress, the general object in view would be attained without
> putting an inordinate strain upon the average human nature, and
> without necessitating recourse to doubtful and artificial devices.
> (*LCA*, p. 151)

His real motivation for endorsing self-control was made apparent in the
next sentence when he went on to observe that "the effort itself,
too, would lead to that Transmutation of sex-force into the higher
emotional elements, of which we have spoken already, and which is
such an important factor in Evolution" (*LCA*, p. 151).

Carpenter's preoccupation with the "law of transmutation" also
explains the attractiveness of Alice Stockham's *Karezza*. Stockham's
book was first published in 1896 but it was not mentioned in *Love's
Coming-of-Age* until the fifth, enlarged edition of 1906. If Carpenter
was unaware of Stockham's work before the turn of the century, she
was well aware of his and had used his distinction between sex and
union to justify non-reproductive methods of intercourse. Union could
be achieved in the following way:

> At the appointed time, without fatigue of body or unrest of mind,
> accompany general bodily contact with expressions of endear-
> ment and affection, followed by the complete but quiet union of
> the sexual organs. During a lengthy period of perfect control, the
> whole being of each is merged into the other, and an exquisite
> exaltation experienced. This may be accompanied by a quiet
> motion, entirely under the subordination of the will, so that the
> thrill of passion for either may not go beyond a pleasurable
> exchange. Unless procreation is desired, let the final propagative
> orgasm be entirely avoided.[53]

The result, as Carpenter described it, was a "more complete *soul-
union*, a strange and intoxicating exchange of life, and transmutation of
elements." The added advantages were "an avoidance of waste, and a
great economy of vital forces – on the one side a more profound, helpful
and satisfying union, and on the other a greater energy for procreation,
when it is desired."[54] Karezza ensured the transmutation of sex-force

into soul-union, but it did not challenge the equation of women with reproduction.

Three things are indicative of an ideology of motherhood implicit in Carpenter's promotion of contraception. First, he was content with the regulation of reproduction rather than the prevention of conception: in neither the rhythm method nor Karezza (for as long as it involved "complete bodily conjunction") were the risks of pregnancy especially mitigated. Second, and conceding Carpenter's hopes that Karezza should prove an effective contraceptive, he did not present it as a preventative of conception, but as an adjunct to motherhood: "it is a preparation for best possible conditions of procreation"[55] once that was desired. Third, and finally, Carpenter failed (both here and elsewhere) to mention abortion, thus limiting his concept of birth control to the moment of conception, not the management of pregnancy. Abortion, as a practice used by women to control reproduction, would have thrown into still sharper relief Carpenter's sentimental and stereo-typical image of motherhood. *Contraception* was far *less* challenging to the stereotype and, as conceived by Carpenter, left quite un-touched social prescriptions concerning women and motherhood. This demonstrates once more how "women as individuals acting in parti-cular social situations are lost on [Carpenter's] stereotypes."[56]

The advantages women gained in the name of sexuality were lost in the name of motherhood. Just as the radical implications of lesbianism were lost by assuming it acted, in the wider sphere, to the social benefit of motherhood, the radical implications of contraception were lost as it became a force for *better* motherhood, rather than women's freedom of choice or rights to control their own bodies. Birth control was about *when*, not whether. It seems clear that the separation of sex and procreation was essential for affirmation of homosexuality, women's sexuality and birth control, so why is it that Carpenter's account of these could be so contradictory, and so effectively undercut by his maternalism?

IV. CONTINUITIES AND DISCONTINUITIES

Carpenter was responding to a Victorian discourse in which there was a complex interplay between concepts of sex and reproduction. The idea that procreation was the purpose of sex was just one part of a matrix of ideas in which sex and procreation were alternately linked and separated in the process of defining female and male sexualities, and female and male procreative roles. The dominant Victorian discourse on sex was pre-eminently one of male-centred, procreative hetero-sexuality. The focus on procreation placed limits on appropriate sexual activity but, nonetheless, never denied male sexual pleasure or male sexual freedom. The dominant discourse on reproduction was mother-centred; it denied women's sexuality while asserting their primary reproductive role. So alongside assertions that the two were inextricably connected we have gender definitions in which sex and reproduction were separate. At heart, the separation of sex and reproduction for men identified them as sexual beings with limited procreative responsibilities; their conflation for women represented us as reproductive beings whose sexuality was eclipsed by maternal desires.

At one level then, Carpenter's separation of sex and reproduction should be particularly significant for women, since the two were already differentiated for men. Nonetheless, as we have seen, Carpenter's .challenge to Victorian conventions was of only limited relevance to concepts of female sexuality. Obviously, and I would not want to argue against this, Carpenter's explicit disavowal of reproduction as the prime purpose of sex legitimated female sexuality and provided an alternative to the conventional idea of procreative sex. But his critique of sexual conventions nonetheless depended on a conventional differentiation of male and female sexuality. Even his defence of homosexuality distinguished between comradely love and normal egocentric sex by reifying female sexuality *as expressed in conventional heterosexual ideology* (lesbian sexuality was implicated by the attack on male heterosexual practice). While his critique was directed at the discourse of male-centred procreative heterosexuality, and his theory of sex-love sought to correct the typically male, egocentric pursuit of physical gratification, his idea that sex could be transmuted into Love through restraint carried few implications for women who already, and naturally, represented Carpenter's ideal type of sexual behaviour.

In conventional Victorian accounts the gendered ambiguities between sex and reproduction were further complicated by biological assumptions. The representation of sexual passion as "animal" rather than "human" strengthened the denial of female sexuality but created paradoxes for male sexuality; at one and the same time it linked men with nature (uncontrollable, brutish) and accorded them primacy. Male sexuality was sanctioned both in spite of and because of its shameful animal nature, and the indulgence of male sexual activity was facilitated precisely because it was assumed to be uncontrollable and spontaneous. The biological view of reproduction was much more straightforward and quite unproblematically women's business. The ideal "Woman" was constituted through her biological role in reproduction. Thus it was commonplace to assume that motherhood came naturally to women; that all women *ought* to be mothers and experienced a great and overwhelming desire to be mothers; that motherhood was the pinnacle of womanly achievement and fulfilment.

Carpenter may criticise Victorian ideology for its double standards but he shares its maternalist vision of Woman, and is equally reliant on a biologistic distinction between human nature and human culture. The ambiguities in Carpenter's use of the nature/culture dualism, however, go far towards explaining the contrary messages of liberation and limitation he gave to women.

The distinction between nature and culture operated on at least two contradictory levels. Put bluntly, Carpenter presumed, on the one hand, that sex as a brute biological/animal drive (in men at any rate) conflicted with the higher, more civilised and human sentiment of Love in which care and concern for one's partner overruled selfish individual needs. On the other hand, Carpenter posited a model in which Nature, in the form of evolutionary imperatives enabling the transmutation of sex into Love, stood in sharp contrast to the dissoluteness of bourgeois society (Culture). This ambiguity operated because Carpenter's view of men and women intersected obliquely with his distinction between Nature and Culture. Carpenter shared with much of the Western tradition of social and political thought the identification of male sexuality with animality *and* men with culture, which was made possible by the presumption that men had two natures. This was evident in the idea that *man* needed to, and could, transmute his animal passions (first nature) into his more truly human, more civilised (second) nature. Woman, however, had only (one) Nature. The animal-human dimension was not used to explain women's nature despite their instrumental role in man's evolution from sex to sentiment. Women were simply expressing their natural capacities, their evolutionary advancement. They had no first and second nature, they had no cultural expression of essence which existed in conflict with a biological given.

Carpenter's view was complicated yet further because he had two notions of Nature and two of Culture, both gendered. Nature was brutish and nasty (biological sex drive – men) and benign and trust-worthy (fundamental evolutionary imperative – women). Culture, on the one hand, was flawed by man's brute biological nature and out of kilter with evolutionary principles expressed in female biological nature; yet it also embodied the higher human sentiments which could only come about in civilised social relations. The key to explaining the complex intermeshing of male–female/Nature–Culture lies in Carpenter's philosophical belief that what was more truly human was in harmony with nature and natural ways of living. Carpenter's ideal Woman embodied this harmony; she was *by nature* an advance on both man's bourgeois culture and man's animal nature.

Carpenter constituted female nature in terms which were romantic and sentimental, reifying both Woman and Nature. He quoted Ellis approvingly:

> In women men find beings who have not wandered so far as they have from the typical life of earth's creatures; women are for men the human embodiments of the restful responsiveness of Nature. To every man ... the woman whom he loves is as the Earth was to her legendary son; he has but to fall down and kiss her breast and he is strong again. (*Woman*, p. 9)[57]

Women restored the balance; they were the source of energy, replenishment and inspiration, the centre of man's life, his haven. The hysterical, over-sensitive Victorian woman was a product of civilisation; in her *true* nature "she is essentially of calm large acceptive and untroubled temperament" (*Woman*, p.40) and, given the freedom to express herself, she would show the way to a free society.

What we see then in Carpenter's treatment of sex, love and essential differences is a radicalism in the face of a male egocentric sexual practice but a conservatism in the means by which he made such a challenge. It depended on an idealisation of Woman, which was much the same as could be found in conservative Victorian belief. Women might be credited with potential influence, but they exerted that influence in conventional terms – passively, as an expression of their moral, ideal nature.

Carpenter's Woman was principally a product of his essentialist concept of reproduction. As a fundamental biological function, reproduction shaped the personal and social life of every woman by inscribing in her biology a concept of femininity inextricably bound up with maternity. There would indeed seem to be little difference between the conventional (liberal) idea of motherhood as the fulfilment of womanhood, and the socialists' claim that motherhood was woman's greatest contribution to social life or, as Carpenter put it, that "a woman has a tremendous work to perform [in] the production and rearing of children" (*Woman*, p.37). The highly idealised, romanticised treatment of motherhood which followed from Carpenter's uncritical espousal of an essentialist reproductive discourse foreshortened all the radical potential his analysis of sexuality had for women.

Ultimately, Carpenter did not break the nexus of reproduction, sex and women. He may have challenged the discourse which held that the primary purpose of sex was procreation but he did not counter the discourse which held that procreation was the primary purpose of (normal) women. His challenge to procreative sex did not implicate procreation itself. Consequently, when he wrote about women, he got thoroughly tangled up between new ideas about sexuality and old ideas about reproduction – ideas which themselves were inextricably connected to a specific concept of women's sexuality. The separation of sex and procreation made it possible for Carpenter to acknowledge women's sexuality and advocate sexual intercourse as a realm of intimacy, reciprocity and mutual pleasure between equals, but both were coloured by women's maternal function. To this extent sexual stereotypes were reinforced, and sexual pleasure itself was described by a "love mystique" which had much more to do with a maternal mystique than Carpenter would ever admit. Carpenter's attraction to the values of heterosexual femininity was an attraction to the *maternal* values of self-effacement, care, compassion and noble sacrifice.[58]

The chances of freedom Carpenter allowed women were curtailed somewhat simply because the nature of the decisions women made about reproduction – the context, both personal and social, in which they made choices – were mystified and obscured. Even if women shared and welcomed a sense of sexuality distinct from its reproductive purpose, their lack of control over fertility gave them a consciousness of sexuality shaped by concerns about reproduction. This experience was invisible in Carpenter's account where, in the absence of a critical perspective on motherhood, women's account of reproduction was either disregarded or entirely blamed on contemporary social conditions. Carpenter reclaimed women's sexuality from oblivion but it was a sexuality removed from common experience, a sexuality dislocated from its context.

Thus, women were both freed to explore their sexuality and thrown into dilemmas by Carpenter's treatment of it: seeing sex as noble and elevating not only legitimated it but also constructed love and sexual experience in forms which were not so far removed from a view of woman as noble and self-sacrificing. Rather than "pursue the radical implications of separating sexuality and procreation as a political question which related to people's actual lives,"[59] Carpenter's idealisation of Love obscured the dilemmas and real life practices of women trying to reconcile their sexuality with their reproductive capacity. Other than the biological, there was no context in which to discuss the significance of women's rejection of motherhood, or the problems they faced as mothers, or the quality of their social experience as mothers (and as women expected by society to be mothers). The separation of sexuality and reproduction in Carpenter's work did not allow for women in whom (hetero)sexuality was strong, but the desire to be a mother was weak, and thus did not reveal the possibility that reproduction made sexual activity problematic for women, or that women might be sexually inactive *because of* the risk of motherhood.

The construction of two separate discourses, then, enabled new possibilities to be revealed (female sexual pleasure generally and lesbianism to a lesser extent) and closed off other possibilities which might well have been revealed if the challenge to Victorian male discourses of sexuality had taken more account of women's experiences. Judged against his historical period Carpenter could be said to have transcended and been limited by his social context, to have challenged and been an apologist for the ideas of his period. As Rowbotham noted, we should not be too harsh in our judgement of Carpenter just because

> he lived and worked in the context of a determinist form of marxism, of eugenic assumptions in which a wide range of acquired characteristics like drunkenness and criminality were still being seen as biologically inherited. Carpenter attempted to assert a dialectic between personal sexual life and the institutions of society in the effort to understand the relationship of subjective consciousness and external social relations, with inadequate theoretical equipment.[60]

The question then becomes: why was it that Carpenter could see through some aspects of his society and make some connections between personal experience and social relations, and not others? In particular, why did he fail to make connections between women's experience of motherhood and sexuality when women were a specific focus of his analysis?

I have suggested a number of explanations for Carpenter's uncritical acceptance of his culture's view of reproduction. The dominance of a paradigm of biological evolution, his own life-long project to make sense of, and then justify, the homosexual experience, his close association with "childless" women, and his class- and sex-based distance from working-class women who had experienced childbirth, miscarriage and child-rearing, all contributed to the deletion of a culturally and humanly significant reproduction. But whatever the reason Carpenter was unable to break away from the theoretical assumptions of his time, his struggle to reconcile the political and personal aspects of sexual life was an important precursor to feminisms' much later study of sexual politics, and his separation of sex and procreation finds an echo in contemporary feminisms' theoretical treatment of these two.

BEVERLY THIELE

NOTES

1. Sheila Rowbotham and Jeffrey Weeks, *Socialism and the New Life: The Personal and Sexual Politics of Edward Carpenter and Havelock Ellis* (London: Pluto P., 1977), p.74.
2. Edward Carpenter, *My Days and Dreams: Being Autobiographical Notes* (1916; rpt. London: Allen & Unwin, 1918), p.195.
3. Robert Blatchford, Letter to Edward Carpenter, 11 Jan. 1893, MS. 386. This and all other unpublished letters and manuscript material cited in this paper are from the Carpenter Collection in the Sheffield City Library, Sheffield.
4. Robert Blatchford, Letter to Edward Carpenter, 11 Jan. 1893, MS. 386, Carp. Coll.
5. Carpenter, *Days and Dreams*, p.196; also Edward Carpenter, Letter to Kate Salt, 13 March 1896, MS. 354.42, Carp. Coll.
6. Carpenter, *Days and Dreams*, p.195.
7. Rev. of *Love's Coming-of-Age*, by Edward Carpenter, *The Academy* (London), 6 June 1896, pp.52–6. N.C.5, Carp. Coll.
8. Robert Blatchford, rev. of *Love's Coming-of-Age*, by Edward Carpenter, *Clarion Reviews*, 1894, p.80. N.C.5, Carp. Coll.
9. "Books and Booklets," rev. of *Love's Coming-of-Age*, by Edward Carpenter, *Justice*, 9 May 1896, p.2; also "Topical Tattle," *Justice*, 26 May 1894, p.5.
10. Lily Bell, "Matrons and Maidens," rev. of *Love's Coming-of-Age*, by Edward Carpenter, *Labour Leader*, 27 June 1896, p.224. MS. C Per. 68, Carp. Coll.
11. Olive Schreiner, Letter to Edward Carpenter, 8 Oct. 1894, MS. 359.73, Carp. Coll.
12. Olive Schreiner, Letter to Edward Carpenter, 24 April 1907, MS. 359.93, Carp. Coll.
13. Isabella Ford, Letter to Edward Carpenter, 28 Jan. 18?, MS. 271.17, Carp. Coll.
14. Among Carpenter's socialist contemporaries writing on the woman question,

Auguste Bebel and Karl Pearson were most notably preoccupied with reproduction.

15. See, for example, Ruth First and Ann Scott, *Olive Schreiner* (London: André
Deutsch, 1980), p.211, and Bell, p.224.

16. Edward Carpenter, *Sex-Love, and Its Place in a Free Society* (Manchester: Labour
Press, 1894), pp.22–3. Further references are incorporated into the text.

17. Not until much later did Carpenter use infertility as evidence for the separation of
sex from procreation: Edward Carpenter, *The Drama of Love and Death: A Study
of Human Evolution and Transfiguration* (London: George Allen, 1912), pp.58–
60.

18. Edward Carpenter, *Love's Coming-of-Age* (Manchester: Labour Press, 1897),
p.5. Unless otherwise indicated citations are from this edition and are incorporated
into the text.

19. Robert Blatchford, rev. of *Love's Coming-of-Age*, p.80.

20. Edward Carpenter, *Marriage in Free Society* (Manchester: Labour Press, 1894),
pp.30–1. Further references are incorporated into the text.

21. Edward Carpenter, *Woman, and Her Place in a Free Society* (Manchester: Labour
Press, 1894), p.9. Further references are incorporated into the text.

22. Havelock Ellis, "The Changing Status of Women," *Westminster Review*, 128, No. 7
(Oct. 1887), pp.818–28, and *Man and Woman: A Study of secondary sexual
characteristics* (1894; rpt. London: Walter Scott, 1902).

23. Rev. of *Love's Coming-of-Age*, *The Academy* (London), pp.52–6.

24. Edward Carpenter, *Homogenic Love, and Its Place in a Free Society* (Manchester:
Labour Press, 1894). Although the imprint date was 1894, in *Days and Dreams*,
p.195, Carpenter recorded that it was actually published in January 1895. Further
references are incorporated into the text.

25. Edward Carpenter, *The Intermediate Sex*, 1908; rpt. in *Edward Carpenter: Selected
Writings, I* (London: Gay Men's Press, 1984), pp.185–246. Further references are
incorporated into the text.

26. Carpenter, *Days and Dreams*, p.30.

27. Carpenter, *Days and Dreams*, p.30.

28. Edward Carpenter, Letter to Walt Whitman, 12 July 1874, cited in Rowbotham,
p.35.

29. Rowbotham, p.80.

30. Havelock Ellis, *Studies in the Psychology of Sex, I* (Philadelphia: Davis, 1900),
p.47. Edward Carpenter's case history is Case VI, pp.46–7.

31. Jeffrey Weeks, *Sex, Politics and Society: the Regulation of Sexuality since 1800*
(London: Longman, 1981), p.104.

32. "Edward Carpenter's Tracts on Sex," rev. of *Homogenic Love*, by Edward
Carpenter, *The Humanitarian*, Aug. 1895, p.155, MS. C. Per. 52, Carp. Coll.

33. Edward Carpenter, preface to Edith Ellis, *New Horizons in Love and Life*
(London: A. & C. Black, 1921), pp.x–xi.

34. Carpenter, *Days and Dreams*, p.197.

35. Rowbotham, p.112.

36. Rowbotham, p.98.

37. Weeks, p.172.

38. Weeks, p.172.

39. Rev. of *Love's Coming-of-Age*, by Edward Carpenter, *The Adult*, Feb. 1898, p.15;
the journal of the Legitimation League which was initially set up to promote equal
legal rights for illegitimate children but later advocated sexual liberalism.

40. First and Scott, pp.213–16, 229–30; Schreiner's surviving correspondence to
Carpenter makes no reference either to miscarriages or to the child's death.

41. Edward Carpenter, Letter to Kate Salt, 27 Nov. 1889, MS. 354.5, Carp. Coll.; also
undated letter, 354.9.

42. George Hukin, Letter to Edward Carpenter, 11 Nov. 1891, MS. 362.30, Carp. Coll.

43. Edward Carpenter, manuscript notes on George Merrill, p.13, cited in Rowbotham, p.96.

44. Rowbotham, p.99.
45. Rowbotham, p.95.
46. Rowbotham, p.112.
47. Edward Carpenter, "Birth Control and Bisexuality" (about 1926), MS. 248, p.9, Carp. Coll.
48. Jeffrey Weeks, *Coming Out* (London: Quartet Books, 1977), p.74.
49. Olive Banks, *Faces of Feminism: A Study of Feminism as a Social Movement* (Oxford: Martin Robertson, 1981), pp.180–204; also Rowbotham, p.17.
50. Margaret Sanger, Letters to Edward Carpenter, 13 April 1918 and 3 Oct. 1921, MS. 375.28, 375.29, Carp. Coll. Sanger asked Carpenter to write something for her *Birth Control Review* during the 1920s and he did write "Birth Control and Bisexuality" sometime after 1926, although it does not appear to have been published.
51. In 1890 Carpenter had visited both India and Ceylon and as his talks on sexual matters date from his return to England it is likely that the concern with wasting seed – and one has to assume the reference is to male semen, since it is here that Nature is most lavish – comes from Eastern philosophical and sexual beliefs about the conservation of vital energies through the retention of semen. There was a discussion in British medical circles on the conservation of sperm and the evils of masturbation which Carpenter may have known about through Havelock Ellis, but the Indian connection is more immediate.
52. Edward Carpenter, *Love's Coming-of-Age* (London: Swan Sonnenschein, 1906), p.174.
53. Alice B. Stockham, *Karezza: Ethics of Marriage* (1896; New York: Fenno, 1903), p.25.
54. Carpenter, *Love's Coming-of-Age* (1906), p.174.
55. Carpenter, *Love's Coming-of-Age* (1906), p.183.
56. Rowbotham, p.112.
57. Citing Havelock Ellis, *Man and Woman*, p.327.
58. Perhaps the struggles of Kate Salt to make sense of herself as a "new woman" best illustrate the dilemmas this posed to women: see Rowbotham, p.98.
59. Rowbotham, p.111.
60. Rowbotham, pp.112–13.

Allegory, Feminist Thought and the
Dreams *of Olive Schreiner*

Olive Schreiner is best known today for her extraordinary novel *The Story of an African Farm* (1883), and for the pathbreaking feminist theory of *Woman and Labour* (1911).[1] Between these two books, however, she published a sizeable quantity of work, ranging from a collection of short allegories, *Dreams* (1890), to a major series of articles on the politics and history of her native South Africa, later anthologised as *Thoughts on South Africa* (1923).[2] Approximately half of her working life was spent in Europe, the site of composition for most of *Dreams*. Schreiner's achievement as a radical writer traverses both metropolitan and colonial cultures, both fiction and theory. To separate these spheres, however, is to lose sight of the fact that they are constantly in dialogue throughout Schreiner's oeuvre. My intention here is to focus upon a relatively neglected, but formative, period of Schreiner's development, her work of the 1880s. *Dreams* enjoyed tremendous and diverse popularity on publication, when it was acclaimed by, and claimed for, both aestheticism (via its chief ideologue Arthur Symons) and feminism (it was a favourite for imprisoned suffragettes), and went through 25 editions in 40 years.[3] The importance of *Dreams* for the late nineteenth century, as Symons and Constance Lytton attest, is equally in terms of aesthetics and political thought.[4] The volume needs to be recognised as a significant feminist intervention in the crises which generated on the one hand the romantic and democratic work of Edward Carpenter and on the other the "scientific" and eugenic work of the social scientist Karl Pearson. Both men were close friends of Schreiner, who liked to characterise them as polar opposites.[5] But whatever their differences, both stand guilty (in divergent ways) of a masculinism which allows no real space or legitimacy for the specificities, and differences, of Western women. It is this space which Schreiner tried to explore in *Dreams*.

However, during the period in which the allegories collected as *Dreams* were being composed, Schreiner was also engaged in a non-fictional work of feminist theory, in the form of an introduction to Mary Wollstonecraft's *A Vindication of the Rights of Woman* (1792).[6] Schreiner was invited to write this work by the publisher Walter Scott in 1886, and she began it in that year; she was still working on it in early 1889. She was unable to complete this work; the structural difficulties inherent in the process of constructing a "scientific" genealogy of Western women's oppression arrested the theoretical project. It remains an unpublished fragment. Some of the allegories of *Dreams* (including its most celebrated, "Three Dreams in a Desert") were produced, as her correspondence indicates, as a direct result of Schreiner's theoretical difficulties; the two writing projects became interdependent. Schreiner never did "complete" her feminist theory; *Woman and Labour*, as she took pains to argue in its introduction, was only a partial analysis, its predominant focus the concerns of contemporary middle-class Western women; it neglected the historical origins and evolution of "sexual difference," in animal and then ancient human societies, which was to have constituted a major part of the book in its entirety. In the Wollstonecraft fragment it is precisely at the point of grappling with "original" human society, in the form of black South African peoples, that Schreiner's project collapses. If the Wollstonecraft fragment constitutes Schreiner's inaugural efforts to outline the "first principles" of sexual difference, the allegories of *Dreams* are equally inscribed in a logic of "first principles": they require to be read as essentially both mediatory and preliminary, narratives whose content lays the foundation for transition to a future ideality but does not attempt a premature and pre-emptive representation of that condition.

As an aesthetic text committed to (discursive and political) emancipation, Schreiner's *Dreams* are perhaps best likened to Edward Carpenter's *Towards Democracy*, a text which she read erratically throughout the 1880s.[7] Like *Towards Democracy, Dreams* is premised upon the belief that subjective transformation is a precondition and a necessary accompaniment of social transformation; the text addresses, likewise, a range of "private" and "public" concerns, featuring narratives about the surrendering of "love" in order to achieve freedom, about the process of aesthetic production, romantic holism and cosmic "unity," and social criticism. But the differences between the texts are significant. One obvious difference is in literary form. Where Carpenter is compendious, Schreiner is minimalist; against Carpenter's omnivorous romantic and Whitmanesque flow is set Schreiner's series of austere narrative episodes, redolent of biblical parable in diction and technique.

The ease with which Carpenter appropriates or incorporates Whitman's poetic is itself indicative of his confident and assimilative ethic, and parallels the assured and dynamic relations of self and other played out within the text: the distance between Carpenter's first person narrator and his objects is variable, but premised upon the possibility of immanent immersion in, or engulfment of, these objects. Where Carpenter's narrator can interact with his objects, Schreiner's narrator is, most obviously by means of the dream structure, given a mediatory position in relation to the action she perceives. Moreover, Carpenter's aesthetic is magnanimous enough to present and juxtapose its own contradictory intellectual modes without embarrassment; Lamarckian evolutionism and platonism, for example, co-exist and even intermingle. In contrast to Carpenter's untroubled relation to his textual precursor, Whitman, Schreiner's relationship with her literary and intellectual precedents – in particular, the Bible – is fraught and interrogative. The diverse literary modes that these precursors imply are strangely juxtaposed against one another, rather than contained.

Carpenter's romantic ego speaks with the confidence endowed by spiritual or democratic authority and is not, in its representation of a celebratory androcentrism, immune from a dominatory turn of phrase:

> The Soul invading, looking proudly upon its new kingdom, possessing the offerings of all pleasures, forbidden and unforbidden, from all created things ...[8]

Schreiner's narrator is not synonymous with transcendental authority but, often graphically and involuntarily, submits to it. While Carpenter's ideal is nameable ("democracy"), Schreiner's is not; the ideal, for example, in "A Dream of Wild Bees," remains deliberately unnamed, beyond the enumeration of qualities ascribed to the other, non-ideal categories (*Dreams*, pp. 87–97).

One could argue their difference to be one of emphasis. Their mutual concern to chart the process of emancipation leads Carpenter to focus on the utopian movement of fusion, while Schreiner instead prioritises the requisite labour, the moment of splitting, disunity and conflict (within and between subjects) that precedes utopia. But the difference goes deeper. Schreiner's correspondence with Carpenter reveals a fundamental disparity on the issue of rationality.[9] Carpenter's romantic anti-intellectualism, for Schreiner, is a product of male privilege, and represents an ideology in which, on grounds both of gender and feminism, she is unable to participate. She shares more of Carpenter's romantic anti-capitalism, but is in general much more ambivalent about the project of technological modernity.

Schreiner's problem with unequivocal romanticism of a Carpenterian kind is partly a problem with the construction of the physical body itself. For Schreiner, the possibility that the body is itself the source of oppression is as strong as the (Carpenterian) suggestion that the *repression* of the body is what is responsible for oppression. In Carpenter's political aesthetic, too, the phenomenal body functions in a metaphorical relation to the noumenon, as is suggested, for example, in his statement that "sex is the allegory of Love in the physical world."[10] (Such a relation is more properly termed "symbolic" than "allegorical," in that it posits an immanent and organic link between "material" and "transcendental" realms. Allegory posits the opposite, that such links are discursively imposed rather than inherent in their subjects. Schreiner's conception, and use, of allegory supports this.)

If in Carpenter Schreiner encounters one kind of restrictive metaphorical discourse, in Karl Pearson she encounters another. It is Pearson who is representative of a social Darwinist and eugenic discourse that was gaining ascendency and was to enjoy hegemony well into the twentieth century. Pearson's sociobiology articulates itself as both a culmination and supercession of what it considers to be the inadequate and artificial laws of liberal political economy; "capital" is now defined as the body itself. The function of scientific reason (itself defined in highly physical and quantifiable terms, usually in variations upon the "brain muscle" idiom) is both analytical and emphatically practical: to map out the evolutionary "laws" of human history and biology and accordingly to prescribe state action for the furtherment of the race. Pearson's eugenicism is a system in which metaphysics doesn't give way to scientific rationality, but become inextricable from it.

The extent of Schreiner's support for the "rational" tenets of Pearson's science should not be underestimated. Nonetheless, in much of Schreiner's (fictional and non-fictional) work can be traced a struggle with the sexist, oppressive and inhumane basis of Pearsonian "scientific rationality," and/or its monopolistic claims on the category of reason itself. Pearson is important (along with Havelock Ellis), for Schreiner, in constituting woman as a category for analysis. But the interests of "the race," as Pearson makes clear in "The Woman Question," predominate over and subsume the interests of the sub-category of the female.[11] If Schreiner's allegory represents a refusal to be contained within the purportedly systematic thought of "science," it is also an eschewal of its corollary, the emergent novelistic naturalism. It is not accidental that the allegory most directly addressed to Karl Pearson, "A Dream of Wild Bees," should problematise the very notion of "the real." Presented with a vision of her future child's trajectory, featured as being a laborious pursuit of the ideal, a pregnant woman asks the presenter "It is real?" "What *is* real?" is the reply (*Dreams*, p. 96). "The real" consists of something more, and other, than the biological reductivism and literalism of Pearson.

Carpenter and Pearson share something more than androcentrism and (on occasion) sociobiological metaphor; they both subscribe to socialism, albeit their constructions of the term diverge – Pearson is interested in the working class as an instrument of the state, and equates socialism with eugenic statism, while Carpenter is interested in the humanitarianism of socialism. Schreiner, however, remained equivocal about socialism, arguing that it could threaten the freedom of the individual.[12] Schreiner's commitment to a labour theory of value was unwavering; but her conception of labour is in some respects fundamentally different from that found in her socialist friends and contemporaries because she comprehends the labour process as one which applies equally to economic production *and* to domestic labour and physical reproduction. Schreiner's ambivalence towards socialism has much to do with its exclusion of women's labour from its theory. This in turn qualifies her avowed individualism. For Schreiner, the individual, like the labourer, is always in the service of something or someone else; it is not an absolute and exclusive category but a mediated and interdependent one. This is not unrelated to her choice of allegory as a fictional form, which retains a modality grounded on the voice of the impersonal and collective, rather than on the individual creative artist (and fictional narrator/protagonist). Allegory challenges, as does Schreiner's labour theory, the rigidity of the distinction between production and reproduction (of a shared "truth").

This may suggest that Schreiner's use of allegory is more cohesive, formally and ideologically, than it actually is. It may also suggest that it is questions of gender which alone determine Schreiner's aesthetic. But this is misleading. For questions of "race" and colonialism are just as crucial; Schreiner's feminism and her aesthetic cannot be conceived and analysed without reference to her colonial foundations and status. Schreiner's early *The Story of an African Farm* testifies, in the episode of "The Hunter" allegory (reprinted in *Dreams*), to the part that racial and cultural otherness plays in her early aesthetic thought.[13] The allegory is told to the boy protagonist, Waldo, by a passing French traveller. The traveller is engaged in a *re-creative*, or repetitive, act: he is in fact interpreting the pictorial narrative engraved on a crude sculpture by Waldo, back to the original producer, who is inscribed as an auditor. We don't get to hear – or to see – Waldo's own pictorial version of the narrative, which remains undescribed; we do see, however, Waldo's amazed and idolatrous response to the Frenchman's allegory, which he "recognises" as the true content of his own narrative. What is produced by the interaction of these two textual layers, and actions, is a strange moment of authorial indeterminacy, in which the distinction between production and reproduction, originality and quotation, is challenged. This indeterminacy is played out between two paradigms.

One is that of nature or biology. It is no accident that Waldo's sculpture is featured as being nine months old. Waldo "mothers" the text, and the French stranger "delivers" it. The other paradigm is that of race, or culture. For it is equally no accident that the deliverer is a Frenchman, a traveller at that, and associated explicitly with the codes of Civilisation. This of course marks him as a suitable agent or (literally) medium of culture, in contrast to Waldo, a hybrid representative of the crude German and colonial–pastoral resident of an African farm. Seen thus, what is involved in the construction and narration of the allegory is not a disinterested and biological process but an example of cultural difference, supporting the ethical/aesthetic claims of an imperial civilisation's "superiority." To deliver or release the potential of the text, its physical origins, through this aesthetic narration is also to legitimate or authorise it. But such a cultural (and biological) transaction is possible only if the agents share a common European stock; as the Stranger's subsequent statement makes clear, aesthetic and epistemological authenticity and "universality" are predicated on the exclusion of black Africa. Because it condenses so many of Schreiner's aesthetic concerns, it is worth quoting extensively from this somewhat long, and highly contradictory, passage:

   "... the attribute of all true art, the highest and the lowest, is this – that it says more than it says, and takes you away from itself. It is a little door that opens into an infinite hall where you may find what you please. Men thinking to detract, say, 'People read more in this or that work of genius than was ever written in it,' not perceiving that they pay the highest compliment. If we pick up the finger and nail of a real man, we can decipher a whole story – could almost reconstruct the creature again, from head to foot. But half the body of a Mumboo-jumbow idol leaves us utterly in the dark as to what the rest was like. We see what we see, but nothing more. There is nothing so universally intelligible as truth. It has a thousand meanings, and suggests a thousand more." He turned over the wooden thing. [Waldo's sculpture.] "Though a man should carve it into matter with the least possible manipulative skill, it will yet find interpreters. It is the soul that looks out with burning eyes through the most gross fleshly filament."[14]

Schreiner starts off here with a recognisable notion of the production of sublimity as the measure of the aesthetic power of an artwork. Interesting here is the weight she gives to the activity of hermeneutics over production. Schreiner wants to validate and uphold individual subjectivism ("you may find what you please") while wanting at the same time to assert the possibility of a single and universal template of truth in its totality (as here the "whole story" of a man's body which can be reconstructed is a singular and exclusive one). No sooner is such a principle raised, however, than it has to be qualified by another principle, of pluralism, which then becomes the condition of "truth" itself ("it has a thousand meanings"). The more "true" an artwork is, it seems, the more generative of a plethora of interpretations it will be. Interpretative action is valued above the stasis of a singular truth; process takes over contemplation. The African fetish represents the (necessary) opposite of this epistemological and aesthetic process. Irreducible and resistant to Western hermeneutics, inaccessible both to the models of rationality and subliminality, it is instead relegated by Schreiner to the level of inanimate matter and of mere illusoriness (truth's other, contrasted with the real fragments of a human body). The half body of the fetish can signify nothing other than itself in its fragmented condition; because it doesn't represent a recognisable concept or evoke a master-narrative (for a Western viewer that is) it is deathly. The association of black and primitive Africa with the realm and laws of the purely material and inanimate (and hence with mortification and reification) recurs (with more ambivalence) in Schreiner's Wollstonecraft introduction. If allegory constitutes the most obvious example of an artwork signifying, and representing, something "more" and other than itself, mediating the universal through its non-naturalistic form, this episode makes clear the degree to which the category of the "universal" is the province of the Western, and the degree to which such categories seem to require and invoke the "opposite." The fetish is the anti-allegorical, or anti-aesthetic, text.

FIRST PRINCIPLES: MARY WOLLSTONECRAFT,
FEMINISM AND AFRICA

It is in Schreiner's Wollstonecraft fragment that the battle between
rationality and physicality is most graphically enacted. The battle
began before the composition did; commissioned to write an introduction to Wollstonecraft's feminist treatise, *A Vindication of the
Rights of Woman*, Schreiner quickly decided that she preferred to
concern herself with Wollstonecraft's own life instead, as constituted
by the memoirs of William Godwin.[15] At this stage, the text *of*
Wollstonecraft's "life and times" was more important than the text *by*
her; the radicalism of Wollstonecraft's activities and practices, and the
example of her egalitarian marriage, is what makes her "great." By the
time Schreiner attempted the introduction, the terms are only slightly
changed; Schreiner's claims for the value of Wollstonecraft's feminist
prescience are ostensibly based on the contents of the *Vindication*, but
are presented in terms which elide the medium of the text and render
the raw vision alone, as emanation of the woman, important:

> The book is a great book because, however vaguely and crudely
> stated, the woman perceived eighty years ago the mighty sexual
> change that is coming upon us; saw the necessity for it, saw its end.
> ... She saw the necessity for this movement. Being a woman,
> perhaps there was no necessity for her to see it; she knew it.
> (*Wollstonecraft*, p. 3)

The last sentence indicates a desire by Schreiner to elide even the
concept of rational vision, or enlightenment, as the basis of Wollstonecraft's feminism, and to replace it by an essential knowledge biologically predetermined and non-rationally experienced. "Necessity,"
it seems, is not compatible with rationality. It is not surprising
that the elevation of Wollstonecraft's physically-based knowledge
seems to require a devaluation of Wollstonecraft's actual practice
of writing, which is how Schreiner begins her introduction, casti-
gating the text for its "lack of genius," or unconvincing, dictatorial and
artificial style. In terms as dictatorial as those she complains of,
Schreiner asserts:

> Her mode of teaching is to assert what appears to her truth; but
> she fails so to assert it that we feel it a necessity. ... One feels
> throughout a sense of duty guiding the woman. She said "Go to, I
> will write me a book" and she wrote it; and the unregenerate soul
> rebels against this form of edification which appears a result from
> choice and not from necessity. (*Wollstonecraft*, p. 2)

Schreiner's comments here recall those that she was busy making (in
her correspondence) on her own writing of this very same introduction.
The exercise of writing non-fictional prose becomes automatically a

problem of rationality itself, which is felt to be moribund and which in its turn just as automatically summons its fictional other, allegory:

> ... My Mary Wollstonecraft is going on. ... There are six or seven allegories in it; I've tried to keep them out, but I can't.
> ... It's the other that's fancy and fiction, and this that is real. It's so easy for a mind like mine to produce long logical arguments, or strings of assertions, but when I have done it I feel such a "valch" [loathing] against it: that is only the material; it has to be combined and made alive.[16]

Schreiner explicitly identifies Wollstonecraft with Enlightenment thought; the *Vindication* "is based on certain broad conceptions of human life common to a small body of philosophic thinkers in France and England at the end of the eighteenth century" (*Wollstonecraft*, p. 1). In projecting her anxieties about her own rationality on to Wollstonecraft Schreiner can convert a methodological and stylistic quandary into a historical trajectory, one which thereby absolves her own work from any taint of artificiality and rationalism. For Schreiner characterises her own period as one in which the evolutionary necessity of feminism is being made manifest:

> Women and men of today, chancing on the old dust-covered volumes, find with delight that this woman, dead eighty years ago, is one of ourselves. Vaguely shaped and not clearly expressed, we still find in the dusty volumes the feelings which are slowly shaping themselves into thought, and the thought which is surely and with suffering shaping itself into action in the world we live in. It is therefore with joy that in a new dress we bring out the old book and lay it again before her fellows. (*Wollstonecraft*, p. 3)

From having fallen "dead," the text is now reborn "in a new dress" with Schreiner herself as the mediator/deliverer, translating its anachronistic terms into present day discourse. What this suggests is that if the *Vindication*'s prose is inauthentic this is the fault not so much of Wollstonecraft but of the period of the Enlightenment in which Schreiner locates her. A dialectic seems to be in operation here, whereby Schreiner's own period is constructed as the logical fulfilment of the Enlightenment narrative of rational liberty, the fulfilment being the conversion of that narrative from concepts such as "choice," "individual liberty" to concepts of "necessity" and "biological/evolutionary determinism" of the whole social body. (The logic here is not dissimilar to that of Karl Pearson, in his revision of liberal political economy.)

The value of the "whole woman" of Mary Wollstonecraft can only be affirmed by splitting Wollstonecraft up, valorising her person over and against her reason/writing. The only way Schreiner can recuperate Wollstonecraft's feminism is by allegorising it, in a sense. Wollstonecraft's rationality becomes physicalised, her dead "literal" material is reanimated (or nullified) as a proleptic symptom of the emancipatory

discourse to come. If the period of the Enlightenment serves, typo-
logically, as did the Old Testament the New, it is hardly surprising that
Schreiner should serve as the fulfilment of Wollstonecraft, simultaneously her scribe and her reincarnation; when after outlining the
significance of the *Vindication* Schreiner proceeds to her own theory,
she is merely, in a sense, enacting or embodying the vindicatory logic of
Wollstonecraft's own theory, its live continuation and demonstration,
writing not out of choice but of necessity (fulfilling the imperatives of
feminism and the ongoing narrative of enlightenment). Schreiner
herself, that is, must be converted into an allegorical figure for the
collective and live (rather than theoretical) project of emancipation.
She is removed from the burden of authority and personality, in her
joint function as vehicle and sign of the imperative of feminism.

When Schreiner commences her own theoretical outline of the
evolution of sexual difference, she begins with the animal or natural
world and proceeds to early society. This scheme accords with the
plan for her "sex book" which she had previously sent to Pearson.
The book was to be in three sections, the first dealing with the
"physiology of Sex" (the origin of sex and sexual difference in the
human race); the second with a historical survey of sexual difference
in early and ancient human societies (beginning with "sexual relations
among savages" and proceeding through early Germany, Egypt,
Greece, Rome, China, India, Arabia); and the final part (considered as
a separate volume) with the "modern position of woman" (covering
"the causes which lead to it," "its evils," "the direction which change
seems tending to take," "the direction which it is desirable that it should
take").[17] Already, in its conception, the book's form raises methodological questions which testify to Schreiner's conflicting theoretical
desires. By sectioning off physiology from sexual difference as constituted within and through society, for instance, Schreiner is already
problematising the very connection between the physical and the
cultural spheres upon which her social-evolutionary scheme depends.
Likewise, the bifurcation of the analysis into "historical" and "contemporary" sites – and the attendant methodological separation of
descriptive "empiricism" (the factual historical outline) and prescrip-
tive critique (the present) – serves to sever rather than synthesise
the two concerns, and to isolate the present instead of situating it
within a historical/evolutionary narrative. "History" is de-historicised,
becoming itself one subject within a discontinuous series. Just how,
if at all, the condition of contemporary Western woman can be read
through a world-wide/comparative and evolutionary discourse, then,
is the question that Schreiner's form immediately begs, even as it
assumes its possibility. In the letter that accompanies this sketch,
Schreiner remarks that

> I like to get even the vaguest sense of having my whole subject in
> my hand before I go to the parts. I don't care how long I work at a

part, but I must realize it's a part of a whole and know what part it is.[18]

The outline here answers to Schreiner's need for a conceptual totality but at the same time the constitution of each part operates along self-subsistent logical lines. Karl Pearson seems to have noted the disjunction between form and content, or the disparities of Schreiner's conceptual scheme; Schreiner answers his question "how I would combine historical facts with a sermon on the iniquity of the present social forms" with an organic image which itself demonstrates more her need for such organic holism to inhere in the scheme than the logical and methodological existence of such holism itself: "I would combine them only as a hand is combined with a foot as parts of one organic whole. I would not mix them."[19]

Whereas Schreiner ostensibly wishes to locate gender within the "objective" evolution of human society, what emerges is a sense that evolutionary narrative, and the concept of the social (or aesthetic) totality are gendered male; the category of woman is a product of, and therefore outside, this narrative.

The inability to make the parts cohere is dramatically demonstrated in the Wollstonecraft fragment itself. Beginning with the non-human world, Schreiner argues that

> the full history of the varying protean shapes which sex assumes in its manifestation on the earth has yet to be written; but it is evident, from the most cursory survey, that nothing is more variable than the forms and functions which their, at core unchanging, principles may assume. (*Wollstonecraft*, p. 7)

She then supplies a catalogue, listing the variety of manifestations of sexual difference across marine life, birds, and mammals. In fact, Schreiner's approach here is highly anti-evolutionary; the examples are constellations, abstracted from their material conditions, removed, that is, from any evolutionary causality – in order to "prove" that indeterminacy and multiplicity is the chief feature of sexual differentiation. Schreiner's method is radical to the same extent that it is conservative: she can assert the fluidity and variability of sexual difference, thereby providing a radical challenge to essentialism and patriarchy, only insofar as she does not suggest any cause for the various processes or phenomena of differentiation, thereby rendering it as metaphysically mysterious as the essentialism she is challenging.

What Schreiner wants, then, and produces, from the purely "natural" is precisely that it is not directly instrumentalisable analogically or allegorically, cannot be surrendered to the particular Darwinian uses of a Karl Pearson (i.e. used to justify human sexual oppression). When, however, Schreiner proceeds with her "evolutionary" outline by turning to ancient and primitive societies, she gives two contradictory bases for women's oppression, one cultural and the other essentially "natural," or animal/physical. The first locates women's oppression with the advent of agricultural cultivation and/or the introduction of slave labour, resulting in women's removal from the public sphere of socially necessary labour. This is the notion which Schreiner was later to develop into her theory of "female parasitism," most fully presented in *Woman and Labour*. The situation is one which occurs in ancient states "where a great degree of civilization has been attained ..." (*Wollstonecraft*, p. 9).

What interests Schreiner more, however, at this stage, is the "natural" situation of "primitive" society, which presents a model of women's oppression as enslavement by, not exclusion from, social labour. And with this Schreiner's social Darwinism comes to the fore, unmediated by any materialist methodology (unlike the first model), and unmediated too by any romantic associations of primitivism and utopia. Schreiner asserts that

> In the early conditions of most society ... it was necessary that women, muscularly inferior individuals, should be enslaved. The races which refused to do this were beaten in the struggle by the races that did. It was necessary that part of the race should become simply a highly specialised fighting organ, it was necessarily the male part; the function of childbearing and rearing is not inconsistent with agriculture, house building, manufacture, it is with operant warfare. The race which first rigorously subjected its female and threw on her the material burden of life, reserving the entire power of the male for warfare, was the dominant race ... (*Wollstonecraft*, p. 11)

On primitivism's "truth" depends the whole of evolution; Schreiner cannot proceed to the rest until she has theorised human origins. The attempt here collapses, however, on a dramatic note, with Schreiner strenuously, almost sadistically, asserting the social necessity and moral duty of the African male to subjugate his female.

At the same time, however, Schreiner characterises primitive society as one in which African women enjoy physical and mental near-equality with their men, if not political equality:

> The Kaffir female is the property of the male; he may kill, fog [sic] or subject her to any use, owing to his superior physical strength; but her functions as builder, manufacturer, cultivator, prevent any deterioration of her mental powers and her physical strength, while less than that of the male in many ways is superior in some, as in the power of carrying weights on the head etc. Among savage races the skulls of the male and female are not so easily distinguishable as among more civilized races. (*Wollstonecraft*, p. 10)

And it is towards a similar state of lesser-differentiation that Schreiner sees contemporary Western society as moving:

Among the most highly civilized races, where mechanical motion has advanced far and muscular power is largely superseded by other forms of force in material production, a comprehensive survey will show us that the process of differentiation is not continuing, and that in such society there is a tendency in the male and female forms to become increasingly similar. (*Wollstonecraft*, p. 10)

That is, the movement of "sex towards sex" which Schreiner describes, and prescribes, is actually a repetition of the early primitive state of relative non-differentiation – but for opposite reasons (technology) and to opposite effect (emancipation). As *Woman and Labour* reveals, Schreiner's argument for feminism is based on a *labour theory of value*: women are to be readmitted to the sphere of socially-useful labour. This is a duty, rather than a right, and is both the sign and condition of women's freedom. It is made possible by the development of technology, in which "nervous" force or non-manual labour, for which women are equipped, is seen to take the place of "muscular" labour, for which Schreiner considers women less well-equipped than men. Here, in the Wollstonecraft fragment, African women are presented as, exactly, the fully-active, socially-labouring agents that she wishes modern women to be. But if African women are a model of active labour, they also exemplify, for Schreiner, degradation, reification, and self-renunciation; they are "beasts of burden," who epitomise their primitive (or animal) culture to the degree to which they are oppressed by it. The "slavery" of the African woman becomes, or is equal to, the freedom of the Western woman. The "freedom" of modernity, however, is necessarily construed in terms of determinism (as an involuntary and inescapable necessity to labour, experienced socially and psychologically). The *negative*, and negation, of the African origin/ other consists, it seems, in a repetition/translation and internalisation of the terms of that other. In other words, the physical or "muscular"-based domain of the African is presented both as the conceptual opposite of, and as the template or paradigm for, the West. When Schreiner alleges racial and evolutionary difference, she cannot help revealing at the same time a notion of the African scene as parallel to, and an influence upon, her theoretical formulation of contemporary white women. If the African woman represents mortification (as we shall see), she also constitutes a sign and source of social *value* for Schreiner.

Schreiner's tentative theorisation here is as much about the origins of her own subjectivity (and unconscious) as it is about the evolutionary origins of human society. Having produced the above social Darwinist assertion, Schreiner immediately shifts into first-hand colonial experience of African society; and it is now, when she attempts to be most "objective," through her utilisation of empirical data obtained in person, that she exposes the most subjective investment in her subject. With this supercession of a metropolitan by a colonial mode comes a radical shift in emphasis, from evolutionism to (metaphysical) fate, from questions of history to issues of female subjectivity. (The shift is also, arguably, from Darwin to Lamarck: here Schreiner is accounting for action not in terms of reaction to external conditions but in terms of a desire which precedes and determines the subject's behaviour.) Arguing that "nowhere is the consciousness of suffering deeper or the sense of injustice stronger than in the savage woman," Schreiner enlists as evidence her own childhood encounter with an African woman. The scene is recorded in detail, with an eloquent speech by the African woman, quoted "verbatim." In this speech the woman gives an outline of her own reification:

> It is a woman; sell it – let us get many oxen for it; let it now bear child and work. See! she has the child – give it milk; she works in the field, she builds the house, she is the servant; let her work. But – now – what is this? She gets old; the lines come up in her face; she cannot have many children – get the young wife. Ah, let her work, let her work, the dog, for the young wife beat her; and he gets a young wife. What is the use of her? Beat her. Do not give her too much food. Ah, throw her away like the dog when it is dead. Hugh, throw it out. We are dogs, we are dogs ... (*Wollstonecraft*, p. 13)

The manner and effect of the engraving of the speech on Schreiner's brain are as fatal as the content engraved, as she comments after the speech's conclusion:

> The strange part of such an outburst is the dead hopeless calm with which it is spoken. It is as though one sat in a house with one's dead and looked at them, but did not dream they could be made alive again. The speech of this woman, a completely uncivilised Betuanna, made an absolutely indelible impression upon my mind as a child. (*Wollstonecraft*, pp. 13–14)

She goes on to outline a theory of social instinct as the explanation for this submission:

> I believe that, deeper yet than this, lies the perception that it is her *duty to submit*. I believe the social instinct which formulates right and wrong, distinctly acts within her, and that her "moral sense," unable as she may be to formulate it exactly, acts as a mighty force upon her urging her to submission. I believe that any act of insubordination or rebellion would inflict on her through her social instincts the same undying remorse which a soldier would feel who on the field of battle refused to shoot a fellow man at the command of his leader. (*Wollstonecraft*, p. 14)

In the best tradition of Christian sacrifice, the African woman stands outside or beneath history in order to produce it; the murder of her subjectivity and autonomy is the condition of "life." Her "social instinct" or unconscious is the prime mover in this submission. In other words, the "superego" and the "id" are constructed as being identical here.

Here, through the figure of the African woman, we have Schreiner encountering problems exactly opposite to those which she confronted through the figure of Wollstonecraft. The difference in rhetorical approach is striking. Whereas Schreiner could not engage with Woll-stonecraft's own words, preferring, significantly, to quote William Godwin rather than Wollstonecraft herself, and positioning herself as spokeswoman for and on Wollstonecraft's behalf, here she speaks *through* the African woman, quoting (or impersonating) her in full. Whereas, too, she was emphatic about Wollstonecraft's *lack* of influence upon her own work, here she acknowledges the formative influence of the African woman (*Wollstonecraft*, pp. 1–2). If one of the dimensions of the Wollstonecraft episode was Schreiner's confrontation with the live demon of her own current rationality (associated with the forces of mortification and oppression), here she can be seen to confront the demon of her missionary past, the mortifying force of the Christian metaphysics and ethics of submission to fate/authority, and its resultant valorisation of oppression, which she projects onto, and ascribes to, the African woman. But it is also a projection of Schreiner's ambivalence about the physical body itself, and the deathliness, as she sees it, of its laws, and of a society whose production and culture is based on such laws. Muscular force gets associated with determinism of all sorts, with social necessity and with involuntary mental submission (through "instinct").

Most complexly, the scene is also to be read as Schreiner's encounter with the origins of her own psyche. How far is it "determined" by this example of the principle of "determinism," in which the unconscious itself is pre-set to collude with the dictates of the race? When Schreiner claims to be describing the African woman's unconscious she "unconsciously" slides into grammatical ambiguity; when she states, of the speech, "It is as though one sat in a house with one's dead and did not dream they could be made alive again," the referent here is equally the subjectivity of both the African woman and Schreiner herself. It stands as a revelation of the degree to which Schreiner's own unconscious is colonised and colonial: her very conceptualisation of (or inability to conceptualise) the origins of her own psyche inevitably takes the route of African otherness. Schreiner's own biographical, subjective, and evolutionary-theoretical "origins" are constitutive and repressive of her "self"; just as the unconscious here is held to repeat the oppressive dictates of material society, so Schreiner's constructions of the present, of emancipation, repeat the repressive terms ascribed to the "original" condition. The force of repression and the force of emancipation are difficult to distinguish, and this is where Schreiner's theory stops, with an impasse produced by a fear of the unconscious that is equal to

Schreiner's fear of rationality. The unconscious – her own, or the African woman's – is as potentially murderous as the physical force or repression that produces it. Schreiner's animism has failed her, it seems – "the dead cannot be made alive again."

THE DRAMA OF FEMININE INDIVIDUATION

The chronological structure of *Dreams* shows Schreiner moving from the terrain of the individual on through the feminine and the cosmic to culminate in the explicitly political and social totality. The Wollstone-craft fragment showed Schreiner desirous to claim for women and their emancipation (through the figure of Wollstonecraft's own person) an intuitive or physically-based knowledge of the necessity of social and individual transformation, submitted to as involuntarily as the African woman submits to her physical unfreedom. Linked with this is an emphasis on individual subjectivity; as Schreiner argues in a letter, "Our first duty is to develop ourselves. Then you are ready for any kind of work that comes. ... It is not against man we have to fight but against ourselves within ourselves."[20] Individual subjectivity is constructed as both a precondition and a goal of individual action. What Schreiner requires of Western woman is that she alone give birth to her proper self, despite the possibility that what has hitherto aborted her has been social/racial dictates. Women, then, have to fight against their own internal forces of self-repression. But it is difficult, in Schreiner's discourse, to distinguish what must be fought for from what must be fought against. Both are characterised in terms of instinctive desire; the instinct of emancipation battles against women's own instinct of sexual desire, and/or the social custom which legislates that middle-class women vicariously thrive through their husbands.[21]

It is entirely appropriate, given Schreiner's concerns, that in the sequence of *Dreams* the two allegories dealing with the drama of female self-birth – "The Gardens of Pleasure" and "In a Far-Off World" – should immediately, and necessarily, *precede* the allegory of feminism in relation to society, "Three Dreams in a Desert." "Gardens" focuses on the process of a woman achieving autonomy through the renunciation of pleasure; "Far-Off World" dramatises how a woman gains freedom through giving up her lover. Both narra-tives freeze, or fetishise, the painful moment of loss, renunciation, and dispossession. These two narratives are, significantly, the only two of the entire collection *not* to contain any geographical and historical specificity, by way of the colophonic signature or topographical detail. The absence of context marks their very lack of precedence: such emancipation has as yet *no history*. If the narrative condition is un-precedented, the narrative action is also unconditional – the woman in the garden surrenders herself entirely to the command of Duty, walking (stripped of all assets save herself) into the indeterminate desert, while the woman on the "far-off" island submits without question to the desertion by her lover (who leaves via the sea, on a boat) which occurs as a result of her wish that he might have whatever is best for him.

In both cases, the woman's access to freedom is presented as involuntary (and in "Far-Off World," a by-product of the freeing of the male partner); the women are vehicles of a transcendental force. The law that is visited upon the women seems to be every bit as patriarchal as that from which it is supposed to be an emancipation. In "Gardens" an aged male figure of Duty compels the woman to exit; in "Far-Off World," the source of authority is a primitive altar before which the woman petitions and wounds herself. Just as in the Wollstonecraft fragment, what emerges here is the powerful association of primitivism, force and subjection with the process of acquiring, and utilising, subjectivity itself.

These are the most enigmatic and uncompromising of Schreiner's *Dreams*, and the most radically ambiguous. A rational explanation or narrative scheme is refused altogether; what this suggests is that the desire for freedom precedes its naming, is as violent and inexplicable as the oppressive condition which produced it.

FEMINISM: FORCE OR REASON

The "Three Dreams in a Desert" are Schreiner's most developed, and celebrated, allegorical representation of female freedom – or its inconceptualisability. The first two between them play out the unresolved antinomies of Schreiner's feminism: the first presents an evolutionary/ determinist account of women's oppression, featuring woman as an object which is released into freedom and agency only through the advent of technology; the second, on the contrary, presents Reason as the motor of women's emancipation (the third is something of a coda, merely asserting the achievability of sexual equality on earth, pictured as a heaven). Woman, in the second, is already, even before her quest, a subject rather than an object of history; her emancipation here is not an end in itself but the privileged vehicle for the freedom of the "entire human race." What should, and does not, link the two is the crucial passage of woman into autonomous status; she remains on the one hand an effect of history and on the other a means of history, never reaching meaning in and for herself.

Just as significant as the gaps between the narratives are the gaps within. The visual logic of both is at odds with its narrative logic. In the first dream, we are presented with the image of two colossal figures of female and male, the former supine and bound. The vision is explained to the dreamer/onlooker (by a male mediator). Woman's oppression has been a historical necessity: ages ago the

> Age-of-dominion-of-muscular-force found her, and when she stooped low to give suck to her young, and her back was broad, he

put his burden of subjection on to it, and tied it on with the broad
band of Inevitable Necessity. (*Dreams*, p. 70)

As the dreamer looks on, the woman's burden falls to the ground; it is
further explained that the "Age-of-muscular-force" has been killed
by the "Age-of-Nervous-force," with the knife of "Mechanical Invention"; the band of Inevitable Necessity has been cut, and the conditions
of possibility for woman's freedom now exist. The woman attempts
to rise but is weak, after ages of physical oppression. Nonetheless
she manages slowly to "stagger" on to her knees. But the narrative's ostensible scheme and teleology – one of evolutionary transformation – is structurally at odds with the scene's static and physical
symbolisation. Schreiner conflates a discourse and language of
Spencerian evolutionism with a metaphysical/Biblical and elemental/
African scene. The result is that the stated medium of emancipation –
technology, or the knife of mechanical invention – is hypostasised; the
condensation of a linear trajectory into a physical image renders the
advent of Nervous Forces as mysterious, and brutal as the primitive
condition which precedes it. It is perhaps the African desert itself which
focuses the ambiguities of the text: it is constitutive of both pre-history
and of history itself, an infinite void signifying all the ages in which
woman has been a beast of burden. It is both geographically specific –
home to the evolutionary origins of man – and ontologically general –
connotative of the metaphysical condition of man as a beast of
burden. To the extent that the figures are "universal" they bespeak the
permanence of an African state or stage of oppression; to the degree
to which they are specifically Western they (unwittingly) challenge
the differentiation of history into a qualitatively superior course of
Western technology. That is the strength of the allegory, and its weakness; the impression given of woman's oppression is overpowering. It
needs to go beyond History, beyond narration, to be overcome.

The second dream betrays a disjuncture between Schreiner's conceptions of personal and collective emancipation. It is originally
featured as an individual's quest for fulfilment through freedom:
woman receives a course of instruction from Reason as to how the land
of Freedom is to be reached, down the banks of Labour, through the
water of Suffering. But this pursuance of enlightened self-interest and
personal evolution has to undergo a discursive transposition; the value
of the quest, for Schreiner, must be turned into a narrative of the
necessity of self-sacrifice for the social whole. To effect this Schreiner
uses a biological image. When "woman" exclaims over her isolation in
undertaking this quest, her guide Reason instructs her to listen to the
sound of the thousands who will follow her:

"Where you stand now, the ground will be beaten flat by ten
thousand times ten thousand feet." And he said, "Have you seen
the locusts how they cross a stream? First one comes down to the

water-edge, and it is swept away, and then another comes and then another, and at last with their bodies piled up a bridge is built and the rest pass over." (*Dreams*, p.82)

The woman becomes one part of a biological machine, guided by instinct rather than reason, prepared to surrender her freedom to provide that of "the entire human race." Even within its own terms the image is incongruous; the locusts' labour is that of a synchronised mass, while the woman is constituted as the leader paving the way for those who will eventually, not simultaneously, follow or traverse her body-bridge. If this narrative is meant to dramatise the inextricability of the individual and the social, the rational and the physical, it does precisely the opposite. What Schreiner seems to suggest is that self-sacrifice is really not compatible with reason; the social totality itself can only be given a mechanical figuration.

HOLISM, HISTORY, AND IDEALITY

The next two narratives raise this tension into a formal principle; rationality is confronted by a material limit or frame (a chapel, a woman's body). The narrative of "In a Ruined Chapel" concerns the effort of a man to transcend his (apparently justified) hatred of another man. The man petitions God to assist him, having found it impossible to effect a Christian forgiveness on his own. With the aid of an angel, the man is finally successful. The desired effect, however, is achieved in a strikingly biological manner: the man is given a lesson in Spencerian first principles, in the form of a backward trip through time and space. It is a trip of de-individuation, the end point of which is the man's confrontation with the "fact" of the essential unity of the entire organic universe and his resultant involuntary realisation of love for his "brother." It is also a lesson in discursive translation: Christian terms of charity, forgiveness, sin, are explicitly traded in for the terms of scientific rationality – "intellectual insight," "intellectual blindness," and necessity take their place. But this (evolutionary Comteian) passage from religion to science takes place in, is contained by, an explicitly Christian setting: the dreamer of this narrative has the dream whilst sitting in the sun outside a chapel in Alassio, Italy. And while the man's passage itself uses the form of biological determinism, the language of his final revelation of the totality, is aesthetic: "how beautiful my brother is!" he exclaims, sublating the discourses both of reason and Christian ethics (or, pure and practical reason).

This, and the fact of the chapel setting, would be enough to suggest that Schreiner is interrogating the exclusiveness of the claims of science, even while affirming it. But the whole undergoes another twist if we look more closely at the details of the context for the dream's narration. The fact that the setting is a defunct chapel is not only significant for Christianity: more important is the fact

that the site serves as an index of European culture and history.
More particularly, ancient Rome, and the vagaries of its imperialism,
become the thematic focus. This is enforced both within and outside the
chapel. Its walls are decorated with frescoes of Roman soldiers, the
infant Christ, Christ bearing his cross, and the Virgin Mary, while

> Behind it runs the old Roman road. If you climb it and come and
> sit there alone on a hot sunny day you may almost hear at last the
> clink of the Roman soldiers upon the pavement, and the sound of
> that older time, as you sit there in the sun, when Hannibal and his
> men broke through the brushwood, and no road was. (*Dreams*,
> p. 100)

The walls of the chapel seem to establish a kind of dialectic between
Imperial occupation (for which ancient Rome is a central trope) and
Christianity, by which it was subsequently overcome. The imperial
power was itself imperialised, its imperial power preserved and
negated at the same time. (Schreiner was steeped in Gibbon's *Decline
and Fall*.) If the walls serve to ironise Roman imperialism of one kind
and affirm another kind of imperialism, the surrounding countryside
does the same; it marks the site both of that Roman hegemony and the
threat to it earlier by a North African force. While the main body of the
dream affirms not only human unity but brotherhood across the natural
globe, a metaphysical cohesion that traverses time as much as it does
space (the sinning man travels through both), such a narrative is
literally contained within, and ironised by, a narrative of the history of
Roman imperialism, or Western civilisation. The democratic holism of
the inside is countered by the military (and religious) contestations,
political conquests, represented by the outside.

The man of the dream, and the dreamer herself, are granted
enlightenment into the meta-physical unity of the world. But Schreiner
cannot affirm an ideology of universalism without invoking its opposite, imperialism, and the general category of biology is qualified by the
specific category of Western history. What this does is to beg questions
about the relation of the former to the latter, and even to question the
nature and function of the process and ideology of "enlightenment"
itself. Enlightenment, even as to "universal" unity, is made uncom-
fortably proximate to, or synonymous with, Eurocentric history and
"civilisation," one which relies upon a process of marginalisation and
exclusion even within its own terrain. At the end of the allegory, when
the narrator/dreamer, descending from the chapel, spots a peasant boy
ahead of her, leading his ass, she is full of the joy of enlightenment into
common humanity, and observes:

> I had never seen him before; but I should have liked to walk by him
> and to have held his hand – only, he would not have known why.
> (*Dreams*, p. 112)

The text's reliance upon a notion of exclusion of the peasant from the domain of enlightenment (he lacks consciousness of his place in the universal brotherhood) suggests that at its core such enlightenment defines exclusiveness as being itself an inevitable condition of universality.

"A Dream of Wild Bees" presents the reverse situation: instead of an ancient setting reoccupied by the new discourses of modern science, the context is novel – a pregnant woman – while the content – her choice of a future for her foetus – has a traditional quasi-medieval mode, as a series of classic allegorical personification-devices, of Wealth, Health, Fame, Love, Talent, ask to be the determinant of the foetal future. The reversal of the method of "In a Ruined Chapel" also inheres in the dynamics between the individual and the totality: whereas "Ruined Chapel" presents the individual subsumed into the totality, "Wild Bees" presents the totality condensed into the individual. The mother is, in taxonomic terms, as "typical" as the foetus, which is explicitly invested with generic significance: it is the ninth child, i.e., the culmination of the nine "months" gestation of the human race itself. The allegory is a direct rejoinder of Schreiner to the "scientific" eugenic theory of Karl Pearson, the (unnamed) "friend" for whom, the title page asserts, the dream was "written as a letter."

The contours of Pearson's eugenicism were already established: a ruthless utilitarianism, based on a notion of biological determinism, the genetic immutability of "stock," a sexism and racism which constructed the white male body as the source and shape of the social totality. Schreiner manages to challenge these within a few pages. The focus of the narrative – the body of a pregnant woman – is itself a decentring of Pearson's androcentrism. The bees, transmuted in her dream into Fame et al, are, significantly, male *drones*, sterile auxiliaries to the queen bee, centre and source of bee society (the dreaming woman takes on a position analogous to the queen bee). Whereas, for Pearson, a foetus's future was fixed by its genetic coding, Schreiner suggests that there is a variety of possible outcomes open to the foetus. She invokes and then problematises the notion of genetic determinism: the foetus's fate is sealed by the end of the narrative, but by the mother's *volition*. And the outcome the mother chooses – the nameless term which promises the child a life of non-specified labour, its only reward being that "the ideal shall be real to it" – is itself a rebuttal of the restrictive and reductive anti-idealism of Pearson.

The challenge to Pearson's determinism inheres also at the level of form. The condition of the pregnant woman is, precisely, an indeterminate one, a state of non-identity. Schreiner's problematising of the boundaries of form is also a problematising of narrative focus: both mother and foetus have equal claims to represent the protagonist of the narrative. Most interesting, perhaps, is Schreiner's pushing of the metaphysics/materialism tension into an equation, at the narrative conclusion. The realisation of the ideal promised to the foetus is given proleptic fulfilment here, with the foetus's "dream" sensation of

Light – that it never had seen. Light – that perhaps it never should
see. Light – that existed somewhere!

And already it had its reward: the Ideal was real to it. (*Dreams*,
p.96)

Schreiner equates idealism with biological reproduction: the "ideal"
has as much substance and potential (pace Pearson) as the foetus with
which it is here associated. The gestation of the one is identical to the
gestation of the other; to "conceive" (a baby, an ideal) is already a form
of achievement. What awaits both the mother and the foetus is the
labour of final realisation. The foetus remains, it seems, the woman's
only form of self-realisation, the condition of her ideal.

THE POLITICS OF LABOUR, CULTURE, AND UTOPIA

"The Sunlight Lay Across My Bed," the final and longest allegory in the
book, is also Schreiner's sole published essay of a "socialistic" kind, an
attempt to formulate a collective utopian vision, based on her theory of
labour, and a critique of contemporary capitalism. The dreamer is
taken by God to visit Hell and Heaven. The dreamer first witnesses the
"insane" system of futile possessiveness and deception: women, in a
parody of their role as nurturers, go around poisoning fruit, so that no
one may eat from them, while men, in a parody of manual labour, dig
pitfalls "into which their fellows may sink," in the hope that they will
thereby rise. The main horror of Hell consists in its cannibalistic
banqueting house, where men, women and children congregate to
feast on wine. The "wine" is the blood of the workers, stationed with
the wine press below the house; the workers both operate the wine
press and constitute its supply of grapes.

The imagery of this representation is as powerful as it is problematic.
Schreiner is involved in a radical demystification of contemporary
society, an exposure of its hypocrisy and exploitation. The course
of her demystification is, in a sense, the opposite to that of "ideology
critique": whereas the latter is concerned to denaturalise social systems
and explode ideology as the instrument of such naturalisation,
Schreiner's method is to "naturalise," to reveal the parasitical appetites
that underlie capitalist production and consumption. That is, she here
applies the biological model to society in order to critique rather than
justify it (unlike Pearson). The most glaring problem of such an
approach is its totalitarianism. The transformation by, or resistance
from within, any of its social elements is impossible. Protesters from
among the feasting class, we are told, are instantly destroyed and
buried beneath marble tombstones – a nice touch of Schreiner's, with
its suggestion that society consecrates and commemorates its critics *in
order to* silence them (or their bones, in this case, which continue to cry
out until covered up).

If the individual critical activity of members of the ruling class is futile, that of the working class is non-existent. The working class (here unrepresented except for a tiny bloodless hand which emerges from below to disrupt the revels) is prohibited, in Schreiner's scheme, from doing anything other than trampling on, and drinking, its fellow members to achieve upward mobility. Schreiner, that is, unwittingly naturalises the oppression of the working class and valorises its function as host to its parasites; the scheme is seamless in its reductivism. When, later, the tomb of Christ is perceived by the dreamer, God explains it as marking a "vine-truss" that got bruised in the press, thereby again justifying his martyrdom (for what else does a grapevine exist except to be used for the making of wine?). The only possibility for social change that Schreiner allows is one based on inevitable self-destruction; the dreamer passes the ruins of banqueting houses which have fallen because the earth was sodden with blood. The message is disturbing and reassuring in equal degree: the system will "organically" reach its end but only after the expenditure of bloody labour (rather than resistance) has reached saturation point.

To biologise the process of capitalist exploitation is also to aestheticise it. Schreiner presents the banqueting hall as the norm, the metaphor of capitalist society. Instead of being based on capital production, this system is based on and around inessential *pleasure* (obtained from the luxury of wine) experienced to excess. The superstructural effects of the economy take the place of that economy. Another way to put this is that Schreiner collapses capitalist system with its surplus, non-systematic, culture. The result is a kind of fetishism, an isolation of, and investment in, a substitute sign; this risks colluding with the very economy it wishes to condemn.

But this is also the scene's strength. Schreiner is at her most powerful when she subverts the sacramental vision. What she does may seem simple: she takes the Christian equation of wine and blood and reverses it, so that instead of actual wine serving as a metaphor for Christ's blood, the workers' blood serves as the actuality of society's "wine." (The banquet even has an officiating priest.) But it represents another example of Schreiner's problematisation of the principle of metaphoricity; by exposing the violence of the literal truth, she is in a sense giving the lie to the innocence of the system of metaphorical – and allegorical – conception.

Heaven in the allegory is structured around a distinction between natural and organic spheres of labour. (It is interesting that evolutionism, as theory and fact, should inhere only in Heaven; Hell is repetitive or cyclical, in contrast.) In the lower sphere, the labour of women and men consists of shining their light upon plants in order that they can grow. Labour, here as often in Schreiner, is basically auxiliary or reproductive, a facilitation and utilisation of that which already has been produced. Interestingly Schreiner again plays off the literal and the metaphorical and converts the latter into the former: the trope of divine radiance becomes a physical source of photosynthesis.

The higher stage of Heaven is Schreiner's most (accidentally) ironic conception of labour. Labour here is of a far more arduous nature than in the organic sphere:

> ... we came at last to a place where a great mountain rose, whose top was lost in the clouds. And on its side I saw men working; and they picked at the earth with huge picks; and I saw that they laboured mightily. ... (*Dreams*, p. 169)

The men are, it turns out, miners of precious stones which although unnamed bear more than a family resemblance to diamonds. Effectively, this site is none other than that of imperialism itself; the association between the mining of precious stones and imperialist activity during this period is unavoidable. As if to enforce the trope, the goal of the miners is itself construed in the image of power: the men labour to set the stones they find into the template of a colossal *crown*, one which, like imperialism, is endlessly expanding. Their work has to occur within the limits (or infinity) of this set pattern.

The higher heaven, then, consists not of freedom, but of the prescribed demarcations of labour, aiming to realise an imperial aesthetic totality. The very apex of heaven follows a similar scheme of domination. At the top of a solitary peak stands a lonely figure, one who has reached heaven's zenith. Predictably, this zenith is expressed in terms of aesthetics: the figure is involved in making music. But the zenith is also one of power, here identified with knowledge:

> God said, "From that lone height on which he stands, all things are open. To him is clear the shining in the garden, he sees the flower break forth and the streams sparkle; no shout is raised upon the mountain-side but his ear may hear it. He sees the crown grow and the light shoot from it. All Hell is open to him. He sees the paths mount upwards. To him, Hell is the seed ground from which Heaven springs. He sees the sap ascending. (*Dreams*, p. 177)

From the disinterested height of heaven one perceives all aspects of the totality from which one has arisen, and is excluded. To grasp the totality is also to recuperate Hell, (literally) to naturalise it as the organic origin of Heaven.

When Schreiner imagines the unimaginable, she ends up with the most extreme example of domination and exploitation then extant. If the miners' self-realisation can only occur within the prescribed outlines of the crown, the same might ultimately be said of Schreiner. Allegory is, like labour itself in Schreiner's theory of value, the activity of freedom, the site of the struggle for the realisation, or freeing, of origins. But it is a freedom that is, in many respects, indistinguishable from oppression. Realisation can only be at the cost of reification – reification of the original matter, of the producing agent. The allegories are not the less important for the impasse that they enact, however; it is on the contrary because of their contradictions that they remain significant. They suggest the very limits of possibility for feminist discourse of that time.

LAURA CHRISMAN

NOTES

1. Olive Schreiner, *The Story of an African Farm* (London: Chapman and Hall, 1883); *Woman and Labour* (London: Fisher Unwin, 1911). References here to *The Story of an African Farm* are based upon the Penguin edition (Harmondsworth: Penguin, 1939). The best recent biography of Schreiner is by Ruth First and Anne Scott, titled *Olive Schreiner: A Biography*, first published 1980, reprinted in 1989 (London: Women's Press, 1989).
2. Olive Schreiner, *Dreams* (London: Fisher Unwin, 1890). References are to the second edition (London: Fisher Unwin, 1891) and are hereafter included in the text. Olive Schreiner, *Thoughts on South Africa* (London: Fisher Unwin, 1923).
3. Arthur Symons considered that "the book is like nothing else in English" in his review of *Dreams*, *Athenaeum*, 10 Jan. 1891, reprinted in *Olive Schreiner*, ed. Cherry Clayton (Johannesburg: McGraw-Hill, 1983).
4. Recent critical assessment of these allegories has been harsh, and largely acontextual. See the judgement of Nadine Gordimer in "The Prison-House of Colonialism," *Times Literary Supplement*, 15 Aug. 1980, reprinted in *An Olive Schreiner Reader, Writings on Women and South Africa*, ed. Carol Barash (London: Pandora Press, 1987). See also Cherry Clayton, "Olive Schreiner, Child of Queen Victoria: *Stories, Dreams and Allegories*," *English in Africa* [Grahamstown], 6, No. 2 (Sept. 1979), reprinted in *Olive Schreiner*, ed. Cherry Clayton. Clayton is appreciative rather than dismissive, but views Schreiner's allegorical aesthetic as constituted exclusively by early and mid-nineteenth-century thought. The view of Barash, in her introduction to *An Olive Schreiner Reader*, is an exception; she relates the allegories, both form and content, to the late-nineteenth-century context in which they were composed.
5. See, for example, Olive Schreiner, Letter to Edward Carpenter, 12 April 1888 (from Alassio, Italy), *Olive Schreiner Letters, Vol. 1: 1871–1899*, ed. Richard Rive (Oxford: Oxford U.P., 1988), p.139.
6. The 15-page fragment "Introduction to the Life of Mary Wollstonecraft, and the Rights of Woman" remains unpublished, in typescript form, and is now the property of the National English Literary Museum, Grahamstown, South Africa; the Museum's permission to quote from thie material is gratefully acknowledged. Efforts to trace the copyright holder have so far proved unsuccessful. References are hereafter included in the text.
7. Edward Carpenter, *Towards Democracy* (1883; rpt. London: George Allen, 1913).
8. Carpenter, *Towards Democracy*, p.9.
9. Olive Schreiner, Letter to Edward Carpenter, 21 Jan. 1889, *Letters*, ed. Rive, p.147.
10. Edward Carpenter, *Love's Coming-of-Age* (1896; rpt. London: Methuen, 1913), p.20.
11. The essay is included in Pearson's *The Ethic of Freethought. A Selection of Essays and Lectures* (London: Fisher Unwin, 1888). See also his "National Life from the Standpoint of Science" (London: Adam and Charles Black, 1901), for a concise articulation of eugenic thought.
12. See for example, Olive Schreiner, Letter to Havelock Ellis, 29 March 1885, *Letters*, ed. Rive, p.63.
13. "The Hunter" is to be found in chapter two of the second part, titled "Waldo's Stranger."

14. Schreiner, *The Story of an African Farm*, pp.151–2.
15. Olive Schreiner, Letter to Karl Pearson, 11 Oct. 1886, *Letters*, ed. Rive, p.106;
    Olive Schreiner, Letter to Karl Pearson, 26 Oct. 1886, *Letters*, ed. Rive, p.111;
    Schreiner to Ernest Rhys, early 1888, *Letters*, ed. Rive, pp.136–7.
16. Olive Schreiner, Letter to Havelock Ellis, 2 Nov. 1888, *Letters*, ed. Rive, p.142.
17. Olive Schreiner, Letter to Karl Pearson, 10 Sept. 1886, *Letters*, ed. Rive, p.104.
18. Olive Schreiner, Letter to Karl Pearson, 10 Sept. 1886.
19. Olive Schreiner, Letter to Karl Pearson, 10 Sept. 1886.
20. Olive Schreiner, Letter to Mary Roberts, January–March 1889, *Letters*, ed. Rive,
    p.145.
21. See for example the discussions of female "self-culture" in the second chapter of
    "Parasitism," in Schreiner, *Woman and Labour*.

Homosexuality and Orientalism: Edward Carpenter's Journey to the East

I

Passage indeed O soul to primal thought
Not lands and seas alone, ...

As fill'd with friendship, love complete, the Elder Brother found,
The Younger melts in fondness in his arms,
Passage to more than India!
     – Walt Whitman, *Passage to India*, 11.165–6, 222–4.

Edward Carpenter's writings on the East evolve from a well-established narrative mode of Orientalism, prevalent in the social, economic, and political framework of nineteenth-century Britain, except that in this case the narrator's discourse is imbued with homoerotic desire. The association between homoerotic desire and the Orient is not unique to Carpenter's work, and occurs in English literature both before and after him, in writers such as Edward Fitzgerald, Sir Richard Burton, Goldsworthy Lowes Dickinson, E.M. Forster, T.E. Lawrence, and J.R. Ackerley. Edward Carpenter's *From Adam's Peak to Elephanta* springs from this tradition of homosexual Orientalism in English literature.[1]

The link between homosexuality and Orientalism is further illuminated by Edward W. Said's distinction between "filiation" and "affiliation," and his analysis of the Western propensity towards the East.[2] Said elucidates "the exaggerated boundary drawn between Europe and the Orient" in terms of the notions of home and place, integral to the Western sensibility.[3] The language of being "at home" or "in place," according to Said, translates into the relationships of "filiation" and "affiliation." Filiation suggests bonds of kinship, and is indicated by an "aggressive" sense of nation, home, culture, community and belonging. Affiliation, on the other hand, arises from a failed possibility of filiation, and denotes an allegiance to a compensatory, "transpersonal," and sometimes subversive order, such as "guild consciousness, consensus, collegiality, professional respect, class, and the hegemony of a dominant culture."[4] The definitions of filiation and affiliation clarify some of the tensions underlying the concepts of home and journey, and these oppositions are rendered most compellingly in the homosexual predicament in nineteenth-century Britain. Against the context of social and religious intolerance, homosexuals invariably turned to places and ideas outside English society that accommodated love between men. Thus they became inveterate travellers to remote and unknown regions, forever in search of a viable lifestyle. Attitudes to homosexuality were more lenient on the Continent than in Britain. Initially France and Italy, and then Greece and Sicily, gave refuge to many homosexuals fleeing from England. John Addington Symonds, Lord Henry Charles Somerset, Oscar Wilde, Frederick William Rolfe or "Baron Corvo," and C.K. Scott-Moncrieff were some of the writers who went to live on the Continent because of their homosexuality.[5]

In writing, as in life, the motif of journey, whether actual or metaphorical, offered a specially enabling mechanism by which an author could escape the rigours of his own age and milieu and flee to another country. The shift could be spatial or temporal, though often the two coincided, so that the geographical change also implied a voyage in time, and entrance into an idyllic and permissive world congenial to the freedom and affections of men. The incidence of journey in nineteenth-century homosexual literature, thus, manifests the writers' impulse to discard given filiations in favour of chosen affiliations. The external, territorial movement in these texts frequently becomes transmuted into a metaphysical and symbolic passage, with rites of male friendship and brotherhood incumbent upon it. Symonds' *In the Key of Blue* (1893), Rolfe's *Stories Toto Told Me* (1898) and *The Desire and Pursuit of the Whole* (1934) fall in the genre of travel narratives where the protagonists' wanderings are fused with homosexual quest and discovery.

Originally, tours across the Continent provided an opportunity for homosexual adventure. Even where the writers did not undertake an actual trip, references to an idealized classical world, when relations between men were the norm, were used effectively as a technique for communicating homoerotic desire. There was a revival of interest during the nineteenth century in the classical past, and within this wider intellectual environment homosexual writers adapted classicism to convey their own emphases and codes.[6] Hence, William Johnson Cory titled his two books of Uranian verse as simply *Ionica* (1858) and *Ionica II* (1877). Theodore William Graf Wratislaw's poem, "To a Sicilian Boy," which appeared in the *Artist* in 1893, touched on a common pederastic theme of homosexual escapades in Sicilian villages. Only two months before, Lord Alfred Douglas had printed his "Sicilian Love Song" in *The Spirit Lamp*.[7] Although Carpenter subscribed to a working-class ideal of homoerotic love, this was preceded by a route taken by several homosexuals, through affiliations with the classical world, as well as modern Greece and Italy. The influence of classical literature is evident in all of Carpenter's work, particularly *Ioläus* and *Towards Democracy*.[8]

The spread of classical learning in nineteenth-century Britain was accompanied by a surge of interest in the ancient civilisations of Asia. The strands of Hellenism and Orientalism ran parallel and overlapped in the Victorian imagination so that the language of classicism expanded to incorporate Orientalism. Jenkyns points out the connotations of the remote and the exotic that the classical era, and also contemporary Greece and Italy, acquired for the English apprehension. The Victorians "were using the past to soften passions and actions by the enchantment of distance."[9] He demonstrates the way in which the north–south contrasts amplified into the west–east metaphors. In *The Stones of Venice*, for example, Ruskin visualises Europe, south to north, from the sky: "a great peacefulness of light, Syria and Greece, Italy and Spain, laid like pieces of a golden pavement into the sea-blue," to where "the orient colours change gradually into a vast belt of rainy green." As Jenkyns explains, "Ruskin, in fact, associates the south with the east; the very name Gothic, he says, implies a degree of sternness 'in contradistinction to the character of Southern and Eastern nations.'" For Byron, too, the Greek islands were "Edens of the Eastern wave. ... Far from the winters of the west."[10] This intermingling of ideas was buttressed by studies like William Jones' *Asiatic Researches* (1799), Edward Pocock's *India in Greece: or, Truth in Mythology* (1852), and Max Muller's *Oxford Essays* (1856) – works that traced the origin of Greek myths to the Aryan religion.[11]

Edward W. Said identifies Orientalism as a tendency peculiar to Western Europe, "a style of thought based upon an ontological and epistemological distinction made between 'the Orient' and 'the Occident.'"[12] The Western involvement in Orientalism, dating from Homer's time to the present day, comprises a pervasive discourse and deep intertextuality, directed towards appropriating the Orient. Orientalism entails not just a manner of speaking *of* the Orient, but an authority of speaking *for* it.[13] Said reveals the attitudes of imperialism and cultural hegemony that shaped Orientalism. The discipline of Orientalism rests on the assumption of superiority; in Western discourse, the Orient is represented as the Other to Europe whilst simultaneously subordinating it to the West. Although Said deals mainly with the experience of the Arabs and Islam, he notes that until the early nineteenth century the Orient had "really meant only India and the Bible lands." From the nineteenth century to the end of the Second World War, "France and Britain dominated the Orient and Orientalism."[14]

The phenomenon of Orientalism had socio-economic and political, as well as psychological and sexual, aspects. On one level, the Orient acted as a repository of escapist sexual fantasies, far removed from the daily realities of ordinary Western life. The "embourgeoisement" and institutionalisation of sex in nineteenth-century Europe prompted Western writers to project sexual freedom onto the Oriental landscape. Said remarks that after 1800, for many European writers, engagement with the East was bound up not with intellectual curiosity, but with the prospect of sexual experiences unobtainable in Europe. He affirms that "What they looked for often – correctly, I think – was a different type of sexuality, perhaps more libertine and less guilt-ridden; but even that quest, if repeated by enough people, could (and did) become as regulated and uniform as learning itself."[15] Consequently, one of the major affiliations sought by homosexual writers, besides nostalgia for the classical ethos, was contact with the Orient. In homosexual writings, the East is construed in the usual imagery of the mysterious and the alien, except that in these instances the Orient stands for the homosexual Other. With Carpenter, Dickinson, Forster, T.E. Lawrence and Ackerley, the pursuit of homosexual love extends from Europe to the East. In these authors, Orientalism is continuous with and culminates the process of affiliation begun with classical scholarship.

Homosexual writers borrowed extensively from Oriental literature, as they had borrowed from classical myths, any instances of homoerotic love. The *Bhagavad-Gita* (first translated into English by Charles Wilkins in 1785), Edward Fitzgerald's adaptation of the *Rubaiyat of Omar Khayyam* (1859), Sir Richard Burton's translation of *Arabian Nights* (1885–88), and extracts from Sufi poetry – especially the verses of Hafiz – are the most prominent of Oriental texts received into the homosexual tradition for exalting friendship between men. Indeed, the transmission of Oriental texts during the nineteenth century forms an interesting bibliographical history. European studies and free translations of Oriental texts validate Said's thesis, that in Western scholarship the Orient was subsumed into Western culture. The *Bhagavad-Gita*, for example, was systematically assimilated into contemporary Western thought, whether it was European Romanticism or American Transcendentalism.[16]

Apart from the intellectual debates that it raised, the *Gita* also had personal and emotional value for many writers, who expressed their alienation from Western mores by giving a qualified acceptance to Indian religion and philosophy. The *Gita* provided a corrective to the pragmatic and rational stance of the West in that it encompassed intuitive and non-rational experience. Sharpe comments that the *Gita* is unusual in that it "strives to unite two conceptions, *jnana* (knowledge) and *bhakti* (loving devotion)."[17] The mysticism espoused in the text is erotic, and it is in this respect that the *Gita* was popular with homosexual writers in the nineteenth century. The title, "Bhagavadgita," means "The Song of the Adorable One," and the adorable one is Krishna; the doctrine of the book teaches Arjuna to love Krishna. Insofar as the *Gita* is a dialogue between a warrior, Arjuna, and a youthful demi-god Krishna, and consecrates the love of Arjuna for Krishna, the Hindu scripture was amenable to homoerotic interpretation.

The other major Oriental text that had an impact on the homosexual tradition in English literature was the *Rubaiyat of Omar Khayyam*. Edward Fitzgerald's translation appeared in 1859, and the poem was immediately seized upon as a declaration of a hedonistic creed.[18] Fitzgerald had eliminated Sufi theology from his translation by treating the images in the *Rubaiyat* literally. Moreover, he added several stanzas to the original one hundred and eleven, some of them containing what another translator, J.B. Nicolas, called "revolting sensualities."[19] Whatever the corruptions of Fitzgerald's version, the religious symbolism of Sufi poetry – the "wine" as a metaphor for "mystical rapture," "*saki*" as "the cup-bearer of God the Lover," and "Friend" as the personification of "divine truth" – was suggestive of homoerotic love. "Saki" is reminiscent of the Greek myth of Zeus and Ganymede, a motif resonant with homoerotic meaning.

Graves defends the religious quality of Khayyam's poem, which Fitzgerald had ignored, by comparing the *Rubaiyat* to the *Song of Solomon*. He says that the Sufis accepted the "divine-love metaphor," like the Hebrews, "but because Mohammedan women were kept in far closer subjection than the Jewish, ... a rapt brotherly love of fellow-initiates was substituted by the Sufis for erotic love."[20] The religious justification of the homoerotic vein in the *Rubaiyat*, however, is irrelevant where the homosexual writers are concerned. The fact remains that the attainment of the divine through love between men, preached in the *Gita* and the *Rubaiyat*, was evocative of the philosophical enterprise in Plato, and as such Oriental texts contained precisely the elements of homoerotic desire. Frederick Rolfe, Baron Corvo, composed an English translation, *Rubaiyat of Umar Khaiyam*, in 1903, from the French of J.B. Nicolas, while Laurence Housman wrote an introduction to one of the reprints of Edward Fitzgerald's editions published in 1928.

Selections from Hafiz also were easily absorbed into the homosexual tradition, for his verses were rich in erotic mysticism characteristic of Sufi poetry. Hafiz was a renowned Persian poet of the fourteenth century, and the interpretation of Hafiz in the eighteenth and nineteenth centuries was monopolised by British scholars.[21] Samuel Elsworth Cottam's (1863–1945?) two books, *Cameos of Boyhood and Other Poems* and *Friends of My Fancy and Other Poems*, include translations from Hafiz.[22] In "Hafiz to the Cup-bearer," a poem in *Towards Democracy*, the poet addresses George Merrill as the "Dear son" who lays down his life at the feet of Hafiz or Carpenter himself.[23] The references to Hafiz and Shiraz, India, China and other countries, give Carpenter's poem breadth and universality. In *Towards Democracy*, the invocations to the Orient are interwoven with the homosexual codes of son, brother and comrade. Carpenter's "anthology of friendship," called *Ioläus*, contains excerpts from Hafiz.[24]

To sum up, during the nineteenth century, there was a vast tradition of Orientalism which, in many ways, grew out of the Victorian interest in the classical world. European authors often tampered with Oriental texts and manipulated them to their own ends. An account of the mutations that Eastern literature underwent in nineteenth-century Britain gives an insight into the kind of activity that constituted Orientalism. The Orient was constructed as the Other to the West, and became a receptacle of empowering affiliations to replace adverse filiations. Edward Carpenter's enthusiasm for the East is entrenched in the nineteenth-century convention of homosexual Orientalism; his writings on the subject reinforce the contemporary stereotype of the Orient.

II

Carpenter's introduction to India was both imperial and philosophical. His elder brother, Charles, had joined the Indian Civil Service in 1857 and he wrote to his family of events in that country.[25] Carpenter's first contact with Indian philosophy appears to have been, somewhat incongruously, in his family home in Brighton. His father seems to have learnt about Indian philosophy through German philosophers. In a letter of 30 January 1876 to a Mrs Cobb, Mr Carpenter expounds the concept of "Nirvana" as it is used by Schopenhauer. He explains the Hindu ideal in relation to Schopenhauer's nihilism:

> By Nirvana, that man must have meant, I suppose, Annihilation; for he regarded existence as an evil. But surely the true meaning of Nirvana is that at some future stage of our being, man will be so conscious of the indwelling and in-working of Deity, that he will ascribe every movement whether of his body or mind to the One Will, the One *Vernunft*, the One Life, and then think of himself as swallowed up by and absorbed as it were in that Being.[26]

Edward Carpenter himself had talked of Nirvana three years before, in a letter to Charles Oates, on 2 April 1873. Carpenter's exposition of the concept, however, is unlike that of his father's. He speaks of the way in which Indian religion might help to resolve the conflicts within an individual. He tells Oates:

> You hint at despair and strangulation yet give me no clue to the cause except the antagonism of action and thought. ... [i]t appears that humanity was constructed especially for the purpose of exemplifying the awkwardness of it; therefore to quarrel with it is as if a house should quarrel with its foundations. Some people certainly don't seem to feel it; but then as they are generally people who never have thought, naturally they can't. I fancy there is a crack all down creation so − Y − and that the more nearly people come to understanding creation the more do they feel this crack in themselves. Life is the bridging of this crack. The Oriental mind says the crack can't be bridged and that the best thing is Nirvana or the retirement from this pontine existence. The Western mind says it can, and that the chain of life is conscience and the moral obligation. At this point the question remains![27]

Carpenter's father, in fact, came closer to understanding the state of

Nirvana, as propagated in Indian philosophy, than Carpenter himself at this point. Carpenter employs the Hindu concept to grapple with his own sense of fragmentation, and the contradiction between public and personal life that he was feeling at this time.

Carpenter was further influenced by Indian philosophy while at Cambridge from 1864 to 1874. He met Ponnambalam Arunachalam, a Tamil Ceylonese, during this period. Arunachalam studied at Christ Church from 1871 to 1875. He was called to the bar the same year, and later joined the Ceylon Civil Service. Arunachalam was knighted in 1915.[28] Carpenter documents his friendship with Arunachalam in his autobiography, and says, "I learned much from him about the literature of India and the manners and customs of the mainland and Ceylon."[29] Arunachalam wrote regularly to Carpenter from Ceylon and these letters were published in *Light from the East*.[30] Arunachalam informed Carpenter on Indian religion and literature and also invited him to visit Ceylon.[31]

Further contact with Indian thought came after Cambridge. For example, on Carpenter's trip to America in 1877, Whitman and Anne Gilchrist talked to him about Indian literature. In the course of the same tour, Carpenter had spent a night at Concord with Emerson, who showed him his translations of the *Upanishads*.[32] Harold Cox, one of Carpenter's Cambridge friends, left for India in 1885, to be a Professor of Mathematics at Anglo-Oriental College in Aligarh. He stayed there for two years and reported on political affairs to Carpenter. He saw a "sea of discontent seething beneath the smooth surface of English rule," while also complaining of the "deadly" dullness of the English people in the station.[33] Cox sent Carpenter two pairs of Kashmiri sandals, and the latter used these as a model to make some at Mill-thorpe.[34] Carpenter made sandals for friends and they were famous in radical circles (see Carpenter's photograph of 1905 in *My Days and Dreams*, facing p.208). Another Cambridge friend of Carpenter, Theodore Beck, was Principal of the same college where Cox had been appointed Professor. Beck had written *Essays on Indian Topics* (1888), in which he warned that some communication between the British and the natives was essential if the Empire was to last in India.[35]

Arunachalam had given Carpenter a translation of the *Gita* some time in 1880–81. Carpenter read the scripture in 1881, when his spirits were at a low ebb. Carpenter records that the *Bhagavad-Gita* gave him "a keynote," and "all at once I found myself in touch with a mood of exaltation and inspiration – a kind of super-consciousness – which passed all that I had experienced before."[36] Previously, reading Whitman's *Leaves of Grass* had generated a similar sense of exhilaration, and it was "with a great leap of joy – that I met with the treatment of sex which accorded with my own sentiments."[37] His reading of Whitman ultimately precipitated Carpenter's first break from his background and led him to seek fresh affiliations outside his class: "... it suddenly flashed upon me, with a vibration through my whole body, that I would and must somehow go and make my life with the mass of the people and the manual workers."[38] Real contact, though, with the working classes had been slow; his extension lectures were attended not by robust manual workers, but by young middle-class ladies and clerks. Seven years of constant travelling and teaching had brought him again to the point of nervous collapse by 1880–81. During his lectures, he met Albert Fearnehough, and through him, Charles Fox. Carpenter went to live with the two men on a farm at Bradway. It was at this point, grief-stricken by his mother's death, that Carpenter read the *Bhagavad-Gita*. The sense of freedom accorded by *Leaves of Grass* and the *Gita* was emotional and sexual, deriving from their emphasis on loves and friendships which were largely discredited or denied in English society. Carpenter acknowledges that for him the contribution of Whitman consisted in "the poems which celebrate comradeship," while the *Gita* "immediately harmonized all these other feelings, giving to them their place, their meaning and outlet in expression."[39] Whitman had been influenced by Indian philosophy, and the *Gita* and *Leaves of Grass* together inspired the conception of *Towards Democracy*. The strains from the former two works flow side by side in Carpenter's long poem.

The *Gita* integrates the earthly with the divine, and individual passion with the love of God. The eroticism of the text is fairly overt even in a nineteenth-century translation by Edwin Arnold.[40] In one of the verses, Arjuna wishes to see Krishna. In answer to Arjuna's request, Krishna says that He is present in the visible world which is a facet of the sacred Whole:

> Behold! this is the Universe! – look! what is live and dead
> I gather all in one – in Me!

Arjuna is held in a trance as Krishna appears before him:

> All this universe enfold
> All its huge diversity
> Into one vast shape, and be
> Visible, and viewed, and blended
> In one Body – subtle, splendid
> Nameless – th' All-comprehending
> God of Gods, the Never-Ending
> Deity!

Krishna guides Arjuna to the path of love:

> Yet not by Vedas, nor from sacrifice,
> Nor penance, nor gift-giving, nor with prayer
> Shall any so behold, as thou hast seen!
> Only by fullest service, perfect faith,
> And uttermost surrender am I known
> And seen, and entered into, Indian Prince!
> Who doth all for Me; who findeth Me

> In all; adoreth always; loveth always; loveth all
> Which I have made, and Me, for Love's sole end,
> That, man, Arjuna! unto Me doth wend.[41] .

The tenets of love between all men, and the individual as a part of the cosmic whole, preached in the *Gita*, would clearly have had an immediate appeal for Carpenter in his loneliness, and for other equally isolated homosexuals.

The teachings of the *Gita* are echoed in *Leaves of Grass*; Arjuna's plea to Krishna to come to him in the *Gita* becomes transformed into a call for comradeship and "brotherhood of lovers" in *Leaves of Grass*:

> Come, I will make the continent indissoluble,
> I will make the most splendid race the sun
>   ever shone upon,
> I will make divine magnetic lands,
>   With the love of comrades,
>   With the life-long love of comrades.[42]

The title of *Towards Democracy* derives from Whitman's *Democratic Vistas* (1871), and Carpenter's poem emulates the American poet in style and content. Carpenter's democracy, we note, brings together "the resplendent-limbed Negro and half-caste ... the glitter-eyed caressing-handed Hindu, suave thoughtful Persian, and faithful Turk." The poet hails them, "Come! And out of your clinging kisses, see! I create a new world."[43] By establishing kinship with men from all over the world, Carpenter is asserting affections that were prohibited both on racial and sexual grounds. The democracy advocated by Whitman and Carpenter has both political and sexual dimensions. Hence their democracy is not based in any actual society; it signals a new affiliation, a new community.

Whitman and Carpenter took from the Indian religion the insight that worldly life is not divorced from the transcendent but that the two are joined together. However, whereas Hinduism instructs the individual to aspire for detachment from material involvement, Whitman and Carpenter reverse that trend in that for them the physical supersedes the spiritual. In *Song of Myself*, Whitman rejoices in every particle of life, "I am the poet of the Body and I am the poet of the Soul. ... therefore I to you give love!/O unspeakable passionate love."[44] So also, Carpenter cherishes the ideal of "the great coherent Whole"; but while in the Indian doctrine the movement is away from the earthly to go "beyond Maya" to find God, Carpenter descends from abstraction "into materials."[45]

For Carpenter, then, the lure of the East was both intellectual and emotional. Carpenter's sympathy for Indian religion and philosophy was intrinsic to his rebellion against the Victorian world view, which in turn was rooted in his homosexuality. As Tariq Rahman explains, "The motivation for creating a congenial value-system and spiritual vision came from Carpenter's alienation from the existing system," and his "metaphysic was a product, as were the social theories, of his homosexual orientation."[46] A journey abroad had always been a mode of escape to which Carpenter had recourse in emotional adversity. In the personal crisis of 1871–3, he visited Italy several times, and took pleasure in looking at the paintings and sculptures of naked male bodies.[47] In 1878, tired and frustrated as an extension lecturer, he travelled to Paris to avail himself of male prostitutes there, but it proved to be a futile trip because he could not get rid of his inhibitions and self-consciousness.[48] In 1887, by which time Carpenter was settled in Sheffield and immersed in Socialist activities, divisions in the Labour movement, both nationally and locally, caused him to become depressed and disillusioned. When his friend, Charles Oates, proposed a holiday together in Italy in April 1887, Carpenter admits,

> I feel tired, and weary of these eternal fogs. Still, it is very doubtful whether I shall get away – some of the people that I am employing in Sheffield are wrangling with each other and if I leave they will break out into open warfare – unless indeed I can put things on a better footing shortly. ...
>
> ... George is as good as ever, and indeed that is one drawback I feel against going to Italy. He is staying here for a day or two, and tomorrow he and I are going for a 2 or 3 days walk among the Derbyshire Hills. His love is so disinterested and so tender – I hardly dare think it true.[49]

But the security that Carpenter found in the friendship of George Hukin disintegrated as Hukin fell in love with a local girl, Fannie, ultimately announcing his intention to marry her.[50] Carpenter's response was to obtain a brief respite from his troubles by travelling to Italy to stay with Oates at Acqui. Carpenter parted with Oates to meet Olive Schreiner in Paris on 7 June 1887. He returned with Schreiner to London the next day, and in his letter to Oates, he voices his despair on approaching England: "at 3 a.m. Miss Schreiner and I were steaming mournfully into Dover! Anything more depressing it were difficult to imagine – a dense fog hanging over the cliffs of Albion, the cold phlegmatic faces of the people." He faced the thought of Hukin's looming marriage with trepidation. In the same letter Carpenter confides, "I keep wondering whether I shall ever settle down in England. If anything were to go wrong between me and George, Italy would be my only hope."[51]

Carpenter's loneliness and unhappiness increased after Hukin's wedding, which fundamentally altered the friendship and intimacy between them. Carpenter's growing isolation from those around him is communicated in his letters to Oates. Again, his attempts at friendship, to establish new affiliations, had failed, leaving Carpenter lonely and confused. Further dissension in the Sheffield Socialist Society caused by the activities of a group of anarchists added to Carpenter's distress and a letter to Oates on 23 February 1890 conveys a familiar feeling of restlessness:

> This long sullen English winter is very trying and I feel a longing every now and then to get away to some place where the sun shines. ... I sometimes think I shall go off to India or some distant region before long – not for good! – but to renovate my faith, and unfold the frozen buds which civilisation and fog have nipped![52]

Carpenter had met George Merrill, who was to be his lifelong companion, in the winter of 1889–90, but their acquaintance was not yet strong enough to keep him in England.[53] So Carpenter had every reason to leave England, and go to another land to invigorate himself, and forge fresh affiliations.

III

Carpenter sailed for Ceylon in October 1890, ostensibly at the invitation of his friend Arunachalam, to meet a Hindu *gnani* (a wise man) and learn about Hindu philosophy. *From Adam's Peak to Elephanta* is the product of that journey. Written as a travelogue, Carpenter's entire narrative is steeped in homoerotic desire. The nature of Carpenter's passage to India is evident from the outset of the journey, in the letters Carpenter was writing home, more obviously than from his account in *From Adam's Peak to Elephanta*. In writing to Charles Oates, for example, Carpenter sees his journey to the Orient as replicating earlier trips to the Continent with his friend, trips on which both he and Oates, away from the constraints of England, had had intimate relationships with Italian youths.[54] On the eve of his departure for Ceylon, he writes to Oates saying, "I shall pass along the route which I travelled 4 years ago when I came to see you at Acqui."[55] In keeping with the Italian journeys, Carpenter developed a friendship with a native he met on ship on the way out to India. In a letter to James Brown, written from the Red Sea, Carpenter talks of "Kaludaseya my little Cinghalese friend" who "came and sat with me last night in the bows of the ship. Such a soft warm air blowing over the sea, moon high up in the sky, every now and then an island quite bare and rocky on the right or left."[56] In a letter to Oates he says:

> There is much that reminds me of Italy in the temperament of the people and climate, but the dark skins and the immeasurable palm trees of all kinds prevent any mistake! On boardship on my way out I got quite friendly with a Cinghalese fellow who was on board – a goodlooking chap of the peasant class – and a day or two ago I went and paid him a visit in his little cabin near Kandy. It reminded me so of our visit to Guido's home near Acqui. Kalua,

my friend – like Guido – had a brother, and we spent a delightful afternoon among the cocoanut groves and rice fields.[57]

Kalua accompanied Carpenter to India and they climbed Adam's Peak together. *From Adam's Peak to Elephanta* contains a vivid recollection of him:

> Kalua is remarkably well-made, and active and powerful. He is about twenty-eight, with the soft giraffe-like eyes of the Cinghalese, and the gentle somewhat diffident manner which they affect; his black hair is generally coiled in a knot behind his head, and, with an ornamental belt sustaining his coloured skirt, and a shawl thrown over his shoulder, he looks quite handsome. (*AP*, p.31)

Elsewhere in the text, Carpenter reveals his reasons for liking Kalua. "His savage strength and *insouciance* are splendid. All over Adam's Peak he walked barefoot, with no more sign of fatigue than if it had been a walk round a garden" (*AP*, pp.77–8).

Repeatedly in the Ceylon section of *From Adam's Peak to Elephanta*, the narrator dwells on the physique and nakedness of the natives. *From Adam's Peak to Elephanta* is rich in descriptions of men, and from early in the text, the author notices in detail the features and appearance of the men around him. Carpenter calls attention to a Cinghalese peasant, "with hairy chest, and nothing on but a red loin-cloth" (*AP*, p.14). A Tamil coolie is shown as "nearly naked except for a handkerchief tied round his head, with glossy black skin and slight yet graceful figure" (*AP*, p.16). Carpenter had come all the way to Ceylon in order to gain divine knowledge from a *gnani* recommended by Arunachalam, but on being introduced to the learned man, Carpenter is more impressed by the learned man's physical qualities than the philosophy he espouses. The *gnani* is lovable and charismatic:

> an elderly man (some seventy years of age, though he did not look nearly as much as that) dressed only in a white muslin wrapper wound loosely round his lithe and even active dark brown form: his head and face shaven a day or two past, very gentle and spiritual in expression, like the best type of Roman Catholic priests – a very beautiful full and finely-formed mouth, straight nose and well-formed chin, dark eyes, undoubtedly the eyes of a seer, dark-rimmed eyelids, and a powerful, prophetic, and withal childlike manner. (*AP*, p.138)

Again, a *yogi* in Benares is approvingly described as "a rather fine-looking man" with "nothing whatever on but some beads round his neck and the merest apology for a loin-cloth." And "there was that look of *insouciance* in his face which one detects in the faces of the animals" (*AP*, pp.261–2). Clearly, not only are the Cinghalese and Indians free of the layers of clothing with which the English are encumbered, they

are also at ease with their bodies, graceful and natural. Free of physical
restrictions, they are portrayed as free of emotional constraints too,
and potentially available for sexual liaisons.

The people and scenes in Ceylon and India evoke memories of Italy
and ancient Greece, with all that that implies for the homosexual
writer. The rice fields in Ceylon recall "the vineyards in Italy" (*AP*,
p. 32), and the houses in Benares present a "picturesque confusion not
unlike the old Italian towns" (*AP*, p. 258). The Cinghalese are, "like
the Italians, easy-going, reasonably idle, sensitive, shrewd, and just a
bit romantic" (*AP*, pp. 19–20). At Delhi, Carpenter finds "about the
Hindus themselves more fling and romance and concreteness; some
handsome faces, verging a little towards the Greek or Italian types – but
looking fine with their dark skins" (*AP*, p. 283). During the festival in a
Hindu temple, the writer catches sight of "a boy blowing two pipes at
the same time, exactly as in the Greek bas reliefs" (*AP*, p. 120). In south
India, he visits a workshop where goldsmiths are making "armlets and
breastplates for the gods, etc. – another touch remindful of the Greeks"
(*AP*, p. 225). As had been characteristic of nineteenth-century English
writers, in Carpenter's writing too, classical images are enlarged to
include Orientalism. The Tamil workers in Ceylon, "with nothing on
beyond a narrow band between the thighs" are "a study of the human
figure. Some of them of course are thick and muscular, but mostly they
excel in a kind of unconscious grace and fleetness of form as of the
bronze Mercury of Herculaneum" (*AP*, p. 17). Carpenter's description
of Tamil men is tinged with remembrance of Greek heroes, and
wrestlers and athletes in a Greek gymnasium. This combination of
classical and Oriental forms occurs again when Carpenter speaks of an
acquaintance in Calcutta:

> Panna Lall is quite an athlete, and interested in anything in that
> line. He took me one day to a little bit of ground where he and
> some friends have their horizontal bars, etc.; they did some
> good tumbling and tight-rope walking, and with their golden-
> brown skins and muscular bodies looked well when stripped. The
> Bengali Babu is often of a lightish-brown colour. The people
> generally wear more clothing than in South India, and at this time
> of year throw a brown woollen shawl over their shoulders, *toga*
> fashion. (*AP*, p. 244)

Carpenter endeavours to formulate an Oriental ideal of male beauty
equivalent to the one found in classical art and literature. The faces of
the men in the streets of Agra are more captivating to behold than the
Taj Mahal itself:

> Very handsome, many of them, with their large eyes and well-
> formed noses. ... but like mermaids they end badly, for when you
> look below you see two thinnest shins with little tight cotton
> leggings round them, and bare feet. ... I have come to the

conclusion about the Hindus generally that their legs are too thin
for them ever to do much in the world. (*AP*, p.296)

The Hindu physique is disappointing for it lacks the muscularity and
symmetry embodied by classical figures, and – in the modern context –
English working-class men.

One of the theories in the nineteenth century for rationalising a
man's leaning towards his own sex saw this as manifesting a feminine
nature in the man. Karl Heinrich Ulrichs, who pioneered congenital
theories in the 1860s, was the leading exponent of this hypothesis. He
argued that the homosexual was neither a criminal nor insane, but a
product of the anomalous development of the human embryo. In the
homosexual, though the genitals developed male characteristics, the
corresponding differentiation failed to take place in the mind, resulting
in "a female mind in a male body."[58] Carpenter uses the biological
explanation of homosexuality in *The Intermediate Sex* and *Love's
Coming-of-Age*, and, in an account of his own homosexuality, he refers
to his disposition in terms of "womanly" traits: "My own sexual nature
was a mystery to me. I found myself with a highly loving and clinging
temperament."[59] Carpenter applies the same phrases for Oriental
men as he does to describe his own homosexuality, and the similarity
of language gives a clue to his covert interest in the Orient. He
emphasises the "femininity" of Cinghalese and Indian men in order
to envisage qualities quite different from English middle-class notions
of masculinity. Carpenter tries to explode the culturally-defined idea of
sex-roles; however, he cannot wholly transcend gender divisions,
and only instals one gender category in place of another. Thus that
which is perceived as sensitive, affectionate, dependent, is immediately
labelled as "feminine." Sheila Rowbotham has pointed to this weakness
in Carpenter's thinking, his inability to overcome gender categories, a
weakness that persists into his later writing on sexual issues.[60]

Whereas Carpenter sees Oriental men as outwardly masculine, in
mental attributes they are indiscriminately described as effeminate
types. The lower class of Cinghalese are "morbidly sensitive" (*AP*,
p.20). Kalua's brother Kirrah has "a clinging affectionateness of
character which is touching" (*AP*, p.31). The docility of the natives
makes them ideally fitted for caring roles. Carpenter says,

> I believe many of these Indian and Cinghalese races love to
> be servants (under a tolerably good master); their feminine
> and sensitive natures, often lacking in enterprise, rather seek
> the shelter of dependence. And certainly they make, in many
> instances and when well treated, wonderfully good servants, their
> tact and affectionateness riveting the bond. (*AP*, p.57)

The narrative abounds in examples of the loyalty of natives to their
white *sahibs* (*AP*, pp.57–8, 79). He agrees with his friend "Ajax" that
the coolies "are so much like children; ... most willing workers

they are. ... and if you are ill, they tend to you just like a woman – never leave one in fact" (*AP*, pp. 84–5). The political soundness of Carpenter's generalisations about the servile character of the natives is questionable, but it has a bearing on the homoerotic desire that permeates the text.

Yet, while submissiveness and pliancy are extolled as virtues in individuals, Carpenter finds them objectionable as racial qualities. The passivity of Cinghalese and Indians outside the boundaries of relationships is denounced as a fault: "The oyster, in keeping with his weaker, more dependent nature, is cunning and lazy – his vices lie in that direction rather than in the Western direction of brutal energy" (*AP*, p. 58). ("Oyster" is a term Carpenter had coined for the natives. He records that Arunachalam had "chaffed me about my way of calling him and the rest of the population, whether Tamil or Mohammedan or Cinghalese, all indiscriminately *natives*, 'as if we were so many *oysters*.' I told this to Ajax, and of course there was nothing for it after that but to call them all oysters!" (*AP*, p. 37).) Carpenter abhors the apathy of Indian people and their reluctance to change:

> Custom undisturbed consolidates itself; society crystallises into caste. The problem of external life once solved presents no more interest, and mechanical invention slumbers; the mind retires inward to meditate and to conquer. Hence two developments – in the best types that of the transcendental faculties, but in the worst a mere outer sluggishness and lethargy. (*AP*, p. 255)

This is a rather sweeping criticism of the religious values that India is supposed to stand for, and which presumably Carpenter had come to learn. Meekness and resignation are, for Carpenter, shortcomings as social or racial qualities, but assets in personality because they denote a capacity for friendship. Here, as elsewhere, the latent desire for homoerotic love sets up conflicts with the political and philosophical surface of the text.

The narrative of *From Adam's Peak to Elephanta* proceeds on a series of contrasts between the natives and the British. Again, the oppositions are not so much political in the narrow sense as between modes of behaviour and capacity for emotional experience. The naturalness of the Cinghalese and the Tamil people offsets the stuffiness of Englishmen, "in tweed suits and tennis shoes ... rather weedy looking, with an unsteady, swimmy look about the eyes" (*AP*, p. 15). The reserve of the British is antithetical to the openness and trusting nature of the natives: "There is something queer about the British and their insularity; but I suppose it is more their misfortune than their fault" (*AP*, p. 37). The instinct of the British to distance themselves, of course, excludes them from the friendship and community of local people. In contrast to the unhampered ways of the natives, the life of the British is organised and passionless. In Kurunegala, the British quarter "is only distinguishable by its court-house and prison and one or two other emblems of civilisation" (*AP*, p.41). Carpenter wrote to Kate Salt from Agra, on 22 February 1891, complaining at length of the monotonously regular plan of the British stations:

> These Anglo Indian towns of the N.W. Provinces are most provoking. You arrive by train, give the name of a hotel, and are driven off to it. When you wake up next morning you find yourself in a trim laid out region of shady roads at right angles to each other, with villa residences, churches, clubs and hotels extending for miles. Except that the houses are only one storey high and that it is warm for February you might just as well be at Wandsworth or Clapham! The native city is 4 miles away!![61]

Carpenter deplores the rigid behaviour of his compatriots because it prevents them from participating in native life:

> In a place like India, where the mass of the people go with very little covering, the spectacle of their ease and enjoyment must double the discomforts of the unfortunate European who thinks it necessary to be dressed up to the eyes on every occasion when he appears in public. (*AP*, p. 62)

He criticises the British values of "suppression of the emotional life," which result in "materialism, capitalistic expansion and imperialism."[62] Speaking of the natives who pull two-wheeled gigs to transport people, Carpenter says, "These Tamil fellows, in the lightest of costumes, their backs streaming under the vertical sun, bare-legged and often bare-headed, will trot with you in a miraculous way from one end of Columbo to the other, and for the smallest fee. Tommy Atkins delights to sit thus lordly behind the toiling 'nigger'" (*AP*, p.16). Building on the oppositions articulated in *England's Ideal* and *Civilisation: its Cause and Cure*, Carpenter posits the simplicity of the East as an alternative to the "civilisation" attained by the West.[63] The local inhabitants of Ceylon are "primitive as savages in their dress, cabins, etc." (*AP*, p.26), and a fisherman sitting on a raft appears to be "a relic of pre-Adamite times" (*AP*, p.25). In nineteenth-century homosexual writing, pre-Christian pastoralism was cherished as a period in which male comradeship was possible. Carpenter's text follows in the tradition of Symonds and Pater where paganism is closely associated with homoerotic desire. Reade notes that, "For John Addington Symonds the word Arcadian meant homosexual, and little more."[64] Carpenter transposes Ceylon and India back to a version of pagan pastoralism, to indicate a culture where sexual mores do not include the Christian taboos against homosexuality. The narrator, in *From Adam's Peak to Elephanta*, sees the landscape of Ceylon and India as a rural idyll.

During his journey across Ceylon and India, Carpenter distances himself from the English society. He makes a pilgrimage to the temple of Chidambaram in South India and notes with pleasure that "though the town itself numbers some 20,000 to 30,000 inhabitants, there is not a single Englishman resident in the place or within some miles of it" (*AP*, p. 221). Moreover, it is to working-class and lower-caste people that, predictably, Carpenter is drawn. He finds "the horse-keepers and stable boys in Ceylon," who "are almost all Tamils (of a low caste)" endearing. He claims that they "are a charming race, dusky active affectionate demons, fond of their horses, and with unlimited capacity for running" (*AP*, p. 18). In another part of the text, he admits, "I like the coolies very much, and one gets quite attached to some of them; they seem instinctively polite" (*AP*, p. 85). Carpenter socialised with "the native 'proletariat' – post-office and railway clerks" in Bombay (*AP*, p. 318). It was unusual for an Englishman to get this perspective on India and its people. Indeed, Carpenter sees the working-class people in India as approximate to their counterparts in Britain. Carpenter says:

> It is curious, but I am constantly being struck by the resemblance between the lowest castes here and the slum-dwellers in our great cities – resemblance in physiognomy, as well as in many unconscious traits of character, often very noble; with the brutish basis well-marked, the unformed mouth, and the somewhat heavy brows, just as in Meunier's fine statue of the ironworker ("puddleur"), but with thicker lips. (*AP*, p. 59)[65]

At one point, Carpenter addresses directly – and movingly – the boys and girls toiling away in the factories back in Sheffield, "Dear children! if you could only come out here yourselves, instead of sending the abominable work of your hands – come out here to enjoy the sunshine, and fraternise, as I know many of you would, with the despised darkie!" (*AP*, p. 49). The word "fraternise" is the key to the passage; the vision is that vision of comradeship and brotherhood that we have in Whitman's *Leaves of Grass* and Carpenter's *Towards Democracy*.

Meanwhile, Carpenter's response to higher caste Cinghalese and Indians is ambivalent. In Ceylon, the *Chetties*, or men from the "Tamil commercial caste," are seen to have "avarice in their faces" (*AP*, pp. 15–16). Later, in India, the author recoils from the money-grubbing Brahmins, who even look predatory, with "sharp eyes, rather close together, and a thin aquiline nose" (*AP*, p. 222). He is revolted by the greed and commercialism that he witnesses in the cities, and censures men in Calcutta, whose "faces are low in type, lazy, cunning, bent on mere lucre. The Bengali is however by nature a versatile flexile creature, sadly wanting in backbone, and probably has succumbed easily to the new disorganising forces" (*AP*, p. 235). In glorifying the Cinghalese and Indian working classes, Carpenter is endorsing Whitman's doctrine of male love for working-class men. Moreover, like Whitman, he argues that the development of civilisation and commercialism is destructive of the natural life and emotional freedom that is the essence of homoerotic love. The onset of modern civilisation brought an ascendency of capitalist, heterosexual society over the classical past which was more permissive of emotional bonds between men. Hence Carpenter backs away from the Cinghalese and Indians of the commercial caste because they share the values of the British colonialists, and as such, are adversaries of male love and friendship.

The evils of civilisation and industrialisation, expressed in *From Adam's Peak to Elephanta*, are reiterated in Carpenter's short story, "Narayan." The tale delineates the encroachment of urban values on rural life and personal relations tragically destroyed by the effects of the commercial world, and this is articulated in a narrative which centres on the love of two boys for one another.[66] Carpenter had heard a story of passionate attachment between two Indian boys who killed themselves on being parted from one another.[67] The protagonists of Carpenter's story are Ganesh and Narayan; the two friends complement each other in character and personality. Narayan is older and stronger, "a well-made youth of about twenty, bright-eyed, with something in his face of the squareness and decision of the Mahratta type." Ganesh is timid and thoughtful in character, "rather younger, darker in complexion and of a milder, more meditative expression" (p.49). In their conversations, each can persuade the other to see the opposite point of view. Narayan and Ganesh together make a striking pair, "The beauty of youth was in their faces and dark eyes" (p.55). The two friends live in a small village at the foot of the hills, cut off from civilisation. The "smoke from the manufacturing quarter of the city" is menacing for it threatens to disrupt their peaceful existence. "The sight of it caused Ganesh to shudder. It was not the first time, of course, that he had seen it; but to-day it looked more detestable than ever – like some devil-stain on the shining garment of a god" (pp.52–3).

Unlike Ganesh, Narayan is excited by the happenings in the big city and the progress it symbolises. He is eager to cast aside their traditional ways and seek his fortune in the city. Ganesh tries to warn his friend as to the dangers of urban life, but Narayan is determined to leave the village. Ganesh, for the sake of his friend, goes along with him. Outside the village, the two boys meet a holy man who advises them to go back to their village, but Narayan is determined to see the city. On reaching Bombay, Ganesh and Narayan are swallowed up by the mechanisation and impersonality of the industrial world. The village boys are dazed by the mindless motions of a factory: "There were the spinning-jennies with their hundreds, thousands, of spindles whirling in endless dance like myriads of living creatures … and then up and down through the midst of this chaos (most amazing!) went crowds of their own country-men and women" (pp.70–1). The capitalist society ultimately extracts the price of the boys' friendship as one day Ganesh's body gets caught in the machines of the mill, and he dies, dripping with blood, in his friend's arms. Devastated by the accident, Narayan turns his back on the city and returns to live with the hermit. The hermit stands not for renunciation, but for greater wisdom. Narayan – and it is his name that is the story's title – goes beyond civilisation to a "higher" consciousness.

Thus, social issues in Carpenter's story are closely allied to the theme of male friendship. Tariq Rahman notes that in "Narayan," "Carpenter has killed two birds with one stone. On the one hand he has affirmed the primacy of personal devotion and on the other hand he has made a significant indictment of imperialism and capitalism."[69] Likewise, the social and political discourse in *From Adam's Peak to Elephanta* attaches to homoerotic desire in the text. Carpenter conceives of Ceylon and India essentially as rural and almost timeless places, rather than historical and political entities, and socio-political matters enter into the text insofar as they impinge on the subject of male friendship. Carpenter admits to an idealised image of the East: "Ceylon is idyllic, romantic – the plentiful foliage and shade everywhere, the easy-going nature of the Cinghalese themselves, the absence of caste – even the English are softened towards such willing subjects" (*AP*, p.228). The pastoral landscape and leisurely pace of Ceylon hark back to the classical era which was perceived by homosexual writers in the late nineteenth century as being the golden age of homoerotic relations, but the factor of colonialism prevents intimacy between the British and native men. Carpenter has to reckon with the political situation because Ceylon is lacking in friendship between the two races: "A perfect social amalgamation and the sweetness of brethren dwelling together in unity are things still rather far distant in this otherwise lovely isle" (*AP*, p.22). Carpenter's vision is socialist and anti-imperialist, but the subtext is that of personal relationships, and primarily homoerotic ones.

On a political level, Carpenter believes that contact with the West, its civilisation and commercialism, will prove liberating for India, "in the way of rousing up the people, giving *definition*, so much needed, to their minds and work, and instilling among them the Western idea of progress, which in some ways fallacious has still its value and use" (*AP*, p.362). At the same time, he regrets the British invasion of Ceylon and India because Western civilisation is encroaching on the older rhythms of Indian life, and gradually eroding the comradeship, naturalness, and harmony the narrator associates with native life. Hence the author attacks the social evils resulting from commercialism – the poverty and greed, the clamour for tips and swindling of tourists – in India (*AP*, pp.228–9). The writer is as derisive of the Western aspirations of Indians as of their own caste divisions and hierarchy. A native policeman presents a ludicrous sight: "A real live oyster in boots! It is too absurd. How miserable he looks; and as to running after a criminal – the thing is not to be thought of" (*AP*, p.50). Carpenter laments the Western progress rife in India which he sees as being the reverse of the socialist movement in Britain (*AP*, p.327 and ch. 9). The British influence on Ceylon and India is pernicious, it seems, chiefly because it threatens to spoil "their naked beauty and simplicity" (*AP*, p.31).

The only interaction that Carpenter is willing to concede between the British and the natives in Ceylon and India is personal. Otherwise the two cultures are totally incompatible. On a socio-economic and political scale, the author dogmatically asserts that the British and the Indians "do not and they cannot understand each other," and the "materialistic and commercial spirit of Western rule can never blend with the profoundly religious character of the social organisation normal to India" (*AP*, p.270). Carpenter dislikes Western influence for it is likely to destroy relationships between men as they exist in the East. Hence the narrator complains that the British officers "will often speak quite warmly of the tenderness and affectionateness [sic] of servants who have nursed them through long illnesses, etc. – but the idea of associating with them on terms of equality and friendship is somehow unspeakable and not to be entertained" (*AP*, pp.37–8). Ultimately, of course, in the context of colonialism, of imperial control of one race by another, the notion of friendships between Briton and Indian is irrelevant and contradicts Carpenter's earlier statements on the incompatibility between the two races; the affinity between men that the author craves is personal and emotional, and occurs regardless of the social and political circumstances.

Carpenter's discussion of Hindu doctrine is selective and, again, is related to the sexual impulses which underlie Carpenter's approach to India. Hinduism is commendable in that it does not comprehend human sexuality as problematic. "On sexual matters generally, as far as I can make out, the tendency, even among the higher castes, is to be outspoken, and there is little of that prudery which among us is only after all a modern growth" (*AP*, p.47). The Hindu attitude to sex is symbolised for Carpenter by the statue of Siva as half-man and half-woman that he sees in the caves of Elephanta. This sculpture of Siva is mentioned again in his essay, "On the Connection between Homosexuality and Divination and the Importance of the Intermediate Sexes Generally in Early Civilisations."[69] The half-man, half-woman, form of Siva recalls the homosexual myth of androgyny in Plato's *Symposium*, and perhaps, too, the nature of the homosexual as a woman's soul in a man's body in Ulrichs. The statue of Siva also depicts the co-existence of male and female in one body and there is, perhaps, some irony in the fact that, while Carpenter can grasp the abstract notion of androgyny, he finds the visual representation of it aesthetically distasteful. He says that the "idea, of the original junction of the sexes, though it may be philosophically tenable, ... is inartistic enough when graphically portrayed; and the main figure of this panel, with its left side projecting into a huge breast and hip, is only a monstrosity" (*AP*, p.315). The enviable components of Hinduism are not spiritual at all. Carpenter describes a Hindu festival in sexual and erotic terms. There "were hundreds of men and boys, barebodied, bare-headed and barefoot, but with white loincloths – all in a state of great excitement – not religious so much as spectacular." He watches "two little naked boys holding small torches"

(*AP*, pp.119–20). The spirit of the ceremony "was thoroughly whole-hearted" (*AP*, p.121). The devotees were "elated and excited," while the "smell of hot coco-nut oil mingling with that of humanity made the air sultry." Altogether, the procession moved forward in a "rampant way" (*AP*, p.128). Carpenter concludes from the event that "the worship of sex is found to lie at the root of the present Hinduism, as it does at the root of nearly all the primitive religions of the world" (*AP*, p.125). Even astrology in India is "a glimmering embodiment of the deep-lying truth that the whole universe conspires in the sexual act, and that the orgasm itself is a flash of the universal consciousness" (*AP*, pp.193–4).

Chapter 10 in *From Adam's Peak to Elephanta* is a long discussion of Indian philosophy. Carpenter speaks of the yogis who train themselves to suppress thought and desire. He approves of their aim of controlling thought, whereby a person loses his ego and gains a finer consciousness that transfers him to another plane. Carpenter's endorsement of the idea of the elimination of thought expresses an anti-rational stance in opposition to the Western obsession with intellectual achievement. The writer reveals the fallibility of a civilisation that hinges entirely on mental effort:

> Nothing indeed strikes one more as marking the immense con-trast between the East and the West than, after leaving Western lands where the ideal of life is to have an almost insanely active brain and to be perpetually on the war-path with fearful and wonderful projects and plans and purposes, to come to India and to find its leading men – men of culture and learning and accomplishment – deliberately passing beyond all these and addressing themselves to the task of effacing their own thoughts, effacing all their own projects and purposes, in order that the diviner consciousness may enter in and occupy the room so prepared. (*AP*, pp.166–7)

Power over thought, exercised in the East, is connected with the subjection of desire. While restraint of desire ensures freedom from fears, doubts and anxiety, Carpenter believes that this principle of Indian religion requires qualification. He assures the reader that "There is no necessity to suppose that desire, in itself, is an evil; indeed it is quite conceivable that it may fall into place as a useful and important element of human nature" (*AP*, p.175). Desire needs to be mastered because it is liable to grow out of proportion and imprison us. Nonetheless, the claims of triumph over desire are treated as exaggerations:

> No doubt certain sections of the Indian and other ascetic philo-sophies have taught the absolute extinction of desire, but we may fairly regard these as cases – so common in the history of all traditional teaching – of undue prominence given to a special

detail, and of the exaltation of the letter of doctrine above the spirit. (*AP*, pp. 175–6)

The purpose of release from thought and desire is to be at one with the universe, which entails a return to the communal order of society and non-differentiation from Nature. One consequence of this liberation is the dissolution of identity and relationships. Though Carpenter sees the virtue of harmony between an individual and his surroundings, he cannot accept the denial of personal relations that such an equilibrium implies.

Carpenter finds the detachment of the gnani, who has reached the goal that the followers of Hinduism must strive after, extreme. His judgement on the discipline practised by the gnani is uncomplimentary:

> I was in fact struck, and perhaps a little shocked, by the want of interest in things and persons around him displayed by the great man – not that, as I have said, he was not very helpful and considerate in special cases – but evidently that part of his nature which held him to the actual world was thinning out. (*AP*, p. 151)

While Hinduism deifies phallic symbols and has an element of sexual ecstasy, it also enjoins individuals to transcend the world. Carpenter cannot accept the self-abnegation recommended in the Indian religion. Similarly, he cannot respond to the austerity of Buddhism, and Buddha's statues "with their sickly smile of Nirvana" leave him cold (*AP*, p. 94). Indeed, Indian religion lays stress on the absorption of the individual into the divine and ultimately excludes personal relations. For Carpenter, Indian teaching and life are inadequate because of "the absence – or less prominence at any rate – of that positive spirit of love and human helpfulness which in some sections of Western society might almost be called a devouring passion" (*AP*, p. 179). Whereas Carpenter concurs with the sexual liberalism of Hinduism, he rejects the negation of self that it prescribes. There is a real ambivalence in Carpenter's attitude to the gnani and Indian philosophy; he is attracted to the tranquillity, and the casting off of material trappings, but the consecutive renunciation of love and individual fulfilment does not appeal to him.

The discourse on Indian philosophy, therefore, finally ends by giving credit to the Western standpoint: "There is one respect in which the specially Eastern teaching commonly appears to us as Westerners – and on the whole I am inclined to think justly – defective; and that is in its little insistence on the idea of Love" (*AP*, pp. 178–9). The whole account of Indian religion has been aimed at the Western society. The narrator concludes that "in the East the Will constitutes the great path; but in the West the path has been more specially through Love" (*AP*, p. 181). Whereas the contact between East and West is disastrous for the East, it can prove fruitful for the West. Carpenter highlights those premises of Indian religion that allow for ecstasy and union between all men, and simultaneously tries to moderate the emphasis on self-effacement. The faculties explored by the East will help the West to develop its potential for love, and "when the Western races once realise what lies beneath this great instinct of humanity, which seems in some ways to be their special inspiration, they will outstrip even the Hindus in their entrance to and occupation of the new fields of consciousness" (*AP*, p.182). Thus the axioms of Indian philosophy are elaborated to enrich the Western sensibility. While many homosexual writers in nineteenth-century English literature counterposed the Orient against the Occident, and paganism and classicism against Christianity, Carpenter ultimately tries to bridge the gap between the two. He attempts to reconcile the individualism of the West with the emotional and sexual energies of the East. Indeed, in later writings like "Sun-worship," Carpenter shows the similarities between pagan sun gods – Osiris, Adonis and Hercules – who are also prototypes of male heroes in homosexual literature, and Christ. Comparisons between pagan rituals and Christianity are again postulated in *Pagan and Christian Creeds.*[70]

The narrative in *From Adam's Peak to Elephanta* constantly refers back to Western society and the image of the Orient serves to mediate the restrictiveness of British society. The habits and practices of the natives hold lessons for people in Britain, and give the author grounds to argue for sexual emancipation. Hence, the scantily-dressed Cinghalese and Indian men become a cause for proposing nudism. Carpenter maintains that the exposure of their bodies to all kinds of weather makes the natives hardy. He then informs his readers at home that he has "taken several sun-baths in the woods ... and found advantage from doing so." Carpenter also certifies that he has "discovered the existence of a little society in India – of English folk – who encourage nudity, and the abandonment as far as possible of clothes" (*AP*, p.61). The best feature of the Orient is the unfettered life of its men, symbolised by their "well-developed broad feet" which are "a mark of distinction and civilisation." As always, Carpenter speaks of the Orient in hyperbole:

> I am never tired of admiring the foot in its native state. It is so broad and free and full and muscular, with a good concave on the inner line ... I sometimes think we can never attain to a broad free and full life on our present day understandings in the West. (*AP*, p.244)

The passage is typical of Carpenter's style in that it depicts the natural freedom and physicality of Oriental values as an alternative to the West, albeit the inferences he draws from the well-developed feet of the natives are unsubstantiated.

Carpenter does not question the presence of the British in India, though he does mention the "National Indian Congress" in the last

chapter of the book. When he is not being moved by the beauty of the
dark races, Carpenter is awed by the immensity of the British empire:

> Certainly the spectacle of our domination of this vast region
> is a very remarkable one – something romantic, and almost
> incredible – the conquest and subjection of so many tribes and of
> such diverse elements ... impressing one no doubt with a sense of
> the power of the little mother-country ten thousand miles away,
> which throws its prestige around one – but impressing one also
> with a sinister sense of the gulf between man and man which that
> prestige has created. (*AP*, pp. 272, 274)

While he does turn attention to the degradation and exploitation of the
colonised people, he is concerned with imperialism because it inter-
feres with friendship between men. Carpenter's attitude to the British
empire is surprisingly fair-minded. He praises the British officials
for their sincerity and dedication to the hopeless task of maintaining an administration, keeping order and wielding justice amongst
impervious natives. A number of English officers are "remarkably
good-hearted painstaking men; but one feels the gulf between them
and the people – a gulf that can never be bridged" (*AP*, pp. 89–90).
Moreover, the native population is none the wiser for all the efforts to
introduce law and order. A British official "never comes near touching
the hearts of the millions, who would probably pay much more respect
to a half-luny *yogi* than to him and all his percentages" (*AP*, p. 90). The
aloofness of the British alienates their subjects: "It struck me indeed
how much a few unpretending Englishmen might do to endear our
country to this people" (*AP*, p. 322). Carpenter does not avert his eyes
from the craftiness of the natives who prey on British tourists: "Good
old John Bull pays through the nose for being the ruler of this country.
He overwhelms the people by force, but they turn upon him – as the
weaker is prone to do – through craft; and truly have their revenge"
(*AP*, p. 229).

Ultimately Carpenter himself is guilty of sexual colonialism in his
treatment of Ceylon and India. The romantic component of his narrative is evident from the moment he is on the ship to Colombo in his
friendship with Kalua. During the course of his journey, Carpenter
uses the language of the dominant culture to describe the Orient,
and applies diminutives, such as "oyster," "darkie," "children," for
Cinghalese and Indian men. Though these terms might have been used
fondly, or to parody other writers, they are nevertheless reductive and
belittling. The Orient is diminished in order to manage the theme of
homoerotic love. Indeed, in spite of the author's claim in the "Preface"
of *From Adam's Peak to Elephanta* that he has had rare access to
ordinary people in Ceylon and India, his perceptions remain con-
spicuously those of a Westerner. Some of his observations are clichés in
Oriental literature – that Oriental men are "lazy" and "cunning" (*AP*,
p. 235); that Indian religion is ridden with superstition and ignorance

(*AP*, pp.65–6); and that "teaching in the East is entirely authoritative and traditional" (*AP*, p.139). The writer finally admits that "It is certainly a very difficult thing to see the real India, the real life of the people" (*AP*, p.268). It is no wonder, then, that the gnani's son, Somasundaram, wrote to Carpenter in 1894, protesting against Carpenter's interpretation of Indian religion and philosophy in chapters 8, 9 and 10 of the book. He points particularly to Carpenter's statement on p.187, that followers of the Siddhantic doctrine "are hopelessly dull, and may be said to carry their own death-warrants on their faces."[71] Arunachalam's letters in *Light from the East* show that Carpenter's knowledge of Indian religion was biased and his enquiries were limited mainly to the Hindu stance on love. The chapters that Carpenter appended to Arunachalam's letters – "The Lingam and Sensual Desire," "The Endeavour to Control Desire," "Birth Control and Bisexuality," "The Mouna Swamis and the Animals" – further illustrate that Carpenter's interest in Indian philosophy related specifically to sexual matters.

IV

From Adam's Peak to Elephanta clearly belongs to a tradition of nineteenth-century English homosexual literature in which the Orient represented a liberating Other, a region free of the constraints of Western sexual taboos. Carpenter's journey, like those of others before and after him, sprang from his disaffection with England, and a search for alternative affiliations. His comments on the political and economic situation in India, it can be argued, stem – as does his attack on "Civilisation" in his earlier essays – from the way that English freedom, personal, emotional, and sexual, is repressed. The political critique in Carpenter has a powerful personal and erotic subtext, and that critique is aimed primarily at English "Civilisation," making a case for a more natural and sexually-liberated way of life.

PARMINDER KAUR BAKSHI

NOTES

1. Edward Carpenter, *From Adam's Peak to Elephanta: Sketches in Ceylon and India* (London: Swan Sonnenschein, 1892). All references are to this edition and page numbers are given in brackets in the text.
2. *The World, the Text, and the Critic* (London: Faber, 1984) and *Orientalism*, 2nd ed. (1985; rpt. Harmondsworth: Penguin Books, 1987).
3. Said, *The World, the Text, and the Critic*, p.8.
4. Said, *The World, the Text, and the Critic*, p.20.
5. See Timothy d'Arch Smith, *Love in Earnest: Some Notes on the Lives and Writings of English 'Uranian' Poets from 1889 to 1930* (London: Routledge & Kegan Paul, 1970).
6. The development of classicism in the nineteenth century has been traced by Richard

Jenkyns, *The Victorians and Ancient Greece* (Oxford: Basil Blackwell, 1980) and Frank M. Turner, *The Greek Heritage in Victorian Britain* (New Haven: Yale U.P., 1981).

7. d'Arch Smith, pp.84 and 53.
8. *Ioläus: An Anthology of Friendship*, ed. Edward Carpenter, 3rd ed. (1902; rpt. London: Allen & Unwin Ltd., 1929), and Edward Carpenter, *Towards Democracy* (London: Swan Sonnenschein, 1911).
9. Jenkyns, p.316.
10. Ruskin, *The Stones of Venice*, II, ch. 6, and 7f., and Byron, *The Giaour*, 11.15 and 28, cited from Jenkyns, p.50.
11. Turner, pp.105–6.
12. Said, *Orientalism*, p.2.
13. Said, *Orientalism*, p.6.
14. Said, *Orientalism*, p.4.
15. Said, *Orientalism*, p.190.
16. Eric J. Sharpe, *The Universal Gita: Western Images of the Bhagavadgita, A Bicentenary Survey* (London: Duckworth, 1985).
17. Sharpe, p.151.
18. Robert Graves, "The Fitz-Omar Cult," *The Rubaiyyat of Omar Khayyam, A new translation with critical commentaries by Robert Graves and Omar Ali-Shah* (London: Cassell, 1967).
19. Graves, p.22.
20. Graves, p.7.
21. A.J. Arberry, *Classical Persian Literature* (London: Allen & Unwin, 1958), p.333.
22. d'Arch Smith, p.186.
23. *Towards Democracy*, pp.416–17.
24. *Iolaus*, pp.113 and 190.
25. Sheffield City Libraries, MSS 349, Carp. Coll.
26. MS. 340.2, Carpenter Collection. Part of this letter is also cited by Edward Carpenter in *My Days and Dreams: Being Autobiographical Notes*, 3rd ed. (London: Allen & Unwin, 1918), p.40.
27. MS. 351.10, Carp. Coll.
28. D.K. Barua, "The Life and Work of Edward Carpenter," Diss. University of Sheffield 1966, p.183.
29. *My Days and Dreams*, pp.250–2.
30. *Light from the East: Being Letters on Gnanam, the Divine Knowledge by P. Arunachalam*, ed. Edward Carpenter (London: Allen & Unwin, 1927), p.68.
31. *Light from the East*, pp.32–3.
32. Edward Carpenter, *Days with Walt Whitman: With Some Notes on His Life and Work* (London: George Allen, 1906), pp.22–3, and *My Days and Dreams*, p.87.
33. Barua, p.192. For Cox's letters to Carpenter from India, see MSS 250, Carp. Coll.
34. *My Days and Dreams*, p.124.
35. Barua, p.194. Carpenter speaks of Harold Cox and Theodore Beck, and also mentions the latter's *Essays on Indian Topics*, in *From Adam's Peak to Elephanta*, pp.276–8 and 356–8.
36. *My Days and Dreams*, p.106.
37. *My Days and Dreams*, p.30.
38. *My Days and Dreams*, p.77.
39. *My Days and Dreams*, pp.65 and 106.
40. *The Song Celestial or Bhagavad-Gita*, translated by Sir Edwin Arnold, 5th ed. (London: Kegan Paul, Trench, Trubner, 1891).
41. Arnold, pp.95, 97–8 and 116–17.
42. "When I Peruse the Conquer'd Fame" and "For You O Democracy," *Leaves of Grass*, notes and introduction by Emory Holloway, 2nd ed. (London: Dent, 1964), pp.111 and 101.
43. *Towards Democracy*, pp.14 and 16.
44. "Song of Myself," 11.422, 446–7, *Leaves of Grass*, pp.41–2.

45. *Towards Democracy*, pp.5 and 66.
46. Tariq Rahman, "The Alienated Prophet: The Relationship between Edward Carpenter's Psyche and the Development of His Metaphysic," *Forum for Modern Language Studies*, 23 (1987), 195 and 194.
47. Barua, pp.250-1.
48. Chushichi Tsuzuki, *Edward Carpenter, 1844-1929: Prophet of Human Fellowship* (Cambridge: Cambridge U.P., 1980), p.37.
49. Charles Oates, Letter to Edward Carpenter, 10 April 1887, MS. 351.38, Carp. Coll.
50. Tsuzuki, p.72.
51. Edward Carpenter, Letter to Charles Oates, 8 June 1887, MS. 351.40, Carp. Coll.
52. Edward Carpenter, Letter to Charles Oates, MS. 351.53, Carp. Coll.
53. Tsuzuki, pp.138-9.
54. See Edward Carpenter, Letters to Charles Oates, 10 April 1887 and 8 June 1887, MSS. 351.38 and 351.40, Carp. Coll.
55. Edward Carpenter, Letter to Charles Oates, 8 Oct. 1890, MS. 351.55, Carp. Coll.
56. Edward Carpenter, Letter to James Brown, 24 Oct. 1890, MS. 372.10, Carp. Coll.
57. Edward Carpenter, Letter to Charles Oates, 7 Dec. 1890, MS. 351.56, Carp. Coll.
58. Jeffrey Weeks, *Coming Out: Homosexual Politics in Britain from the Nineteenth Century to the Present* (1977; rpt. London: Quartet Books, 1983), p.27.
59. Carpenter explains Ulrichs' theory in the "Appendix," *The Intermediate Sex: A Study of Some Transitional Types of Men and Women*, 2nd ed. (London: Swan Sonnenschein, 1909), pp.157-9, and also uses it in *Love's Coming-of-Age: A Series of Papers on the Relation of the Sexes* (Manchester: Labour Press, 1896). The case study of Carpenter's homosexuality is included in Havelock Ellis, *Studies in the Psychology of Sex*, I (London: Watford U.P., 1897), p.46; see Tsuzuki, p.11.
60. Sheila Rowbotham and Jeffrey Weeks, *Socialism and the New Life: The Personal and Sexual Politics of Edward Carpenter and Havelock Ellis* (London: Pluto P., 1977), pp.110-12.
61. Edward Carpenter, Letter to Kate Salt, MS. 354.12, Carp. Coll.
62. Tariq Rahman, "The Literary Treatment of Indian Themes in the Works of Edward Carpenter," *Durham University Journal*, 80 (1987), 77.
63. Edward Carpenter, *England's Ideal, and Other Papers on Social Subjects* (London: Swan Sonnenschein, 1887) and *Civilisation: its Cause and Cure, and Other Essays* (London: Swan Sonnenschein, 1889).
64. *Sexual Heretics: Male Homosexuality in English Literature from 1850 to 1900*, ed. Brian Reade (London: Routledge & Kegan Paul, 1970), p.8.
65. Constantin Meunier (1831-1904) was a Belgian sculptor and painter who found his subjects among miners, factory workers and stevedores. See *The Oxford Companion to Art*, ed. Harold Osborne (Oxford: The Clarendon P., 1970), p.714. The statue Carpenter speaks of shows the puddler in repose.
66. "Narayan: A Tale of Indian Life," *The New Age*, 16, 23, 30 Nov. and 7 Dec. 1899, pp.172, 187-8, 203-4, and 220. Collected in *Sketches from Life* (London: Allen & Unwin, 1907), pp.49-85. All references are to this edition and page numbers are given in brackets in the text after the quote.
67. MS. 93 in the Carpenter Collection. This manuscript forms part of the notes for *Ioläus*, though Carpenter did not include the story in his anthology.
68. "The Literary Treatment of Indian Themes in the Works of Edward Carpenter," p.81.
69. In *The American Journal of Religious Psychology and Education* (July 1911), pp.219-43.
70. *The Christian Commonwealth*, 8 and 15 Dec. 1909, pp.194 and 212 and *Pagan and Christian Creeds: Their Origin and Meaning* (London: Allen & Unwin, 1920).
71. Letter dated 9 July 1894, MS. 270.198, Carp. Coll.

Writing the Body: Edward Carpenter, George Gissing and Late-Nineteenth-Century Realism

INTRODUCTION

The writing of Edward Carpenter and the realism of George Gissing meet at a point which can be termed "writing the body." It is the term used by Ann Rosalind Jones in her account of *l'écriture féminine*[1] (not necessarily written by women) and is exemplified by a text like *La Jeune Née* by Hélène Cixous and Catherine Clément. In the introduction to the English translation of *La Jeune Née*, Sandr̆ Gilbert describes Cixous' concept of *l'écriture féminine* in terms of bodily pleasure, or *jouissance*:

> Woman must challenge "phallo-logocentric" authority through an exploration of the continent of female pleasure, which is neither dark nor lacking, despite the admonitions and anxieties of patriarchal tradition. Out of such a repossession and re-affirmation of her own deepest being, woman may "come" to writing, constructing an erotic aesthetic rooted in a bisexuality that is not a "fantasy of a complete being which replaces the fear of castration ... a fantasy of unity" but rather – as Clément has suggested – a delight in difference, in multiplicity, in continuous awareness of "the other" within self.[2]

Both Jones and Gilbert warn of the dangers of a bodily essentialism in *l'écriture féminine*, but there are good historical reasons for citing the body as central motif in late-nineteenth-century writing. Evolutionism had, for the first time, marked out the body as an historical entity. Social Darwinism provided a language in which society could be understood in biological terms. This language was used, by criminologists like Cesare Lombroso,[3] and "sexologists" like Havelock Ellis, to analyse social crises. Elaine Scarry describes how the body can serve as a source of security amid social uncertainty:

> At particular moments when there is within society a crisis of belief – that is, when some central idea or ideology or cultural construct has ceased to elicit a population's belief either because it is manifestly fictitious or because it has for some reason been divested of ordinary forms of substantiation – the sheer material factualness of the human body will be borrowed to lend that cultural construct the aura of "realness" and "certainty".[4]

These two positions usefully define the parameters of a dilemma in nineteenth-century writing which centres on "writing the body." I have used the term to discuss the overt writing of sexual identity in Carpenter's *Towards Democracy*, a text which has its moments of *jouissance*, and I argue that it is possible to use Carpenter's utopian writing to analyse the construction of male sexuality in George Gissing's realism. For Gissing, the body provides precisely that "realness" and "certainty" which, I argue, reveals a crisis within the text.

Gissing's realism needs to be distinguished from the term "naturalism," with which it has some affinity, because, with the possible exception of George Moore, English novelists cannot be characterised as direct followers of Zola. Instead, it is possible to talk about Gissing's use of a "scientific realism" within the context of a tradition of the nineteenth-century novel. For Gissing, Charles Dickens was the father of this tradition, exemplifying the "old England," in contrast with the "new England ... which tries so hard to be unlike the old."[5] In the "new England" it seemed less and less possible to write of an organic society as a totality in the way Dickens achieved.

Science, in the shape of social Darwinism, is deployed, in Gissing's writing, to intervene in the fractures opening up between classes and to account for the emerging new subjectivities of feminists and "Uranians" like Edward Carpenter. In the face of the collapse of an organic society, Gissing's texts turn to a bodily organism for reassurance. Science is not seen as a solution in itself. It is a necessary evil in conflict with a nostalgic social and aesthetic whole, no longer available amid the class and gender conflicts of the 1880s and 1890s. In *The Private Papers of Henry Ryecroft* (1903), Ryecroft looks back to "the generous hopes and aspirations of forty years ago! Science, then, was seen as a deliverer; only a few could prophesy its tyranny, could foresee that it would revive old evils and trample on the promises of its beginning."[6]

In order to explore this aspect of Gissing's novels in relation to Edward Carpenter, I intend to look first at an explicitly scientific text, Havelock Ellis' *Sexual Inversion*, and the correspondence that preceded its publication. The correspondence between Edward Carpenter, John Addington Symonds and Havelock Ellis demonstrates the process whereby the masculine homosexual subjectivities of Carpenter and Symonds are objectified as "other" by Ellis' scientific realist text.[7] It is a process whereby Ellis is himself constructing a heterosexual describing subject, writing himself as objective in opposition to the threat of oppositional subjectivities. It reveals the realist novel as highly mediated, and allows us to read it as "writing the body."

PRIVATE DISCOURSES: CORRESPONDENCE BETWEEN MEN

Sexual Inversion[8] is a text which aspires to objectivity as a mark of legitimation; while nominally about bodily desire, the text attempts to distance itself from the intimacies and contradictions which that desire entails. The 1897 edition moves towards the science of eugenics; one of its conclusions reads:

> So far as the really congenital invert is concerned, prevention can have but small influence; but in a large proportion of cases there is little obvious congenital element, sound social hygiene should render difficult the acquisition of homosexual perversity.[9]

The term "social hygiene" combines clinical distance with the power of state control over reproduction and upbringing.

Yet despite its tone of scientific objectivity the contradictions contained in the text of *Sexual Inversion* are illuminated by the correspondence between Carpenter and Symonds, who identified as homosexual, and Ellis, who identified as heterosexual.

In his first letter to Carpenter, Symonds makes clear the value of Ellis the doctor, as well as his own, non-scientific, vulnerability: "I need somebody of medical importance to collaborate with. Alone, I could make but little effect – the effect of an eccentric."[10] The first conflict over the text of *Sexual Inversion* was between Symonds' view of homosexuality as a social and cultural phenomenon and Ellis' definition, using the terminology of evolutionist science, of "inversion" as an "abnormality."[11] In his first letter to Ellis, Symonds writes: "The so-called scientific 'psychiatrists' are ludicrously in error, by diagnosing as necessarily morbid what was the leading emotion for the best and noblest men in Hellas."[12] An exchange of letters ensued in which Ellis agreed that "inversion amongst the Greeks" was not "necessarily morbid," but insisted that, under what Symonds had described as modern "adverse conditions," sexuality had to be seen as "a process of selection."[13] Symonds rapidly became infuriated with Ellis' social Darwinism, arguing for the influence of "custom and example" and, in the tradition of Shelleyan radicalism, the autonomous role of the imagination:

> I apprehend that, while I have been growing to regard these anomalies as sports, that is to say, as an occasional mal-arrangement between the reproductive function and the imaginative basis of desire, *you* still adhere to the neuro- or psychopathical explanation.
>
> I should be inclined to abolish the neuropathical hypothesis and also suggestion, on the ground that impaired health in ancestors and suggestion are common conditions of all sexual development, normal and abnormal.[14]

In December of 1892, Ellis wrote to Carpenter, who he knew identified as a "Uranian," requesting his help in the project:

> Symonds has given much study to this subject, both in old Greek & in modern times (has himself printed pamphlets about the matter), & feels very strongly about it. I have been independently

attracted to it, partly through realising how wide-spread it is, partly through realising, also, how outrageously severe the law is in this country (compared with others), & how easily the law can touch a perfectly beautiful form of inversion.[15]

As heterosexual and as a scientist, Ellis situates himself in a position distinct from both Symonds and Carpenter. That his attraction has been formed "independently" is in contrast to the fact that Symonds "feels very strongly about it." In a later letter to Carpenter, written after Symonds' death, Ellis wrote:

I only recognise two classes – complete inversion & psychosexual hermaphroditism. I call them both "abnormal" (in the sense in which genius & criminality are abnormal) which does not involve morbidity though it permits of more or less morbidity in any particular case. This is not quite your way of presenting the matter but I do not think it is a way to which you would seriously object.[16]

For Ellis "morbidity" is the scientific aspect which justifies the public discourse of the book rather than "inversion" as an aesthetic – "perfectly beautiful" – or as constructed socially. In the same letter he writes, "I shall make my cases the kernel of my book, insisting on the fact that they are more of them medical cases, & shall simply argue, so far as I argue, from the cases I present." Medical language and the key term "morbidity" construct his own identity as normal, in contrast to "inversion" as "abnormal," and his position as author as objective. Yet in his correspondence with Symonds he had made clear his personal interest, using very similar terms to those in his letter to Carpenter, "through often finding how it exists to a greater or less extent in many persons whom I know, or know of, and whom I much love and respect."[17]

One of those persons was Ellis' wife, Edith Lees.[18] Edith's revelation about her lesbianism after their marriage had exacerbated Ellis' pre-occupation with his own sexuality; like many of the case studies in *Sexual Inversion* he was troubled by "spermatorrhoea," the condition which described a masculine anxiety about the loss of sperm from the biological economy.[19] His anxiety about Edith finds textual utterance in the section on lesbianism. He writes, "The man who is passionately attracted to an inverted woman is usually of rather a feminine type,"[20] although, even here, the word "passionately" leaves some leeway for his self-estimation as a masculine man. Some biographers have specu-lated as to whether Ellis was himself homosexual.[21] As a speculation it tends to assume a preconceived heterosexual/homosexual opposition, whereas the question in relation to *Sexual Inversion* is one of written subjectivity, of self-identification. In July 1892, Ellis wrote to Symonds: "I have not written, partly because I think it is a mistake to begin by identifying oneself with these questions, and still more because I have not felt qualified to do so."[22] The two factors of scientific distance and science as qualification give Ellis the confidence to involve himself, even though the publishers of *The Contemporary Science Series* would not;[23] yet he wrote himself outside the subject matter. In November 1895, Carpenter wrote, "I doubt whether you *quite* appreciate the 'true inwardness' of this kind of love."[24]

The correspondence between Symonds and Carpenter is one of the hidden discourses behind *Sexual Inversion*. Each had a quite different relationship to the text. Symonds as aesthete emphasises "custom and example," considering "sexual inversion...due to mental imaginative aesthetical emotional peculiarities of the individual."[25] Symonds knew of Carpenter, however, as a Whitmanite, through his poem *Towards Democracy*, so behind their dialogue lies another episode in the formation of a written homosexual identity.

In the 1880s Symonds had been in correspondence with Walt Whitman, and his letters illustrate the conflicts within his own writing about men's desire for men. In contrast to the formal, classical aesthetic of love between men, Symonds rejoiced in the naturalism of Whitman's *Leaves of Grass*: "At home I found in them pure air and health – the free breath of the world – when often cramped by illness and the cares of life."[26] The letters from Symonds to Whitman go on to expand upon this conflict which centres on the body as register for his reaction to the poetry. Symonds presses Whitman to be more naturalistic and to explain exactly what he means by "comradeship," but Symonds expresses his interest in terms of his attempts fully to realise the aesthetic project of *Leaves of Grass*. The descriptions of the effect of the poems on Symonds, "the powerful force with which you have entered into me," are explained by this loftier desire: "Of course I do not care much about it, except that ignorance on the subject prevents me from forming a complete view of your life-philosophy."[27] The ambiguity in Symonds' attitude allowed Whitman to make fun of his attempts to "get to the bottom of Calamus." He described Symonds as a "great one for delving into persons and into the concrete, and even into the physiological, the gastric – and wonderfully cute."[28]

Symonds' aestheticism leaves him open to Whitman's subversion through an alternative canon, the grotesque. The grotesque canon is a concept used by Mikhail Bakhtin as another approach to "writing the body." He stresses the subversive potential of the "obscene" body to the official canon, where "laughter degrades and materializes":[29]

> We understand the word "canon" not in the narrow sense of a specific group of consciously established rules, norms and proportions in the representation of the human body. (It is still possible to speak of the classic canon in such a narrow sense at certain stages of its development.) The grotesque image never had such a canon. It is non-canonical by its very nature. We here use the word canon in the wider sense of a manner of representing the body and bodily life.[30]

The "laughing chorus" of the grotesque canon sets up an opposition to the monologic or one-sided, official version, creating a dialogue between the two, which Bakhtin sees as an element of "novelistic discourse." Here, the profundity of Symonds' "bottom of Calamus" becomes the grotesque but pleasurable bottom in opposition to an ideal of "Greek love." Although evasive with Symonds himself (to prove his virility, he claimed he had six illegitimate children), Whitman shows himself to be well aware of the scope of the fantasies within the naturalism of *Leaves of Grass*. He too is conscious of the dangers of the obscene bottom, fears which were fulfilled by the court case involving *Sexual Inversion*. In the culture of late-nineteenth-century Britain, where homosocial bonds structured power relations, the discourse of pleasure between men is the most dangerous.[31]

Carpenter, as an exponent of Whitmanesque poetry, had a different attitude from that of Symonds towards a science which would define his desires as morbid, and had written a critique of modern science in his collection of essays *Civilisation: its Cause and Cure*. Like Symonds, Carpenter is critical of scientific reductionism which would exclude the question of the social construction of sexuality:

> In the search for exactness then science has been continually led on to discard the human and personal elements in phenomena, in the hope of finding some residuum as it were behind them which should not be personal and human but absolute and invariable.[32]

Science is not, however, rejected as an explanatory medium, but between Symonds and Carpenter its use is in explaining the physical benefits of sex between men:

> You raise a very interesting question with regard to physio-logical grounds for this passion. I have no doubt myself that the absorption of semen implies a real modification of the physique to the person who absorbs it, & that, in these homosexual relations, this constitutes an important basis for subsequent conditions – both spiritual & corporeal.[33]

In the letters between Carpenter and Symonds bodily pleasure is discussed, but guardedly, as the hidden agenda. In the same letter, Symonds writes, "It is a pity we cannot write freely on the topic" and, in contrast to the projected public discourse of the book, this letter is marked "Private." Symonds continued to emphasise the example of the Greeks to Carpenter as utopian: a society in which the aesthetic aspect was joined with the social. Both believed, as followers of Whitman, in the potentially democratising effect of "masculine love," seeing "Uranianism" as an ideal, and science as a medium through which that ideal could be publicly discussed.

Sexual Inversion was an attempt to write publicly about men's desire for men in a way which, through its realism, could change the public perception of that desire. However, that intention was overcome by the complex relationship of the contributors (direct and indirect) to writing the body. Ellis found himself in a problematic position because he was writing as a self-identified heterosexual to change a system which invests power in that identification. The necessary textual contact with the "other" – the "inverted" – those who would turn things bottom up, who would let in anarchy, overpowered the text in Britain. Symonds' writings about homosexuality were kept private and his memoirs were locked away for years after his death.[34] Carpenter, however, attempted a form of writing pioneered by Whitman as a way of writing the body.

TOWARDS DEMOCRACY: THE IDEAL BODY

Carpenter's reading of Whitman was an uplifting experience, one which influenced his whole life as well as being the dominant influence on *Towards Democracy*. The effect of *Leaves of Grass* on Symonds is described above. By contrast, the first reaction of Olive Schreiner, on hearing Whitman read, was to laugh,[35] although, in the company of Havelock Ellis and others, she soon learnt to like him "very much."[36] To Whitmanite enthusiasts, like Carpenter and Symonds, *Leaves of Grass* provided a new way of seeing; but to the uninitiated it appeared ridiculous and inaccessible. Similarly, *Towards Democracy*, placed within a movement associated with Whitman, gathered an audience around itself as a minor work in that tradition; but compared with the realist novel, the writing is unexpected and even "unreadable" in its lack of narrative form or poetic structure.

It is, however, possible to "make sense" of *Towards Democracy* by relating it to the textual positions outlined above in relation to *Sexual Inversion*. As such it can be seen as part of a discourse between men. This method of reading can then be related to the way gender positions are similarly inscribed into the realist text.

Carpenter builds on Whitman's corpus of poetry to write a masculine identity for himself, calling all "confessed passionate lovers of your own sex":

> When a new desire has declared itself within the human heart, when a fresh plexus is forming amongst the nerves – then the revolutions of nations are already decided, and histories unwritten are written.[37]

In contrast with the objective narrative of *Sexual Inversion, Towards Democracy* is written outside conventional narrative and from the perspective of the subjective "I." This "I" is inclusive where the third person, "independent" observer is exclusive, distancing and defining through classification. The grotesqueness of the body's interiority is celebrated. That grotesqueness, which the realist text needs to refer to as exterior, to legitimate the subject–object distinction, is made universal in Carpenter's poem. The reader accepts the subjectivity of the "I" and then its dissolution; in "A Note on 'Towards Democracy'"

Carpenter wrote: "It seems to me more and more clear that the word 'I' has a practically infinite range of meaning – that the ego covers far more ground than we usually suppose."[38] Carpenter aims at a utopian universality, the inclusiveness of which will dissolve division and difference. The reader is invited to engage in the breaking down of determinist structures and to embrace a democratic world.

> For this world you see around – these trees, mountains, these high city streets and the myriad faces that pass among them – are not all these but images?
> Images, to the Heart of which with restless longing you have indeed so often sought to penetrate ...
> For deep down there is, may-be, no difference –
> And when the desires that are born of Hate and Fear and Distrust are gone, there is no difference.[39]

Democracy is the corporeal world in which "sex goes first." This utopian ideal is written in opposition to the scientific prose of Ellis' *Studies in the Psychology of Sex*, where women are attracted by the "manly" qualities in men and men by the "womanly" qualities in women. The content of the work is about direct bodily contact, bursting open the rigid, determinist definitions of Ellis' evolutionism. Carpenter talks about drinking the semen of Democracy, about desiring an erection, but he locates this writing the body in his own scientific framework.

In his critique of evolutionist science, in *Civilisation*, Carpenter counterposes a radical human will to the fetishisation of disease he perceives to be a product of "civilisation." The dissociation of love – which is universal – and desire – which is specific and fetishised – is seen as a historical process, where Ellis sees it as scientific fact.

Carpenter stresses "exfoliation" rather than evolutionism. This is a type of Lamarckian evolutionism where the stress is on a personal and spiritual approach to change, one which permits self-definition: "Desire, or inward change, comes first, action follows, and organisation or outward structure is the result."[40] This stress later allows Carpenter, in *The Intermediate Sex*, to define his own sexuality as both congenital, and therefore irreversible, and as historically willed, in opposition to medical or scientific definitions of deviance. While Carpenter uses biological examples to illustrate this, in his later essays he makes it clear that he doubts their validity except as an "allegory" of the processes of human desire.[41] Carpenter, unlike Ellis, recognised that evolutionism was a formal structure which provided the models through which sexuality was understood at the end of the nineteenth century. He did maintain the idea of biology as base, but not as necessary causality:

> The ground floor in a house is not the cause of the first floor, nor the first floor of the second floor, nor that of the roof; but these

actualities and the whole house itself stand in strict relationship to a mental something which is not in the same plane with them at all, nor an actuality in the same sense.[42]

The central contradiction of Carpenter's radical individualism is that his assertion of a homosexual identity, while challenging the biological heterosexuality of scientists like Ellis, is in opposition to his own criticism of the differentiation of desire. Differentiation is, as we have seen, a negative aspect of civilisation. Carpenter's concept of utopia thus involves a stage beyond civilisation in which individuality is dissolved, but by way of further contradiction, this is seen as a subjective process:

> Of course the ultimate reconcilement of the individual with society – of the unit Man with the mass-Man – involves the subordination of desires, their subjection to the true self.[43]

The limitations of Carpenter's radical individualism become clear when his system requires that alternative constructed identities are incorporated into that "true self." The universal subjectivity of *Towards Democracy* ("I am the lover and the loved") threatens to dominate the celebrated pluralism.

This can be related to his essay on masculinity, "Man the Ungrown," in which Carpenter uses biologistic assumptions of race and gender, going back to Ellis' *Man and Woman* (1894) to support his analysis. He suggests, for example, that the middle-class man is "the tool of the Jew and the speculator."[44] Carpenter's solution to the problem of the nineteenth-century middle-class man is not far from the ideal of imperial masculinity, except that that role should incorporate leading both the working-class and the women's movement: he should "organise the world for them."[45] The "English ruling classes [have] a similar role in the world to the Romans of the early Empire."[46] Women, above all, provide a refuge where men can recuperate from civilised alienation and find their "true self":

> It is to her that Man, after his excursions and wanderings, mental and physical, continually tends to return as to his primitive home and resting-place, to restore his balance, to find his centre of life, and to draw stores of energy and inspiration for fresh conquests of the outer world.[47]

The new man of *Love's Coming-of-Age* represents a recognition of the divisions of class, gender and race which construct his masculinity, but those divisions are not seen as social. Working-class men, women, Jews and colonised peoples, who are to Carpenter explicitly "inferior races," are still seen as fundamentally, that is biologically, different.[48]

A similar process occurs in *Towards Democracy*. Celebration of a plurality of difference slips into domination by inclusion, as opposed to domination by exclusion and definition: "The peoples of the earth;

the intertwining many-colored streams" are incorporated into a consuming text, as part of a universal list:

> China, gliding seemingly unobservant among the crowd, self-restrained, of her own soul calmly possessed; the resplendent-limbed Negro and half-caste (do you not see that old woman there with brow and nose and jaw dating conclusively back from far away Egypt?); the glitter-eyed caressing-handed Hindu, suave thoughtful Persian, and faithful Turk; Mexico and the Red Indian (O unconscious pleading eyes of the dying races!) ...[49]

Although Carpenter asserts that Democracy has "relations to these,"[50] described thus, they are part of *his* utopia, "unconscious," "pleading" and even "dying." This inclusiveness is reflected in the structure of *Towards Democracy*. We are not provided with the "realist" reference points which would contextualise Carpenter's transgressions. Instead the idealisation of the body prevents transgressive desires from becoming publicly dangerous.

The cataloguing technique, which Carpenter takes from Whitman's poems such as "Crossing Brooklyn Ferry," includes, without ordering, long lists of tactile images:

> trickling slime-places and ponds and bogs and mangrove marshes and chattering shale-slopes and howling deserted ridges and heaps of broken glass and old bones and shoes ...[51]

These images, were they taken out of one of Dickens' urban descriptions, would have a particular function of time and space within the narrative structure. The dust-heaps in *Our Mutual Friend* are a metaphor for accumulation which moves the narrative on or provides a site where its contradictions can be partially resolved. In *Dorian Gray*, images of degeneration are sited on trajectories of both decline and pleasure, a dangerous and transgressive combination in the public discourse of the novel; but Carpenter is describing "the solid earth in the midst of which I am buried."[52] The inclusivity of *Towards Democracy* in a form without narrative works to replace what Bakhtin calls the novelistic chronotopes with a celebration of plurality which is timeless. At the same time, the timelessness of *Towards Democracy* is itself a chronotope. Bakhtin describes how:

> In literature and art itself, temporal and spatial determinations are inseparable from one another, and are always colored by emotions and values. Abstract thought can, of course, think time and space as separate entities and conceive them as things apart from the emotions and values that attach to them. But *living* artistic perception (which also of course involves thought, but not abstract thought) makes no such divisions and permits no such segmentation.[53]

However, unlike the novel, where chronotopes of time and space compete in dialogue with one another, *Towards Democracy* preserves one timeless space in which a new subjectivity can be explored. This timelessness is made explicit in the last section:

> Do not wander too far into time at all, lest with the everlasting Now – the centre of all life and experience, and your own true lover –
> You fail to keep your first appointment.[54]

The aphoristic phrasing of this poem, "The Everlasting Now," written in the present tense, disallows a teleological reading. In "Now is the Accepted Time," teleological desire is seen as futile:

> The effort to catch the flying point of light, to reach the haven of Peace – always in the future –
> Amid all, glides in the little word Now.[55]

The writing of *Towards Democracy* is oppositional to the teleologies of both evolutionist science and the narrative structure of the novel. As Carpenter was to put it in *Love's Coming-of-Age*,

> The dissatisfaction is not in the name of pleasure itself but in the nature of *seeking*. In going off in pursuit of things external, the "I" (since it really has everything and needs nothing) deceives itself, goes out from its true home, tears itself asunder, and admits a gap or rent in its own being.[56]

Evolutionist science and the novel are both public discourses, whereas *Towards Democracy* is shaped by the knowledge that the desires contained within it are part of a discourse disbarred from public utterance. The text is full of references to forbidden love, to secret exchanges, to private languages in public places: poems like "To a Stranger" in which Carpenter writes "I know the truth the tenderness the courage, I know the longings/hidden quiet there."[57] These longings risk definition if they extend beyond the now to have their own specificity in history, and Carpenter employs textual strategies to avoid such negative definitions as "morbidity."

The repeated use of the vocative to evoke liberation from determinist structures – "O laughter!", "O freed soul!", "Freedom!", "Joy!" – paradoxically delineates an enclosed space from which it is difficult to intervene historically against the oppressive social relations from which the text has escaped. It is a problematic situation, but one which illustrates the difficulties of the uninitiated reader. Without the familiar reference points of time or subject–object distinction provided by a realist text, *Towards Democracy* is often difficult and inaccessible. The process of creating the space in which a homosexual identity can exist without fear of attack, excludes the familiarly social.

Shaped in the context of a discourse between men, in the late-nineteenth-century atmosphere of strong homosocial bonds and public homophobia, *Towards Democracy* writes an ideal, atemporal subjectivity. It is an ideal which expands rather than defines the limits of masculinity. In this sense it is first and foremost a masculine discourse, and Schreiner's laughter is not a surprising reaction. Where Carpenter trangresses the hierarchies of evolutionist science is in his writing of the male body as pleasurable. Irigaray writes, "When the penis itself becomes simply a means of pleasure, and indeed a means of pleasure among men, *the phallus loses its power*."[58] Carpenter writes the body in a way which at least allows the possibility of egalitarian sexual relations. His use of language, when understood as oppositional, celebratory and pleasurable is transformative in the way it redefines images. Within the historical limitations described above, Carpenter invites us to a utopian sense of self:

> Believe yourself a Whole.
> These needs, these desires, these faculties –
> This of eating and drinking, the great pleasure of food, the need of sex-converse and of renewal in and from the bodies of others;[59]

Carpenter experienced the difficulties of getting published and the persecution suffered by all men and women who transgressed sexual norms at the turn of the century (the references to the police in *Towards Democracy* are unusual for late Victorian literature in that they speak of the enforcement of social norms, rather than of the upholders of law and order.)[60] Carpenter managed to preserve his identity as a Uranian through mysticism. In his account of a utopia he talks of "a cosmic world of souls," returning to the idea of an evolution of consciousness present in *Civilisation: its Cause and Cure*.[61] It is one of the ways in which the desire for certain "sexual qualities" is incorporated into a larger narrative of biological evolution. The formal framework of evolutionism is both resisted and usefully deployed.

Reading historically, the inaccessibility or difficulty of the non-canonical text provides us with a way of placing the realist texts of the period within the context of contemporary debates about male sexuality. The non-canonical throws light on the canonical and allows us to re-examine the familiar which appears as the real. Given the rigidities of Gissing's realism as a form, it is possible to read Carpenter's celebration of the body against Gissing's novels as a form of the grotesque "laughing chorus" which Bakhtin sees as a part of the narrative structure of the novel. Where Carpenter was "writing the body" as a focus for the liberation of sexual identity, Gissing uses it as a defence against the legitimation crisis of a heterosexual masculine identity.

GISSING'S REALISM

In the last twenty years of the century, the difficulties facing a novelist as conscious of "tradition" as Gissing are clear in a novel like *Demos: A Story of English Socialism* (1886). In *Demos*, class conflict is not resolvable within a framework of organic society. The cracks and strains which are apparent at moments in novels like *North and South* prove unbridgeable.[62] The East End is another world (and an "other" world in the sense that it is constructed as "other" than the describing subject of the text), its inhabitants are not necessarily human, and can even become monstrous: a fate which afflicts Richard Mutimer, the working class protagonist who inherits a suitably gothic mansion.

As is commonplace in the Victorian novel, the strain of keeping society together is thrown onto a marriage, and within that marriage it is the construction of femininity which is required to provide resolution. In *Demos*, the character of Adela is given the task of proving that the organic society of Wanley is irreconcilable with the East End.

Realism was not, of course, the only novelistic strategy open to late-nineteenth-century novelists; romance, melodrama and horror were all employed. The sensationalist "new woman" novels, like Rhoda Broughton's *Belinda*, were enormously popular, concentrating on the limits of allowed behaviour within gender relations and carried forward by the growing women's movement. Realism, however, especially for the male novelists who employed it, had a sense of itself as the tradition of serious novel writing even though writing "life as it is" was no longer a consensual activity. Associated with French writing, it was often reviled for concentrating unduly on the "sordid."

In this sense, the "scientific realism" of *Sexual Inversion* can be seen as an aesthetic strategy as well as an attempt to intervene in public discourse. Rachel Bowlby in her book *Just Looking* has described how naturalism as a style in France, England and the United States arose at about the same time as the Darwinist social sciences. She relates this to the growth of a consumer-orientated capitalist economy:

> The period of naturalism (1880–1920, approximately) is contemporary with the rise of the social sciences, and there are significant parallels between the two practices. Their common project of showing the "facts" of society in a plain, unembellished form marked off naturalism as radically inartistic in the established sense, in which science and art were considered two poles as different from one another as machines from feelings.
>
> In terms both of their place in the field of literary production and of the methods and subjects which they took on, naturalist novels are thus on the borders between art and industry, which makes them *a priori* a promising ground for considering questions of commerce and culture in the late nineteenth century. These questions are also addressed directly and implicitly within the novels themselves, where they occur as part of the social reality which the novels seek to reproduce.[63]

Commercialism is reviled in the work of George Gissing; the coverage of walls with advertisements for soap and God is treated with disgust as an example of the general devaluation of culture. In contrast, Whitman, writing earlier, celebrates the plurality of small ads in newspaper columns. The lists of wants, needs and items on sale becomes another example of a democratic pluralism. In Gissing's realist prose the possibility that the needs of the many could be integrated into a new ideal of culture is rejected. Democratic ideals are written as Demos, the mob which destroys Richard Mutimer, as it destroyed his Chartist father, or the crowds which sweep along Nancy Lord in *In the Year of Jubilee*. Human desires cannot be celebrated in Gissing's novels; once you have succumbed you are caught up in forces which are predetermined and which leave you either isolated, like Nancy, or in the grip of the dominant social values, for example, the business motive of Crewe, who is able to use the laws of the crowd like the laws of physics to make his own way, and who loves nothing better than to watch the unreserved display of commodity desire in a riot.

The relationship between Gissing's writing and the nascent social sciences is most clear in the early novels. Booth's social surveys were started in response to the claims of the Social Democratic Federation that a third of London's population lived in conditions of extreme poverty. In novels like *Demos* and *The Nether World* social classes are zoned into geographical areas. The city is mapped out horizontally; in Booth's maps, colours delineated areas, black being "vicious, semi-criminal."[64] The rapid growth of the urban working-class in London led to widespread middle-class anxiety that the organic connections of patronage and charity had been severed. The casualised labour force which predominated in the East End lacked even the imposed working discipline of large-scale manufacturing industry. This "residuum," as it was known, was seen as a threat to the fabric of society and its unknowability, its "otherness," was compared in equal terms to the "otherness" of Africa:[65]

> Hoxton, a region of malodorous market streets, of factories, timber yards, grimy warehouses, of alleys swarming with small trades and crafts, of filthy courts and passages leading into pestilential gloom; everywhere toil in its most degrading forms; the thoroughfares thundering with highladen waggons, the pavements trodden by working folk of the coarsest type, the corners and lurking-holes showing destitution at its ugliest. Walking northwards, the explorer finds himself in freer air.[66]

Hoxton, in the East End, serves as the figure for the "otherness" of working-class life. The process of description is objectified; there is a sharp distinction between that which is exterior and the describing subject, "the explorer." We can compare Carpenter's inclusivity, where the subject is part of the material, integrated with the text. Yet, Gissing's text is a narrative, there is movement. Instead of the construction of an atemporal inclusive identity, the describing subject interacts with the process of description, smelling the streets, brushing against the warehouses and the workshops, being deafened by the traffic, delving into corners and holes and passing into the gloom. Here, the visible distinction between the subject and object disappears; instead of a medico/scientific distance the pestilence is close enough to be caught; but it remains outside the subject who is in danger of being infected by it. The passage contains a written corporeal subjectivity which is diminished by bodily contact with the objects which make up Hoxton, dirtied, coarsened, made ugly; and, conversely, Hoxton itself is a body to be explored, one of the forbidden internal parts of the body which nevertheless has the capacity to give pleasure in exchange for the diminution of the subject. Gissing's realism relies on the exclusivity of the subject, so that it can enter the "passages" and "lurking holes" and then withdraw in order to legitimate its own construction as distinct.

Whereas in *Towards Democracy* there is a willed identification with the "other," in Gissing identification is in opposition to that "other." In a poem like "The Carter," a working-class man is represented as an emblem of hope and of desire:

> Thus in the din and dirt of the city, as over the mountain tops and in the far forest alone with Nature,
> I saw the unimaginable form dwelling, whom no mortal eye may see,
> The unimaginable form of Man, tenant of the earth from far ages seen of the wise in all times –
> Dwelling also in the youthful carter.[67]

In Gissing, distance is maintained by the intervention of science. For example, Kate in *Demos*, a working-class woman, is described in anthropological terms:

> He did not offer to relieve her of the bundle – in primitive societies woman is naturally the burden-bearer.[68]

The textual strategy, here, can be described in the language of spending and thriftiness which Peter Cominos describes as part of the sexual ideology of Victorian respectability.[69] The masculine economy of holding back, penetration and loss is written into the text, much as it is written into the case histories of *Sexual Inversion*. The masculine subject spends, in its recognition of a sordid "otherness," but it maintains a scientific distance, thriftily saving the libidinal return in an objectification of the object desired. Images of pestilence invoke masculine fears of syphilis and feminist resistance to the Contagious Diseases Acts. A masculine bodily subjectivity is distanced by the subject–object relationship within the text and by the morality which finds dirt, coarseness, noise and darkness objectionable; but this inscribes an identity into the text, one which does not celebrate Bakhtin's grotesque, with its pleasurable transgressions, but which keeps those transgressions in a subordinate position.

Gissing's realism can be read as a textual strategy used to confront the threat to a traditional hierarchy of sex and class, and to meet it in the arena of public, fictional discourse employing the most serious form he knew, the tradition of the novel. A scientific realism attempts to reassert a relationship between the subject and a potentially chaotic object in which that object can be made comprehensible; but the combination of Gissing's conception of that tradition and the sense of crisis within society, produces a form which operates in a contradictory fashion. The will to restore an ideal of social cohesion is opposed by the sense that that ideal is inoperable. The effect of Gissing's use of scientific realism is to deconstruct the ideal behind its use. The Darwinist origins of late-nineteenth-century social science reduce social relations to biological make-up. Instead of enabling the reconstruction of an ideal of society, there is a tendency towards an individualist psychology. Characters in the realist text are distanced and empirically assessed as hysterical women, criminal proletarians, degenerate aristocrats or protagonists in an environment of competing individuals, where only the fittest survive.

In *Demos*, the social ideals of Hubert, which have their premise in the old society of Wanley, have no meaning in the industrialised environment of New Wanley. As Hubert's decision to destroy the factories and the new community cannot be justified in terms of the new organisation of society, it becomes a purely aesthetic gesture, which in terms of scientific realism is decadent, even degenerate. Yet, the scientific realism employed is equally removed from an organic society; its justification in the novel can only be aesthetic, as a discourse of pleasure. The analysis of society provided by Gissing's realism lies on the borderline between encompassing society's divisions in an artistic whole, and exploiting science (scientific realism) to celebrate deviance. The accusation levelled indirectly at *Sexual Inversion* hangs over the realist text, that its aims are not medical or legal, that the text is in fact directed at the satisfaction of lewd or obscene desires. This would mean that, for all its rhetorical strategy to distance the subject matter, the text is in fact writing the body, inscribing a sexual identity which allows us to understand the construction of masculinity in the late nineteenth century.

If we return once again to the correspondence with which we started, it appears that the accusations can be verified. The three collaborators in the text of *Sexual Inversion* can be treated, without too much distortion, as paradigms through which we can interpret Gissing's novels. Symonds, the aesthete, wants to understand male sexuality as part of an organic whole; unable to integrate his own desires into society as it stands, he uses renaissance art and "Greek love" to present an alternative vision in the field of criticism. When it comes to changing society, however, he is forced, like Gissing, to compromise with science. Ellis writes as a scientist, specifically requesting that Symonds does not include literary references,[70] which might suggest the dimension of pleasure, yet in his exclusiveness, anxious to make clear the differences between himself and Symonds, writing himself and his own anxieties into the text. The analytical approach turns upon itself, deconstructing the very categories it proposes. Carpenter's writing celebrates heterogeneity in the context of an ideal atemporality.

Gissing's realism writes these chronotopes of organicism, science and *jouissance*, but the "dialogic imagination", which, according to Bakhtin, should allow each to speak to the other producing polyphony,[71] is repressed. Instead, Gissing, in an attempt to achieve an aesthetic which is an organic whole, deploys the determinations of science, constructing a masculine subject which negates bodily pleasure.

In his novels of the 1890s, Gissing moved from writing on exclusively working-class themes to novels which focused on gender relations, reflecting the public interest in (and the market for) the new woman. *Eve's Ransom*, published in 1895, describes the relationship between two characters who have, through financial windfalls, an opportunity of escaping the drudgery and monotony of a waged existence.

In *Eve's Ransom* the emphasis has shifted to the construction of character and, more overtly, to sexuality. Hilliard's "pass" is described as

> one of desperation centred in self. Every suggestion of native suavity and prudence was swept away in tumultuous revolt. Another twelvemonth of his slavery and he would have yielded to brutalising influences which rarely relax their hold upon a man. To-day he was prompted by the instinct of flight from peril threatening all that was worthy in him.[72]

Hilliard is balanced on the edge of incorporation by his environment, close to becoming a part of the mechanised world which, as a trained but uncreative draughtsman, it is his job to draw. The money which falls into his hands gives him the distance to recreate an identity which is separate and from which he can assert some control. That identity is explicitly gendered; it is his chance to be a "man."[73] Subsequently he does not hold back from London's "grossest lures";[74] but his position of control means he does not succumb to "brutalising influences", he has money to spend, capital enough not to be diminished.

The plot of *Eve's Ransom* has the aesthetic form and brevity more characteristic of Gissing's later novels. Hilliard sees a photograph of Eve before going to London and forms an idealised image of her as silent and submissive. In London he finds her, where her smaller windfall has left her compromised. Rachel Bowlby has described the contradictory position of the independent woman worker in the 1890s.[75] Her ability to earn, plus the extra money she acquires, allow her to buy clothes and to go to the theatre, to create a new independent identity; but her consumption is part of the spectacle of commercialism. Her clothes are to be seen in; she is at the theatre to see and to be seen. Eve is both consumer and consumed. This compromised position is furthered by a suitably mysterious relationship, which has left her needing money. Hilliard is the voyeur of Eve's spectacle, but with more money and not compromised by consumption in the same way, he can ransom her. The act of ransoming threatens to destroy Eve's independence and her resistances to Hilliard's power are written as bodily. She is too ill, at first, to go to Paris with him. When they return to Birmingham she becomes more and more ill, unable to find work in the less emancipated Midlands. Eventually Hilliard discovers that she has started an affair with his friend Narramore, a successful but indolent businessman; but in the meantime Hilliard too has been "ransomed." He has used the rest of his money to buy into an architect's firm, where he can learn to use his skill creatively. Ransomed, and detached, Hilliard happily exchanges Eve for his freedom. He meets her again, as married, in a garden, an English Eden, where she is magically transformed to health and happiness. The closing paragraphs leave Hilliard walking alone in the countryside in a state of mind which, if not blissful, at least involves a working relationship with his environment.

A comparison of the masculine subjectivity constructed in Hilliard with that in *Towards Democracy* demonstrates an inclusive/exclusive opposition. Incorporation, in Gissing's realist prose, is equated with a loss of control, the destruction of a specifically gendered identity, the grip of "brutalising influences." Hilliard's relationship with Eve is part of the process of constructing a positive and distinct masculine identity, but sexuality is itself a determining and destructive influence. Sexuality here is not, of course, constructed as unitary. Hilliard's sexuality is constructed in opposition to that of Eve. He is powerful and dominating while he has money. He requires her dependence. She has the independent sexuality of the "new woman," but her independence exists in no concrete social institutions. Her psychology is individualised; she is unstable, depressive, until she is made part of a social unit, married to Narramore. The sexualised relationship between Hilliard and Eve carries with it the dangers which accompany the instabilities of both their identities. Sexuality, as an independent phenomenon,[76] is a potentially degenerative process,[77] and the impossibility of a heterosexual relationship on equal terms is reiterated throughout Gissing's novels in the 1890s. Hilliard's final gesture, and the form of the novel as a whole, is an aesthetic gesture. Society is deemed to be an insufficient basis for social creativity. Realism itself has to be detached from the social process, as a form in its own right, an artistic dilemma which Oscar Wilde resolved by using paradox as the only way of articulating the relationship between identity and the writing of the real, which, he claimed, *is* Art.

Paradox, in contrast with contradiction, holds an opposition in suspension. At certain points in Gissing's novels the determinist narrative threatens to degenerate into the abyss which Hilliard fears. The paradox, as a textual non-resolution, keeps an aesthetic distance between the constructed male identity and chaos; it is an exclusive relationship. Chaos, is not, however, just the unarticulated other, but also the articulated threats of industrialised, "mechanised" society – in *Demos* organised labour, in *Eve's Ransom* the perceived threat to social cohesion of the women's movement.

The utopianism of Carpenter's body writing lay in its ability to utilise the biological and evolutionist model and produce a form which celebrates possibility and, within an ahistorical context, the potential of changing identities, of new desires. Gissing resists the historical body which evolutionist science brings into being as part of an inevitably determinist narrative whose only result must be the destruction of culture. In *The Private Papers of Henry Ryecroft* science is regarded with "dread." Both writers, Gissing and Carpenter, can be seen to be taking up different positions of masculine subjectivity in relation to a debate on sexuality in which, if the impetus for reappraisal came from the women's movement and socialist ideas, the discourses were supplied by science.

The biological processes which Carpenter and Symonds discussed, where the exchange of sperm had mutually beneficial effects, serve as a metaphor for the sexual relations each envisaged, Carpenter working in a biological framework, Symonds in the cultural. In contrast the sexual practice analogous (Carpenter's term is allegorical) to the written subjectivity of realist prose is penetrative. The distance of scientific realism is used to enter as part of a process of self-affirmation; to withdraw confirms the distinct identity of subject as opposed to object, but the masculine economy constructed is also seen as diminished.

The position of Eve can be related to the representation of women by other realist writers in the 1880s and 1890s. Eve is in some ways unique because she is both a new woman and working-class. The conjunction should not be so surprising, however, because the writing of working-class women as central characters is widespread amongst the male realists. It is as if the threat of the new woman, and in particular the literary new woman, provokes a reaction where men attempt to represent the real experience of women, as opposed to the artificial experience of middle-class feminists.

In George Moore's *Esther Waters* a direct comparison is made between the lifeless novels of a middle-class "spinster" and the raw reality of the life of her servant, Esther. Women represent a dangerous interiority which has to be represented from the outside. Women, as a privileged register, indoors, susceptible to stimuli according to Ellis, have to be exteriorised, put on display as commodities, to be consumed; but this sets up a written anxiety about a type of bodily knowledge associated with women.

When Nancy Lord in *In the Year of Jubilee* (1894) attempts novel writing, she is patronised for her pains, but the patroniser is Tarrant, her husband, whose commercial writing is disdained by him and which, like advertisements, is constantly seen as part of the devaluation of culture in the novel. In Gissing and Moore, romance, as the writing of women, is replaced by reiterated reference to a material reality. The inevitable determinations of the narrative deny the fulfilment of romantic satisfaction.

CONCLUSION

The question of satisfaction, of pleasure, takes us back to the problem raised in the introduction, of the dangers of essentialism when discussing "writing the body." We have looked at how the crisis of realism manifests itself as centred on the body, but bodily pleasure is not a given, but a historical phenomenon. Darwinist social science provided the discourse for some aspects of new subjectivities. In particular, evolutionism provided a way of writing the body as historical, and as divorced from society. As such, it was a discourse in conflict with a nostalgic idea of society as an organic whole, even while it was being used to sustain a hierarchy of discourses, in order to preserve unity.

Carpenter's resolution of these contradictions was, using the form of *Leaves of Grass*, to write an atemporal subjectivity, which, seen historically, resisted the determinist narratives of evolutionism. Gissing's realism is an example of the use of evolutionist science as a way of bringing new historical identities under the control of the text; but as an artistic venture it is fraught with the danger of becoming another "writing of the body." The textual resolutions of both writers impose ideological horizons which are informed by their positions as white middle-class men and, within the limitations of their class, gender and race, each negotiates a written sexuality.

The crisis which manifests itself in this way in Gissing's realism takes place amid the beginnings of modernism. The texts of Joyce and Woolf which followed start from a premise of subjectivity in their construction of the social, and Carpenter's work can be seen as a precursor of this modernism. When Gissing was writing, the threat of a feminine subjectivity was present in the highly visible form of popular romance.

Realist narrative is displaced from its hegemonic position after the turn of the century, reappearing as one form deployed with others, as much in the mass cultural forms of journalism, film, radio, television and best-sellers as in "high" culture. Gissing's realism can be seen as an attempt, by a male novelist, to defend his position by making the novel a "high" cultural form. To do this he had to write in a form which fended off the threatening bodies of those who would usurp that cultural dominance.

SCOTT MCCRACKEN

NOTES

1. Ann Rosalind Jones, "Writing the Body: Toward an Understanding of *l'Écriture féminine*," in *The New Feminist Criticism* ed. Elaine Showalter (London: Virago, 1986), pp. 361–77.
2. Hélène Cixous and Catherine Clément, *The Newly Born Woman* (Manchester: Manchester U.P., 1987), p.xv.
3. Cesare Lombroso, *Crime: Its Causes and Remedies* (Boston: Little, Brown, and Company, 1911).
4. Elaine Scarry, *The Body in Pain* (Oxford: Oxford U.P., 1985), p. 14.
5. George Gissing in *The Immortal Dickens* (London: Cecil Palmer, 1925), pp.5–6.
6. George Gissing, *The Private Papers of Henry Ryecroft*, ed. Mark Storey (Oxford: Oxford U.P., 1987), pp.163–4.
7. Jeffrey Weeks has described, in relation to public events like the trial of Oscar Wilde in 1895, how homosexuality was constructed as an individual identity through the discourses of law and science, and through resistance to those definitions. See *Sex Politics and Society* (London: Longman, 1981), pp. 99–101.
8. As *Sexual Inversion* is not well known, a brief history of the text might be helpful. *Sexual Inversion* was finally published in 1897 under the names of Ellis and Symonds. Symonds had originally suggested collaboration to Ellis, but had died before publication in 1893 and his family wanted to suppress his involvement with the book. The control of the text passed into the hands of Ellis after Symonds' death; but it was not entirely Ellis' at any stage. He still required Carpenter's help with regard to available literature and case histories (Carpenter was producing his own pamphlets, ultimately incorporated into *Love's Coming-of-Age*). Ellis could not manage to get a reputable scientific publisher for the book, and it was eventually published, in 1897, by a firm with anarchist connections. Following its publication in English (there was a German edition published first to prepare the way, as Germany was more favourable to scientific works on sexuality), there was a court case in which the book was described as obscene. As a result of this experience Ellis had *Sexual Inversion* and the rest of his series, *Studies in the Psychology of Sex*, published, only under his name, and only in the United States. See Phyllis Grosskurth, *Havelock Ellis* (London: Allen Lane, 1980), Vincent Brome, *Havelock Ellis* (London: Routledge & Kegan Paul, 1979), Chushichi Tsuzuki, *Edward Carpenter* (Cambridge: Cambridge U.P., 1980).
9. Havelock Ellis and John Addington Symonds, *Sexual Inversion* (London: Wilson and Macmillan, 1897), p.141.
10. John Addington Symonds, Letter to Edward Carpenter, 29 Dec. 1892, *The Letters of John Addington Symonds*, Vol. III, ed. Herbert M. Schueller and Robert L. Peters (Detroit, Wayne State U.P., 1967–69), p.797.
11. Symonds had already written two books on the subject, *A Problem in Greek Ethics*, and *A Problem in Modern Ethics*. Both texts were published privately and only circulated to those known to be sympathetic. *A Problem in Modern Ethics* was polemical, arguing against scientific definitions of "inversion" as morbid. "Morbidity" was the scientific term denoting homosexuality as criminal or as a hereditary defect. Symonds envisaged the project of *Sexual Inversion* as one of legal reform. In this case, he felt collaboration with a scientist was necessary if the book was to be taken seriously. He approached Ellis as editor of *The Contemporary Science Series* and a doctor, writing that he felt the subject "ought to be scientifically, historically, impartially investigated."
12. Symonds, Letter to Ellis, 20 June 1892, *Letters, Vol. III*, pp.693–4.
13. Ellis, Letter to Symonds, 1 July 1892, copy in Symonds Collection, Bristol University Library, D.M. 375. In the 1897 text Ellis uses the the term "morbid" when in doubt, particularly with reference to the social acquisition of "inversion": "Whatever the mechanism of the process may be, there is certainly a tendency for a morbidly feeble impulse to become inverted" (*Sexual Inversion*, p. 41).
14. Symonds, Letter to Ellis, 29 Sept. 1892, *Letters, Vol. III*, p.787.

15. Ellis, Letter to Edward Carpenter, 19 Dec. 1892. MSS. 357, Carp. Coll.
16. Ellis, Letter to Carpenter, 22 Jan. 1894, MSS. 357, Carp. Coll.
17. Ellis, Letter to Symonds, 18 June 1892, copy in Symonds Collection, Bristol University Library, D.M. 375.
18. See Brome, pp. 109–17, and Grosskurth, pp. 154–64.
19. Edward Brecher, *The Sex Researchers* (London: André Deutsch, 1970), p. 18; Peter T. Cominos, "Late Victorian Respectability and the Social System," *International Review of Social History*, 3 (1963), 216.
20. The passage continues: "For instance, in one case present to my mind, he was of somewhat neurotic heredity, of slight physique, not sexually attractive to women, and very domesticated in his manner of living – in short, a man who might easily be attracted to his own sex" (*Sexual Inversion*, p. 98).
21. Brecher considers this possibility but rejects it; Brome finds himself able to come to a certain conclusion that Ellis was a "repressed homosexual" (Brome, *Havelock Ellis*, p. 240).
22. Ellis, Letter to Symonds, 1 July 1892. Symonds Collection.
23. "Several of the volumes approach forbidden topics, as nearly as is desirable and I am inclined to agree with the publisher [Walter Scott Ltd] that there is still too much at stake to involve the Series in any risky pioneering experiment," Ellis, Letter to Symonds, 1 July 1892. Symonds Collection.
24. Carpenter, Letter to Ellis, 28 Nov. 1895, quoted in Grosskurth, *Havelock Ellis*, p. 183; original in Humanities Research Centre, University of Texas.
25. Symonds, Letter to Ellis, 29 Sept. 1892, *Letters*.
26. Symonds, Letter to Walt Whitman, 7 Oct. 1871, *Letters*, Vol. *II*, p. 167.
27. Symonds, Letter to Walt Whitman, 3 Aug. 1890, *Letters*, Vol. *III*, pp. 483–4.
28. Quoted by Ellis in *Sexual Inversion*, p. xiii.
29. Mikhail Bakhtin, *Rabelais and His World* (Cambridge, Mass: MIT P., 1968), p. 20.
30. Ibid., p.30.
31. "Homosexuality is the law that regulates the socio-cultural order. Heterosexuality amounts to the assignment of roles in the economy: some are given the role of producing and exchanging subjects, while others are assigned the role of productive earth and goods," Luce Irigaray, "When the Goods Get Together," in *New French Feminisms*, ed. Elaine Marks and Isabelle de Courtrivron (Brighton: Harvester, 1981), p. 107.
32. Edward Carpenter, *Civilisation: its Cause and Cure, and Other Essays* (London: Swan Sonnenschein, 1889), pp. 78–9.
33. Symonds, Letter to Carpenter, 29 Dec. 1892, *Letters*, Vol. *III*, p. 798.
34. They have now been published: *The Memoirs of John Addington Symonds*, ed. Phyllis Grosskurth (London: Hutchinson, 1984).
35. Olive Schreiner, Letter to Ellis, 2 May 1884, *Letters 1871–1899, Vol. 1*, ed. Richard Rive (Oxford: Oxford U.P., 1987), p. 39.
36. Olive Schreiner, Letter to Ellis, 30 May 1884, *The Letters of Olive Schreiner 1876–1920*, ed. Samuel Cron Cronwright-Schreiner (London: T. Fisher Unwin, 1924), p. 21.
37. Edward Carpenter, *Towards Democracy* (London: Gay Men's Press, 1985), p. 45.
38. Ibid., p. 413.
39. Ibid., pp. 398–9.
40. *Civilisation*, p. 133.
41. "[The] explanation of these processes does not lie in any concatenation of the things themselves, but in some plane of being of which these concatenations are an allegory or symbolic expression," Edward Carpenter, *Love's Coming-of-Age* (London: Allen & Unwin, 1923), p. 50.
42. *Civilisation*, pp.144–5.
43. *Civilisation*, p. 126.
44. *Love's Coming-of-Age* (Manchester: Labour Press, 1896), p. 33.
45. Ibid.
46. Ibid., p. 29.

47. Ibid., p. 40.
48. "... as a general rule, in the evolution of the human race, as well as of the lower races, the female is less subject to variation and is more constant to and conservative of the type of the race than the male," *Love's Coming-of-Age*, p. 39. This is footnoted with references to Ellis' *Man and Woman* (London: Walter Scott, 1894), which describes "race" and gender in terms of biological difference.
49. *Towards Democracy*, p. 22.
50. Ibid.
51. *Towards Democracy*, p. 24.
52. Ibid.
53. Mikhail Bakhtin, "Forms of Time and of the Chronotope in the Novel," in *The Dialogic Imagination* (Austin, Texas: University of Texas P., 1981), p. 243.
54. *Towards Democracy*, p. 384.
55. Ibid., p. 385.
56. *Love's Coming-of-Age*, pp. 13–14.
57. *Towards Democracy*, p. 140. Whitman's "To A Stranger" speaks of a similar unspoken desire.
58. Luce Irigaray, "When the Goods Get Together," p. 108.
59. *Towards Democracy*, p. 392.
60. Ibid., p. 245 and p. 320.
61. *Love's Coming-of-Age*, "The Free Society."
62. John Goode remarks, "*Demos* is really a novel of the 1840s cunningly disguised as a story of the 'eighties," "Gissing, Morris and English Socialism," *Victorian Studies*, 12 (Dec. 1968), 203.
63. Rachel Bowlby, *Just Looking* (London: Methuen, 1985), p.10.
64. Charles Booth, *Life and Labour of the People*, Vol. 10 (Maps) (London: Macmillan, 1892–97).
65. Gareth Stedman Jones, *Outcast London* (Oxford: Oxford U.P., 1971).
66. George Gissing, *Demos: A Story of English Socialism*, ed. Pierre Coustillas (Brighton: Harvester, 1982), p. 26.
67. *Towards Democracy*, p. 267.
68. *Demos*, pp. 245–6.
69. Cominos, "Late Victorian Respectability and the Social System," p. 216.
70. Ellis, Letter to Symonds, 19 Feb. 1893, copy in Bristol University Library, D.M. 375.
71. Bakhtin sees the work of Dostoevsky as the best example of the polyphonic novel: "A plurality of unmerged voices and consciousnesses, a genuine polyphony of fully valid voices is in fact the chief characteristic of Dostoevsky's novels." *Problems of Dostoevsky's Poetics* (Manchester: Manchester U.P., 1984), p. 6.
72. George Gissing, *Eve's Ransom* (New York: Dover Publications, 1980), p. 15.
73. "I have become possessed of enough money to live upon a year or two. At the end of it I may find myself in the old position, and have to be a living machine once more. But I shall be able to remember that I was once a man," *Eve's Ransom*, p. 30.
74. Ibid., p. 20.
75. Bowlby, *Just Looking*, pp. 10–11.
76. "The psychoanalytic demonstration of the sexual dimensions of overtly nonsexual conscious experience and behaviour is possible only when the sexual 'dispositif' or apparatus has by a process of isolation, autonomization, specialization, developed into an independent sign system or symbolic dimension in its own right; as long as sexuality remains as integrated into social life in general as, say, eating, its possibilities of symbolic extension are to that degree limited, and the sexual retains its status as a banal inner-worldly event and bodily function," Frederic Jameson, *The Political Unconscious* (London: Methuen, 1981), p. 64.
77. Ellis is characteristically ambivalent about degeneration, admitting the definitive qualities of the term, while, as in his letters to Symonds disclaiming any moral, pejorative connotations: "Strictly speaking the invert is degenerate, he has fallen away from the genus. So is the colour-blind person. As it now stands we gain little or no information by being told that a person is a 'degenerate,'" *Sexual Inversion*, p.136.